UK MONETARY POLICY

Also by Paul Temperton and published by St. Martin's

A GUIDE TO UK MONETARY POLICY

UK Monetary Policy

The Challenge for the 1990s

Paul Temperton

St. Martin's Press   New York

332.49
T28u

First published in the United States of America in 1990

Printed in Great Britain

ISBN 0–312–05569–2

Library of Congress Cataloguing-in-Publication Data
Temperton, Paul, 1958–
    p. cm.
Includes index.
UK monetary policy : the challenge for the 1990s / Paul Temperton.
ISBN 0–312–05569–2
1. Monetary policy—Great Britain.   I. Title   II. Title: United
Kingdom monetary policy.
HG939.5.T46   1991
332.4'6'0941—dc20   90–44810
                                                       CIP

4b

Contents

List of Tables		*ix*
List of Figures		*x*
Preface		*xii*

1		**The Development of UK Monetary Policy, 1949 to 1990**	**1**
	(i)	1949 to 1967: a fixed $/£ exchange rate	1
	(ii)	1967 to 1971: the IMF, broad money and deregulation	3
	(iii)	1972 to 1973: floating exchange rates and fiscal expansion	4
	(iv)	1974 to 1976: evolution towards targets for broad money	4
	(v)	1976: first published targets for broad money	6
	(vi)	1977 to 1978: control of sterling conflicts with the broad money target and is abandoned	6
	(vii)	1979 to 1980: the development of the Medium Term Financial Strategy	8
	(viii)	1980 to 1983: problems with £M3	12
	(ix)	1983 to March 1987: attention shifts to narrow money	15
	(x)	March 1987 to March 1988: 'capping' sterling at DM3.00/£	17
	(xi)	March 1988 to mid-1988: the DM3.00/£ cap is removed but interest rates fall further	19
	(xii)	Mid-1988 to end-1989: progressive rise in short-term interest rates	19
	(xiii)	Conclusions	20
2		**Measures of Money in the UK**	**23**
	(i)	A range of financial assets with varying degrees of 'moneyness'	23
	(ii)	Relationships between the monetary aggregates and their components	24
	(iii)	Narrow money	24
	(iv)	Broad money	29
	(v)	Divisia money	34

3   **Analysing Narrow Money**   37
 (i)   M0 as a measure of transactions balances   39
 (ii)   M0 and inflation   41
 (iii)   Explaining the behaviour of M0   44
 (iv)   Controlling M0 by interest rate changes   47
 (v)   The counterparts to M0   48
 (vi)   Monetary Base Control   49

4   **The Counterparts Approach to Analysing Broad Money** 55
 (i)   The balance sheet of the UK banks and building societies   55
 (ii)   Financing the PSBR   56
 (iii)   The definition of M4   58
 (iv)   The counterparts to M4   58
 (v)   The counterparts to M4 in practice   59
 (vi)   External and foreign currency counterparts   61
 (vii)   Net non-deposit liabilities   62

5   **Funding Policy**   65
 (i)   The full funding rule   65
 (ii)   The funding rule in practice   65
 (iii)   The different funding instruments   70
 (iv)   The gilt market in decline   76
 (v)   Possible changes to the full funding rule   76
         Appendix: Significant developments in UK
         funding policy, 1980 to 1989   79

6   **Problems with Broad Money**   81
 (i)   Broad money and inflation   82
 (ii)   Credit demand by the private sector - the most important
         counterpart to broad money growth   83
 (iii)   Relationship between broad money and money GDP   84
 (iv)   Structural changes, deregulation and innovation
         in the financial system   85
 (v)   Deregulation and financial innovation - how much
         of a concern?   89
 (vi)   Financial innovation and real interest rates   90

(vii)   The sensitivity of credit demand to changes in interest rates   92
(viii) Could direct controls on the banking system work?   92
(ix)   Controlling credit demand without direct controls in a
        financially sophisticated world   93
(x)   A return to targets for broad money?   93
(xi)   A return to overfunding?   94
(xii)   A reintroduction to the reserve assets ratio   94
(xiii) Control of the Bank of England's balance sheet   95
(xiv)   Conclusions   97

7   **European Economic and Monetary Union**   99
(i)   What is meant by European Economic and
        Monetary Union?   99
(ii)   The Delors plan for Economic and Monetary Union   100
(iii)   Controversial aspects of the Delors plan and the UK's
        attitude   102
(iv)   Treaty changes in Stages Two and Three   103
(v)   The relationship between Economic and Monetary Union   104
(vi)   Surrender of national sovereignty   105
(vii)   UK alternatives to Stages Two and Three of the
        Delors plan   107
(viii) Developing the use of the ECU   109
(ix)   Other obstacles towards EMU   111

8   **The Exchange Rate as a Monetary Indicator:**
        the experience of the 1980's   **115**
(i)   Early use of the exchange rate in the MTFS   115
(ii)   Targeting the DM/£ rate   117
(iii)   Why the DM3.00/£ cap was abandoned   120
(iv)   DM/£ exchange rate after the cap was removed   121

9   **UK Membership of the European Exchange**
        Rate Mechanism   **127**
(i)   Benefits and costs of UK membership of the ERM   127
(ii)   The timing of UK entry to the ERM   131
(iii)   The mechanics of ERM entry   135
(iv)   Effects on policy of joining the ERM   144

10 **Bringing together the information on monetary conditions** **151**
(i) Assessment of a range of factors 151
(ii) The method used in aggregating the information 151
(iii) The exchange rate 152
(iv) Narrow money 153
(v) Broad money 154
(vi) Asset prices 156
(vii) Real interest rates 157
(viii) Assigning weights to the different measures 159
(ix) Relationship between the index and inflation 159
(x) Conclusions 160

11 **Bank of England Operations in the Money Market** **161**
(i) Administered versus market related interest rates 161
(ii) The role of the Bank of England in the money market 163
(iii) The objective of money market operations 166
(iv) Techniques for relieving money market shortages 167
(v) Techniques for absorbing a money market surplus 169
(vi) Relationship between money market flows and the government's funding policy 170
(vii) Relationship between Bank of England interest rates and market interest rates 171

12 **Conclusion** **177**
Appendix 1: Official Interest Rates, 1932 to 1989 181
Appendix 2: Monetary Policy Developments 185
Glossary of term 197
Index 209

List of Tables

1.1 Inflation trends, 1958-1981   2

1.2 Monetary targets set in the UK and results achieved   7

1.3 MTFS target ranges for the growth of broad money, £M3   9

1.4 Targets for the PSBR/GDP ratio   11

1.5 MTFS target ranges for the growth of narrow money, M0   17

1.6 MTFS target ranges for the growth of money GDP   18

2.1 Monetary aggregates, amounts outstanding at the end of 1989   28

4.1 Consolidated balance sheet of UK banks and building societies   56

4.2 Counterparts to M4 growth   60

5.1 Funding of the PSBR   66

5.2 Composition of the National Debt   71

5.3 Treasury bills   73

5.4 Profile of gilt maturities   77

8.1 Behaviour of the DM/£ and FF/DM exchange rates (20 March 1987 to 4 March 1988)   124

9.1 Estimates of appropriate level of DM/£ rate, end-1990   136

9.2 Composition of the ECU   140

9.3 Exchange Rate Mechanism grid with sterling included   141

9.4 Calculating the effect of a 2.25% rise in sterling against all other currencies in the ECU   143

9.5 OECD estimates of UK general government financial balances   149

11.1 Influences on the cash position of the money market and official offsetting operations   172

11.2 UK money market term structure   174

List of Figures

1.1   Ratio of general government expenditure to GDP   2

1.2   Broad money and inflation, 1964 to 1979   5

1.3   Velocity of broad money   12

1.4   Velocity of M0   16

2.1   Relationships among the monetary aggregates
      and their components   25

2.2   Classification of bank deposits   31

3.1   M0 and inflation, 1976 to 1983   41

3.2   M0 and inflation, 1970 to 1990   42

3.3   M0 and target range   43

4.1   External and foreign currency counterparts to M4
      and the current account   63

5.1   Public sector finances and the yield on long dated gilts   78

6.1   Broad money growth and inflation   83

6.2   Growth of sterling lending to the UK private sector   86

6.3   Real one year interest rate   91

8.1   DM/£ exchange rate and official intervention   119

8.2   DM/£ exchange rate and one year moving average   122

8.3   Volatility of the DM/£ exchange rate   122

8.4   DM/£ exchange rate, March 1987 to March 1988   123

8.5   French franc/DM exchange rate, March 1987 to March 1988   123

9.1   Italian-German and French-German inflation differentials   129

9.2   Domestic demand growth in Germany, France and Italy   133

9.3   Domestic demand growth in Germany and the UK   133

9.4 UK-German inflation differential   135

9.5 DM/£ purchasing power parity   137

9.6 The conventional adjustment process within the ERM   145

9.7 The Walters critique   146

10.1 Exchange rate tightness indicator   153

10.2 Narrow money tightness indicator   154

10.3 Broad money tightness indicator   155

10.4 House price and retail price inflation   156

10.5 Asset prices tightness indicator   157

10.6 Real interest rates tightness indicator   158

10.7 Monetary tightness index and inflation   160

11.1 Money market structure and flows   164

11.2 Base rates and three month interbank rate   173

Preface

Over the last year, when I have told enquirers the subject of this book, the most common response has been: 'is there still a UK monetary policy?'. The question is understandable, given that the 1980s saw a marked changes in the conduct of UK monetary policy and, especially, the abandonment of targets for the growth of broad money. Indeed, data for sterling M3-the cornerstone of UK monetary policy at the start of the last decade-are no longer published. But this change in the role played by broad money does not mean that there is no monetary policy. There is one, and it is important that we continue to have one. The discussion of the development of UK monetary policy over the last thirty years in Chapter 1 points out that, although the presentation of monetary policy has changed markedly, there have been relatively few periods in which there has been little concern with monetary developments. Monetary policy has taken various forms including maintainance of a fixed exchange rate, a target for broad money, simultaneous targets for several monetary aggregates, an unannounced exchange rate target and conditional targets for the exchange rate and monetary growth. Although periods without a clearly defined policy have been few, they have without exception led to macroeconomic problems-in particular, rising inflation.

During the 1990s, the most important issue facing UK monetary policy makers will be progress towards European Economic and Monetary Union (EMU). If full EMU were to be achieved then there would be no role for an independent UK monetary policy - short-term interest rates would be set at the EC level. This, and the other diverse issues raised by the question of EMU, form the subject of Chapter 7. Although full EMU is not an immediate prospect, progress towards it is of utmost importance. In particular, UK membership of the Exchange Rate Mechanism (ERM) of the European Monetary System forms an important part of Stage One of the Delors plan for EMU. The issues raised by ERM entry are discussed in Chapter 9, after an examination in Chapter 8 of the practical problems the UK authorities had with using the exchange rate as a monetary indicator and an intermediate target of monetary policy in the 1980s. In particular, Chapter 8 examines the period from March 1987 to March 1988 when the UK authorities 'capped' sterling's value against the Deutschemark.

Given that the form of UK monetary policy has often changed in the last decade, it would be foolhardy in a book which looks at the issues facing policy in the 1990s to concentrate just on the one issue of the exchange rate. An important section of the book is, therefore, allocated to the role of the monetary aggregates. The changing measures of the money supply form the subject of Chapter 2; and Chapters 3 and 4 discuss the analysis of narrow and broad money, respectively. Chapter 5 focuses on funding policy, which will be of special importance as the UK faces the prospect of a continued public sector debt repayment. A full chapter - Chapter 6 - is taken up in discussing the problems that have been experienced in setting targets for, and assesing the behaviour of, broad money.

A pragmatic approach to aggregating the information on monetary conditions - embracing the role of the exchange rate, narrow and broad money, real interest rates and asset markets - is launched in Chapter 10. The aim is to provide a method of quantifying the 'lets look at everything' approach which currently characterises the Treasury's view.

The subject of greatest day-to-day importance for observers of UK monetary policy - the operations of the Bank of England in the money market - is discussed in Chapter 11.

Although the intention is for each of the chapters to stand alone as discussions of the key issues facing policy, overall conclusions are drawn together in the final chapter.

Thanks must go to the many people who helped in the production of the book. First, and foremost, Nicky, my wife, who not only managed to cope with a resident author for the best part of a year - latterly whilst expecting an addition to the Temperton household - but who also proved to be a tireless critic and proof reader. Without her it really would not have been possible. Philip Reece must be praised for being the last in a line of desk-top publishing operators struggling to shape the text into the confines dictated by Ventura. Amongst the people who read and commented on a draft version of the book Roger Clews at the Bank of England, Peter Lilley at the Treasury and Sir Alan Walters must be thanked not only for speedily checking references but also for offering additional helpful comments. Charles Goodhart went even further than could reasonably be expected in his examination of the draft and it is regretted that not all his suggestions could be incorporated given the time constraint; that will have to be the task for any second edition. I do, of course, take full responsibility for any errors which remain.

Paul Temperton   June 1990

1 The Development of UK Monetary Policy, 1949 to 1990

(i) 1949 to 1967: a fixed $/£ exchange rate

During the 1950s and early 1960s, the UK economy grew at a rate which was sufficient to keep unemployment at a very low level. Economic policy was aimed at 'managing demand' so as to achieve a level of economic activity which was sufficient to obtain 'full employment'. The principal constraint on this demand management policy was the maintenance of the value of the exchange rate at $2.80/£. When economic growth became too rapid and the balance of payments deteriorated, economic policy would become more restrictive in order to moderate demand, correct the balance of payments position and hence moderate pressure on the exchange rate. In the period of correction, any balance of payments deficit was met largely by running down the official foreign exchange reserves.

The policy of maintaining economic activity at (or close to) the full employment level led to a steady increase in the public sector's involvement in the economy. One indication of this is given by the ratio of general government expenditure to GDP: as is shown in Figure 1.1, this rose from 38% in 1955 to around 50% in the early 1970s (and subsequently reached almost 55% in the mid and late 1970s).

Inflation, in large part pulled by the continually high level of demand in the economy, also displayed a clear upward trend. Comparing the levels of inflation reached at comparable times in each of the business cycles since the mid-1950s inflation rose steadily, as can be seen from Table 1.1.

Figure 1.1: Ratio of general government expenditure to GDP

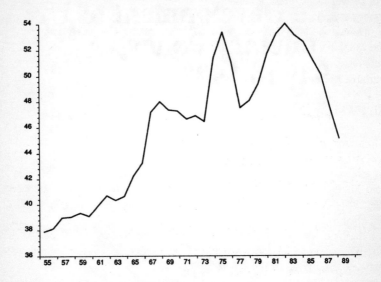

SOURCE : DATASTREAM

Although later on in the 1960s monetary policy was concerned primarily with the management of the level of nominal interest rates and the control of bank lending to the private sector, policy decisions were still driven by the need to maintain the fixed exchange rate. From 1964 the authorities imposed quantitative ceilings on bank lending to the private sector. Within these ceilings, guidance was given as to which sectors of the economy available credit should be channelled: broadly, companies which required finance for

Table 1.1: Inflation trends, 1958-1981*

Date:	Inflation Rate (% p.a.):
December 1958	1.9
January 1963	2.7
March 1967	3.5
February 1972	8.1
August 1975	26.9
May 1981	11.7

* the dates chosen are those corresponding to the troughs in each of the business cycles

exporting or investing were favoured at the expense of the personal sector. Policy was not explicitly concerned with the growth of any measure of the money supply.

Monetary data were collected from 1959[1] but the accepted view was that the relationship between the money supply and prices and incomes in the economy was so unpredictable that it was highly unlikely to be a useful variable to examine for policy purposes.

(ii) 1967 to 1971: the IMF, broad money and deregulation

Maintenance of the dollar/sterling exchange rate at $2.80/£ lasted from 1949 to 1967. In 1967, when a prolonged period of restrictive policies had failed to produce any correction of the balance of payments deficit, the exchange rate was devalued from $2.80/£ to $2.40/£ and the UK obtained a loan from the IMF in order to bolster the foreign exchange reserves. The conditions attached to the loan obliged the UK to restrict the public sector borrowing requirement (PSBR), restrain finance to the private sector and hence bring about more moderate Domestic Credit Expansion (DCE). The relationship between the PSBR, bank lending, government debt sales and DCE could be expressed within the new flow of funds accounting framework in a way which brought a greater coherence and consistency to the analysis of fiscal and monetary policies. As the size of the PSBR was constrained by the need to meet this restriction on DCE, the use of discretionary changes in the government's budgetary position to manage demand became more restricted. Although control of this credit measure was thus forced upon the UK by the IMF, two other key developments also led to greater attention being placed on money and credit.

First, as inflation rose and became more volatile, the behaviour of nominal interest rates became a much less reliable guide to the stance of monetary policy. The expected real interest rate is equal to the nominal interest rate less the expected rate of inflation and is a better guide to the stance of monetary policy. When inflation is low and stable, changes in nominal interest rates are associated with commensurate changes in real interest rates; but in times of high and volatile inflation, inflationary expectations become much more difficult to assess. Hence, the authorities cannot know with any degree of certainty the prevailing real interest rate. In the late 1960s, this problem led to the search for an alternative guide to monetary conditions.

Second, econometric work which had been carried out on the monetary data collected since 1959 came up with the conclusion that the demand for money could be satisfactorily explained by a few other economic variables - prices, incomes and interest rates. Moreover, the studies implied that control of the growth of the money supply could be achieved by acceptable variations in short-term interest rates. Thus money could be controlled by changing interest rates and direct controls may not be needed. At the time, there was a general movement towards favouring more competition in banking. Given this background and the evidence of the econometric studies, direct controls on lending were abandoned in September 1971: the authorities placed greater emphasis on changes in interest rates as a way of influencing the demand for credit.

(iii) 1972 to 1973: floating exchange rates and fiscal expansion

At around the same time, the US authorities suspended the dollar's convertibility into gold, and the postwar system of fixed exchange rates was abandoned. After a short experiment in the 'snake' (the European fixed exchange rate system), the UK authorities decided to 'float' sterling on 23 June 1972. Shortly before that, the Conservative government had embarked on a highly expansionary fiscal policy in the March 1972 Budget. The combination of such a stimulative fiscal policy and the new-found freedom of the banks to meet a strong demand for credit (financed by the increasingly popular liability management technique of bidding for deposits) produced a high level of demand in the economy and severe inflationary pressures ensued.[2] Despite sharp rises in interest rates, rapid growth of money and credit persisted. Bank lending to the private sector grew by 33%, and M3 by 28%, in 1973. The econometric relationships based on the data of the 1960s (suggesting M3 could be brought under control by varying interest rates) had clearly 'broken down' in the face of the structural change in the banking system. Narrow measures of money, however, grew only modestly during the period: M1, for example, grew by only 5% (perhaps because money shifted from sight deposits to time deposits in response to the higher level of interest rates). Given the divergent movements of broad and narrow measures of money, interpretation of monetary conditions was not straightforward. With hindsight, however, the rapid growth of M3 in 1972 and 1973 was seen to provide a good advance indication of the behaviour of inflation in 1974 and 1975 (see Figure 1.2).

(iv) 1974 to 1976: evolution towards targets for broad money

Even without that evidence, and in the face of the 'breakdown' of the econometric equations for M3, 'the course of M3 was a fairly strong policy constraint after 1973'.[3] Containment of M3, however, once again came to rely on a form of direct control on the banking system; the Supplementary

Special Deposits Scheme (SSD or, more commonly, the 'corset') was introduced in December 1973. M3's key attribute appeared to be the way in which it could be expressed in terms of its 'credit counterparts' - DCE (in turn reflecting the PSBR, the extent to which it was financed by debt sales to the non-bank private sector and bank lending to the private sector) and the influence of external flows. The counterparts framework has been the central feature of the analysis of developments in the UK broad money supply since that time.

Figure 1.2: Broad money and inflation, 1964 to 1979

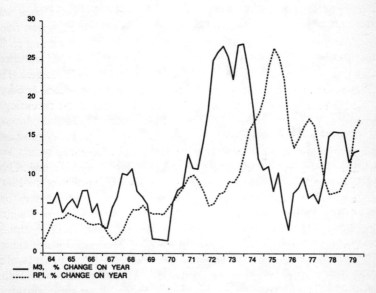

M3, % CHANGE ON YEAR
RPI, % CHANGE ON YEAR

SOURCE : DATASTREAM

The first monetary targets were informal, specifying guidelines and anticipated outturns for broad money growth and domestic credit. In the Budget of 6 April 1976, Denis Healey (Chancellor of the Exchequer) said that 'after two years in which M3 has grown a good deal more slowly than GDP, I would expect their respective growth rates to come more into line in the coming financial year'. Later on in the year, statements about the expected behaviour of the monetary aggregates became more definite. According to Fforde 'the UK authorities had become caught in a spiral of declining confidence' in 1976.[4] Exchange rate weakness, coupled with continuing concern about the government's fiscal stance and the size of the PSBR, led to concern about the viability of the government's incomes policy and, hence, future inflation. In this environment, the government's funding programme was particularly difficult: this in turn led to problems with controlling M3. When it became clear that financial confidence would not be obtained without it, a published M3 target was announced.

(v) 1976: first published targets for broad money

On 22 July 1976 the Chancellor announced that the target rate of increase in M3 was to be 12% during the 1976/77 financial year. This was viewed as consistent with the likely £9 billion DCE originally forecast in December 1975. In December 1976, as part of the 'letter of intent' to the IMF, the monetary objectives were again restated. Although DCE was still expected to be £9 billion in 1976/77, the monetary expansion compatible with this was expressed in terms of Sterling M3 (£M3 i.e. M3 minus UK residents' foreign currency deposits): growth of £M3 for 1976/77 was expected to be 9-13%.

(vi) 1977 to 1978: control of sterling conflicts with the broad money target and is abandoned

External confidence improved markedly following the December measures; indeed, there was strong upward pressure on the exchange rate. Two methods were used to control the appreciation. First, heavy official sales of sterling were made in the foreign exchange market. Although some of the increase in the foreign exchange reserves was used to repay loans taken out over the previous three years, the external flows still proved to be a highly expansionary influence on £M3. Second, interest rates were cut sharply. Minimum lending rate (MLR) fell from a peak level of 15% in October 1976 to 5% in October 1977 (see Appendix 1 for a list of the dates of MLR changes). Again, this was found to be undermining control of the domestic monetary aggregates.

Until the end of October 1977 the pound was allowed to move against the dollar in such a way as to keep its effective exchange rate steady, and the index was held within the range 61.7 to 62.6; market purchases of sterling were heavy. On 31 October, official intervention to prevent a rise in the index was withdrawn because it was feared that such intervention would, if continued, prevent achievement of the authorities' monetary objectives.[5] The measures to control the appreciation of the exchange rate 'had collided with the overriding monetary constraint; and they were abandoned'.[6]

Table 1.2: Monetary targets set in the UK and results achieved

Period	Measure	Target Set	Outturn	
1976/77 (fin. year)	£M3[1]	9-13	8.0	
1977/78 (fin. year)	£M3	9-13	15.1	
1978/79 (fin. year)	£M3	8-12	11.4	(10.9 to October 78)[2]
October 78/October 79	£M3	8-12	13.7	(12.4 to June 79)[3]
June 79/October 80[4]	£M3	7-11	17.2	(9.9 to February 80)[5]
				(10.4 to April 80)
February 80/April 81[6]	£M3	7-11	19.4	
February 81/April 82	£M3	6-10	12.8	
February 82/April 83:	M1	8-12	12.4	
	£M3	8-12	11.2	
	PSL2	8-12	11.6	
February 83/April 84:	M1	7-11	14.0	
	£M3	7-11	9.5	
	PSL2	7-11	12.6	
February 84/April 85:	M0	4-8	5.4	
	£M3	6-10	11.9	
1985/86	M0	3-7	3.4	
	£M3[7]	5-9	16.7	
1986/87	M0	2-6	4.4	
	£M3[8]	11-15	19.0	
1987/88	M0	2-6	5.6	
1988/89	M0	1-5	6.1	
1989/90	M0	1-5	6.3	
1990/91	M0	1-5	—	
1991/92	M0	0-4	—	
1992/93	M0	0-4	—	
1993/94	M0	-1-3		

Notes:
[1] On 23 July 1976 a target rate of increase for M3 of 12% was announced, but was superseded by the 9-13% target for £M3 in the 'letter of intent' to the IMF.
[2] New target after six months.
[3] New target after eight months.
[4] Original target was to April 1980. Target was extended in October 1979 for one year.
[5] New target after eight months.
[6] For 1980/81 and subsequent years, targets were also set out for the medium term growth of the monetary aggregates - see Table 1.3.
[7] Target suspended in October 1985.
[8] Target suspended in October 1986.

The importance of the overriding monetary constraint was further demonstrated in the summer of 1978 when the government's fiscal policy was corrected and direct credit controls reintroduced once market confidence in the containment of £M3 growth became undermined. Control of inflation, however, still depended to a large degree on direct restraint of prices and incomes.

(vii) 1979 to 1980: the development of the Medium Term Financial Strategy

After the election in May 1979 of the Conservative Government, economic and financial policy was changed radically. The measures taken in the first Conservative Budget, only six weeks after the election, fell into three broad groups. First, there was a major shift from direct to indirect taxation. The top marginal rate of tax on earned income was cut from 83% to 60% and the basic rate from 33% to 30%. To help pay for this, the rate of VAT was raised from the split level of 7% and 12 1/2% to one uniform level of 15%. Second, a wide range of controls were ended: pay, price and dividend controls were abolished and a phased removal of exchange controls was announced. Indeed, only three months later (on 23 September) it was announced that all remaining exchange controls were to be removed with effect from 24 October. Notably, however, the 'corset' was retained. These two groups of measures were designed to stimulate the 'supply side' of the economy by improving incentives to work and by eliminating some of the bureaucratic obstacles to the efficient working of markets. Third, the money supply was moved to the centre of economic and financial strategy. The ultimate objective was to reduce inflation: control of the money supply was seen as the indispensable intermediate goal to achieving this final objective. £M3 was retained as the chosen measure of money. Its target growth rate was reduced from 8-12% to 7-11% for the period June 1979 to April 1980 (the target period was extended in October 1979 for one year). To reinforce the new government's counter-inflationary resolve, MLR was raised from 12% to 14%.

The Medium Term Financial Strategy (MTFS) made its appearance in the Conservative government's second Budget on 26 March 1980. The government's objectives for the medium term were 'to bring down the rate of inflation and to create conditions for a sustainable growth of output and employment'.[7] The importance of the control of money was reaffirmed: the government believed that 'control of the money supply will over a period of years reduce the rate of inflation'[8] and an important change of emphasis was made. Plans for a progressive reduction in monetary growth over a number

Table 1.3: MTFS target ranges for the growth of broad money, £M3 (%)*

Target set in:	80/81	81/82	82/83	83/84	84/85	85/86	86/87	87/88	88/89
Mar 80	7-11	6-10	5-9	4-8					
Mar 81		6-10	5-9	4-8					
Mar 82			8-12	7-11	6-10				
Mar 83				7-11	6-10	5-9			
Mar 84					6-10	5-9	4-8	3-7	2-6
Mar 85						5-9	4-8	3-7	2-6
Mar 86							11-15		
Outturn:	19.4	12.8	11.2	9.5	11.9	16.7	19.0	20.9	21.1

* In the 1982 and 1983 Budgets the identical target ranges were applied to M1 and PSL2, now renamed M5. The outturns for these two measures were:

	82/83	83/84
MI	12.4	14.0
PSL2	11.6	12.6

of years were made public. Thus, as is shown in Table 1.3, the March 1980 Budget envisaged monetary growth declining from 7-11% in 1980/81 to 4-8% in 1983/84. Control of monetary growth was to be linked to control of the size of the PSBR in relation to GDP (the relationship between £M3 and its credit counterparts, discussed fully in Chapter 4, provided a framework within which the two were linked). The 1980 Budget envisaged that ratio falling from 3¾% in 1980/81 to 1½% in 1983/84 (see Table 1.4).

The MTFS was 'monetarist' in the sense that it was based on the quantity theory of money. This theory is founded on the identify that

$$MV = PT$$

where M is the stock of money and V its velocity of circulation (the number of times it changes hands in any particular period), P is the average price and T the total number of transactions in the economy. Thus the total amount of money spent in a particular time period must be identical to the value of transactions which it finances. If the velocity of circulation of money is reasonably stable and predictable, then there will be a close relationship between the growth of money and nominal expenditure in the economy. Traditionally, quantity theorists had thought that the output of the economy was also relatively fixed in the short run, thus leading to the conclusion that any rise in M would automatically raise P.

The MTFS made the assumption (more realistic in the 1980s) that with monetary growth set on a declining path, the course of output in the economy would depend on how quickly inflationary expectations were changed. The government was resigned to the fact that these would not change instantly and thought that 'the process of reducing inflation almost inevitably entails some loss of output initially'.[9] In the labour market, in particular, it was thought that with monetary growth restricted, excessively high wage demands would simply price people out of work. As a corollary, it was pointed out that 'the sooner inflation comes down, the faster the rate of economic growth that can be accommodated within the monetary guidelines'.[10]

The announcement of medium term monetary growth guidelines was, in itself, thought to be a key influence on inflationary expectations. The Green Paper on Monetary Control[11] had pointed out that 'no single statistical measure of the money supply can be expected fully to encapsulate monetary conditions, and so provide a uniquely correct basis for controlling the complex relationships between monetary growth and prices and nominal incomes'. Nevertheless, on grounds of clarity, it was thought appropriate to formulate monetary targets on the basis of one single aggregate, £M3. The use of more than one monetary aggregate for targetry was considered inappropriate as it 'would make it much more difficult for the market and the public to appraise the determination of the authorities to meet their monetary objectives'.[12]

The gradual movement of government policies away from 'Keynesian demand management' that had started in the mid-1970s, thus appeared to have been completed. The postwar use of macro-economic policies to obtain full employment and micro-economic policies (various forms of price and wage restraint) to control inflation was overturned. Indeed, Lawson, commenting in 1984 on the MTFS said that 'it is the conquest of inflation, and not the pursuit of growth and employment, which is or should be the objective of macro-economic policy. And it is the creation of conditions conducive to growth and employment, and not the suppression of price rises, which is or should be the objective of micro-economic policy'.[13]

Although the statement of the objectives of the MTFS changed only marginally between 1980/81 and 1990/91, the representation of monetary policy in the achievement of such objectives was substantially revised. As noted above, the 1980/81 MTFS stated that the government's objectives for the medium term were to bring down inflation and to create conditions for sustainable growth of output and employment. The same statement of policy

Table 1.4: Targets for the PSBR/GDP ratio (%)

Target set in:	80/81	81/82	82/83	83/84	84/85	85/86	86/87	87/88	88/89	89/90	90/91	91/92	92/93	93/94
Mar 80	3.75	3.00	2.25	1.50										
Mar 81		4.25	3.25	2.00										
Mar 82			3.50	2.75	2.00									
Mar 83				2.75	2.50	2.00								
Mar 84					2.25	2.00	2.00	1.75	1.75					
Mar 85						2.00	2.00	1.75	1.75					
Mar 86							1.75	1.75	1.50	1.50				
Mar 87								1.00	1.00	1.00	1.00			
Mar 88									-0.75	0.00	0.00	0.00		
Mar 89										-2.75	-1.75	-1.00	-0.50	
Mar 90											-1.25	-0.50	0.00	0.00
Outturn	5.4	3.5	2.9	3.2	3.1	1.6	0.9	-0.9	-3.0	-1.5	—	—	—	—

Note:
A negative public sector borrowing requirement (PSBR) is referred to as a public sector debt repayment (PSDR).

continues to be made in the MTFS. In 1984/85, however, a change of detail
was made: the government's ultimate objective became the achievement of
'stable prices with lower interest rates'. Thus the rate of inflation was to fall
to zero, and a reduction in interest rates in itself became an objective.

(viii) 1980 to 1983: problems with £M3

Difficulties with using £M3 as the chosen measure of money to target were
encountered very soon after the 1980 Budget. The abolition of the corset in
June 1980 led to a substantial increase in £M3. In July and August the
increase was 6½%, compared with a target rate of growth of 7-11% for the
year as a whole. In the 1981/82 *Financial Statement and Budget Report
(FSBR)* it was considered that '£M3 has not been a good indicator of
monetary conditions in the past year'. Nevertheless, £M3 was retained as the
sole target monetary aggregate: there appeared to be three main reasons for
this. First, its velocity was thought to be stable in the medium term: the fast
growth in relation to money GDP in 1980/81 and the fall in £M3's velocity
of circulation (see Figure 1.3) could be considered a temporary aberration.
Second, through the 'counterparts relationship', £M3 could be linked to the
stance of fiscal policy, the extent to which the fiscal deficit was financed by
sales of debt to the non-bank private sector, the private sector's credit demand
and external flows. Third, £M3 was well understood in financial markets.

Figure 1.3: Velocity of broad money

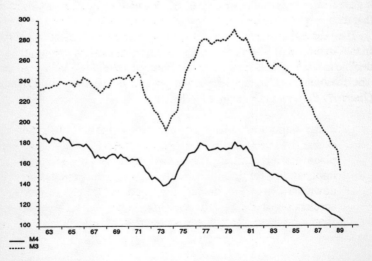

—— M4
······ M3

SOURCE : DATASTREAM

In coming to the conclusion that financial conditions had been tight in 1980/81, the government looked at four other indicators. First, other measures of money; it was noted that narrow money had fallen in real terms and that PSL1 (which includes private sector holdings of bills as well as money and was less distorted by the removal of the corset) had grown more slowly than £M3. Second, the exchange rate had been particularly strong, reaching peak levels of $2.45/£ on 4 November 1980 and 105 on the effective exchange rate index (1980 = 100) on 28 January 1981. Third, interest rates had been high, and fourth, there had not been any marked upward movement in the prices of houses or other real assets.

In the next financial year (1981/82) £M3 again grew rapidly - well above the top of its target range. The 1982/83 *FSBR* highlighted three factors which had made interpretation of £M3's behaviour particularly difficult. First, £M3 (as well as other monetary aggregates) had been affected by 'innovations and structural changes in financial markets'. The abolition of the corset and the removal of exchange controls had been important influences on bank behaviour: for example, the banks started to lend on a significant scale for residential mortgages. Second, the demand for liquid balances as a means of saving increased. These two factors had tended to reduce the velocity of £M3, by around 4% in 1981/82. Third, the civil service dispute had seriously disrupted the pattern of financial flows in the economy, making interpretation of £M3 and its counterparts more difficult.

In this environment, other indicators of the stance of policy were again taken into consideration. The behaviour of narrow money and nominal GDP, high real interest rates and weak asset prices were all considered as indicating that monetary conditions had remained restrictive.

The year had, however, seen the first of a series of exchange rate crises. In the Autumn of 1981 the authorities became seriously concerned about the decline in sterling's exchange rate and initiated a sharp rise in interest rates. The reasoning behind the move was set out in the Bank of England's *Quarterly Bulletin* in December 1981:

> ... the authorities were concerned that a further fall in the exchange rate, following the decline that had already taken place earlier in the year, would have serious adverse implications for inflation. Failure to respond rapidly to downward pressure on sterling appeared likely to risk accelerating sterling's fall, and a rise in the general level of short term interest rates therefore seemed appropriate.

In the light of the structural changes in the banking system and the increased desire to hold liquid balances as savings media, the target range for monetary growth was set at 8-12% for 1982/83, some two percentage points higher than the illustrative range for that period set down in the previous Budget. Moreover, the range was to apply to M1 and PSL2 as well as £M3. Growth of the monetary aggregates at the centre of this range (10%) would be equivalent to the anticipated rise in nominal GDP, leaving velocity unchanged. It was again stressed that the 'interpretation of monetary conditions will continue to take account of all the available evidence, including the behaviour of the exchange rate'.[14]

The explicit use of three target monetary aggregates was a departure from previous practice, apparently contradicting the view of the 1980 Green Paper on the desirability of using just one aggregate for reasons of clarity.

Nominal GDP grew much more slowly than expected in 1982/83 (7 ½% compared with a 1982 Budget forecast of 10%) as inflation turned out lower than forecast. Retail price inflation fell sharply - from 10.4% per annum at the time of the 1982 Budget to 4.6% per annum at the time of the 1983 Budget. Thus, even with a continued fall in velocity, £M3 finished the year within its target range. PSL2 grew at the upper end of, and M1 slightly above, the target range. The Chancellor was, therefore, able to claim in his 1983 Budget speech that monetary conditions had developed broadly as intended. Despite this, other indicators of the stance of monetary policy gave less convincing evidence of restrictive conditions. In particular, the end of 1982 had seen another sharp fall in the value of sterling, leading to some reversal of the fall in interest rates during the year. Base rates rose from 9% to 10-10^1/4% on 26 November 1982 and then again to 11% on 12 January (Appendix 1 gives details of the changes in official interest rates).

The same three monetary aggregates were targeted in 1983/84, with a common range (7-11%) that was one percentage point lower than in the previous year. Again the authorities would 'continue to take account of all the available evidence including the exchange rate, structural changes in financial markets, savings behaviour, and the level and structure of interest rates' when assessing monetary conditions.[15] £M3 grew well within the target range during the year but PSL2 and M1 were above the range. It had been considered when M1 was introduced as a target monetary aggregate in the 1982 Budget, that lower interest rates and inflation might lead to rather faster growth in the aggregate; the 'cost' of holding M1 deposits (which were predominantly non-interest bearing) fell as interest rates fell and so demand for M1 might be expected to be correspondingly higher. The fast growth of M1, however, appeared to be due less to this factor than to the growing share of interest bearing deposits within the M1 measure; again, this was due to structural change in the banking system. PSL2 had grown rapidly due to the attractiveness of building society deposit rates.

(ix) 1983 to March 1987: attention shifts to narrow money

After the re-election of the Conservative government in June 1983, Nigel Lawson, the new Chancellor of the Exchequer, initiated a review of the MTFS. In particular, the question of the choice of target aggregates was addressed once more. The upshot of the reappraisal seemed to be a renewed emphasis on the use of monetary aggregates as intermediate targets of policy, with something of a move away from the more pragmatic approach which had developed over the previous three years. The preliminary results of the review were announced in October 1983.[16] On the fundamental question of the ability of monetary aggregates to predict future inflation, it was now considered that narrow monetary aggregates were better predictors than broad aggregates - a finding at variance with the conventional wisdom of the 1970s. Furthermore, it was thought that M0 bore a reasonably close relationship to developments in nominal GDP (i.e. that its velocity was stable, see Figure 1.4) and that it could be controlled by variations in short-term interest rates. The three essential attributes of a monetary aggregate which is suitable for targetry - that it predicts future inflation, has a stable velocity and can be controlled by the authorities - seemed to be possessed by M0. Although £M3 was still considered important, it was thought that it might be more useful in guiding the authorities' funding policy than in giving the signals for setting short-term interest rates.

In both the 1984 and 1985 Budgets, M0 and £M3 were given equal weight in the assessment of monetary conditions. Separate target ranges were set for the aggregates, with M0's range two percentage points lower than that for £M3, reflecting historical differences in the trends of velocity of the two aggregates. In 1984/85, M0 grew comfortably within its target range (at the end of the period it had grown by 5.4% compared with a target range of 4-8%) but £M3 overshot its target for the first time since 1981/82 (see Tables 1.3 and 1.5). Despite this relatively satisfactory picture of monetary developments given by the monetary aggregates, the first eighteen months of the Conservatives' second term of office saw two more exchange rate crises - in July 1984 and January 1985. In both, a sharp rise in interest rates occurred as a result of exchange rate weakness. Although for a time in 1984 there was an attempt to downplay the importance of the exchange rate in the assessment of the stance of monetary policy and hence the appropriate level of interest rates, this proved relatively short-lived. By March 1985 Nigel Lawson claimed that 'benign neglect [of the exchange rate] is not an option'.[17]

Figure 1.4: Velocity of MO

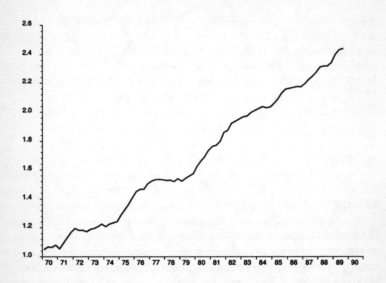

SOURCE : DATASTREAM

The 1985 Budget thus placed new emphasis on the behaviour of the exchange rate as an indicator of the stance of monetary policy. It also made clear the government's forecasts for nominal GDP in the medium term, presenting these alongside the projections for monetary growth. These money GDP projections are shown in Table 1.6.

Although the 1985 Budget gave equal weight to broad and narrow money in the assessment of monetary conditions, by October 1985 the target range for £M3 was suspended. A new target of 11-15% growth was set in the March 1986 Budget: this was well above the earlier MTFS target for that year of 4-8%. However, this higher target range was itself suspended in the Chancellor's October 1986 Mansion House speech. The reasons for this were set out in a speech by the Governor of the Bank of England at Loughborough University[18] and are discussed fully in Chapter 6. The final abandonment of an explicit target range for £M3 in the 1987 Budget left M0 as the only monetary aggregate targeted by the authorities.

Table 1.5: MTFS target ranges for the growth of narrow money, M0 (%)

Target set in:	84/85	85/86	86/87	87/88	88/89	89/90	90/91	91/92	92/93	93/94
Mar 84	4-8	3-7	2-6	1-5	0-4					
Mar 85		3-7	2-6	1-5	0-4					
Mar 86			2-6	2-6	1-5	1-5				
Mar 87				2-6	1-5	1-5	0-4			
Mar 88					1-5	1-5	0-4	0-4		
Mar 89						1-5	0-4	0-4	0-4	
Mar 90							1-5	0-4	0-4	-1-3
Outturn:	5.4	3.4	4.4	5.6	6.1	6.3				

(x) March 1987 to March 1988: 'capping' sterling at DM3.00/£

The demise of broad monetary targeting in the UK coincided with a growing movement internationally to place greater reliance on exchange rate movements in guiding monetary policy decisions. A landmark in this process was the Plaza Accord of September 1985, the primary concern of which was to bring about a further decline in the value of the dollar. This Accord was superseded in February 1987 - once the required fall in the dollar's value had been achieved - by the Louvre Accord which aimed at broad stability of key exchange rates. As far as the UK was concerned, it was the latter agreement which was most influential in the formulation of policy.

Statements by the Chancellor of the Exchequer soon after the meeting of the Group of Six Finance Ministers in Paris between 21 and 22 February gave the strong indication that the authorities were pursuing an unannounced exchange rate target. Immediately after the meeting, which came to be known as the Louvre Accord, Lawson said he did not want sterling 'to fall nor rise substantially' but gave an indication that a fall in sterling's value would be a greater cause for concern than would a rise. On the day after the March 1987 Budget, however, Lawson said that sterling's appreciation since the meeting meant the formulation had changed so that it was no longer as 'lopsided' as between downward and upward shifts. Immediately after the Louvre Accord sterling stood at DM2.82/£; on the day after the Budget at DM2.95/£. The development of policy during this period (which is crucial in understanding the current debate about UK membership of the Exchange Rate Mechanism (ERM) of the European Monetary System) is discussed in detail in Chapter 8.

Table 1.6: MTFS target ranges for the growth of money GDP (%)*

Target set in:	85/86	86/87	87/88	88/89	89/90	90/91	91/92	92/93	93/94
Mar 85	8.50	6.50	5.75	5.00					
Mar 86		6.75	6.50	6.00	5.50				
Mar 87			7.50	6.50	6.00	5.50			
Mar 88				7.50	6.50	6.00	5.50		
Mar 89					8.00	7.50	7.00	6.50	
Mar 90						7.50	6.75	6.25	5.75
Outturn	9.70	6.80	9.80	11.00	8.50				

*Although money GDP forecasts were implicit in earlier versions of the MTFS the 1985 Budget marked the first time these were set down explicitly alongside projections for monetary growth. The money GDP forecasts are not strictly targets: for the 'next' year the number is a forecast; for subsequent years, projections in line with the government's medium term objectives.

Although 1987 saw greater emphasis being placed on the exchange rate, the 1987 *Financial Statement and Budget Report* stated that:[19]

> ...if the underlying growth of M0 threatens to move significantly outside its target range in 1987/88 there is a presumption that the Government will take action on interest rates unless other indicators clearly suggest that monetary conditions remain satisfactory.

As M0 was not threatening to move outside its target and as the exchange rate remained firm (the most important 'other indicator') there was, for some time, no apparent conflict between the two in the message they gave about the stance of monetary policy. During 1987, however, policy became increasingly directed towards maintaining a DM3.00/£ 'cap' on sterling's value.

In October 1987 any potential conflict between the messages from the two indicators on the stance of policy became relatively unimportant as the emphasis of the world's monetary authorities shifted to maintaining financial stability in the face of the global stock market crash. The world wide concern was that a global recession of the type that had been experienced after the stock market crash of 1929 might ensue if monetary policies generally did not become more accommodative. Interest rate reductions in the UK in

November and December 1987 were due predominantly to the desire to avoid recession and the message from the domestic monetary aggregates was temporarily overridden.

(xi) March 1988 to mid-1988: the DM3.00/£ cap is removed but interest rates fall further

Perhaps because of such swift action by the world's central bankers, the threat of such a global recession had significantly receded by early 1988 and in March the DM3.00/£ cap on sterling's value was removed. The immediate reason for abandoning the DM3.00/£ cap was that the scale of foreign exchange intervention required to hold sterling down against the Deutschemark had became unacceptable to the authorities. An alternative way of offsetting the pressure on the exchange rate would have been to allow interest rates to fall again. This, however, would have conflicted with the desired stance of domestic policy. The UK economy grew strongly in 1987 (with real GDP rising by more than 5%); towards the end of the year wages started to rise more quickly and the balance of payments began to deteriorate sharply. Concern about overheating of the economy, which temporarily abated after the stock market crash, resurfaced with a vengeance. The dilemma faced by the authorities at various times over the previous year thus became increasingly acute: domestic factors argued for a rise in interest rates; pressure from international capital flows was for lower rates. Something had to give: in the end, the DM3.00/£ cap rather than the domestic objectives were sacrificed.

Nevertheless, after the cap was removed, sterling appreciated strongly, moving up to a level of DM3.12/£ by the end of March and further reductions in short-term interest rates were made, so that base rates fell to a low point of 7.5% in mid-1988.

(xii) Mid-1988 to end-1989: progressive rise in short-term interest rates

As 1988 progressed, however, domestic considerations took on greater importance in the determination of short-term interest rates. Given rising inflation and a sharp deterioration in the current account position, the government embarked on a progressive rise in short-term interest rates with the ultimate aim of slowing the growth of domestic demand in the economy. Throughout the period, M0 remained above its target range and there was little evidence of a slowing in the growth of broad money or in the pace of lending to the private sector. For some time it appeared that the authorities were attempting to keep sterling's exchange rate against the Deutschemark within an unannounced band. Membership of the ERM of the EMS thus became an important topic for discussion. Indeed, disagreement between the Chancellor of the Exchequer, Nigel Lawson - who favoured entry to the ERM and stabilising sterling's value against the deutschemark - and Sir Alan Walters, the Prime Minister's personal economic adviser - who preferred to rely on domestic indicators to guide policy - led to the resignation of Nigel Lawson in October 1989. The widespread view that his successor, John Major, attached less emphasis to the achievement of exchange rate stability was reinforced by the steady fall in sterling against the deutschemark between the time he took office and the end of the year.

(xiii) Conclusions

What can we learn from this examination of developments in monetary policy during the last thirty years? There are a number of points, which can be mentioned briefly at this stage, and which will be developed further in the remainder of the book. First, there have been relatively few periods during the thirty years without a clearly defined monetary objective, whether in the form of a fixed exchange rate or a monetary target. But periods without such a clearly defined objective have been ones of great difficulty in the management of the economy and have been followed by higher inflation. The period from 1971, when the fixed exchange rate was abandoned, to 1976, when monetary targets were introduced was one such period. Similarly, since 1985 there has been no effective target range for broad money growth and although one has been set for narrow money it does not appear to have been a constraint on policy. Furthermore, the government has not had (with the exception of the period March 1987 to 1988) a firm objective for the exchange rate. It is perhaps no coincidence that this later period also saw a return to higher inflation. An intermediate objective of some sort - whether it be a firm exchange rate or a monetary target - seems to be an essential ingredient of counter-inflation policy.

Second, there have been two periods in which broad money has been seriously affected by structural changes and deregulation in the financial system: 1971 to 1973 and 1980 to 1983. In both periods, the authorities attempted to downplay the importance of developments in broad money, arguing that such structural changes and deregulation made the broad money aggregates difficult to interpret. Both periods, however, saw such financial changes have very real effects on the availability of credit and hence on the behaviour of the real economy. Financial innovation and structural change are no excuse for ignoring the behaviour of money and credit.

Third, narrow money has never provided anything more than a coincident indication of developments in the economy and must be accorded a dubious status as a financial indicator. Fourth, attempts to cap sterling's value at an unannounced rate - as in 1977/78 and 1987/88 - led to reductions in interest rates which did not appear warranted by the behaviour of domestic fundamentals. This suggests that it might be important for any exchange rate objective to be announced although such inconsistencies in policy may, even then, not be avoided. Fifth, controlling the demand for credit in a deregulated financial system may be impossible to achieve by acceptable changes in interest rates. But in a financially sophisticated world, direct controls on credit are unlikely to be effective. This leaves the authorities in a particularly difficult position as far as the control of domestic credit is concerned.

The conclusion must be that an announced target for the exchange rate - which can most appropriately be expressed in terms of a band for sterling within the ERM - may be the only meaningful way of setting guidelines for the conduct of UK monetary policy in the 1990s.

Notes and References

1. Following the Report of the Radcliffe Committee: *Report of the Committee on the Working of the Monetary System*, Command 827, (London: HMSO,1959).
2. Fforde, J.S. 'Setting Monetary Objectives', *Bank of England Quarterly Bulletin*, June 1983, p 202.
3. Fforde, J.S., op. cit., p.203.
4. Fforde, J.S., op. cit., p.203.
5. *Bank of England Quarterly Bulletin*, December 1977, p. 437.
6. Fforde, J.S., op. cit., p.203.
7. *Financial Statement and Budget Report*, 1980/81.
8. *Financial Statement and Budget Report*, 1980/81.
9. *Financial Statement and Budget Report*, 1980/81.
10. *Financial Statement and Budget Report*, 1980/81.
11. 'Monetary Control', Command 7858, (London: HMSO,1980), p.iii.
12. 'Monetary Control', op. cit., p.iv.
13. Lawson, N., 'The Fifth Mais Lecture: The British Experience', (H. M. Treasury, 19 June 1984).
14. *Financial Statement and Budget Report*, 1982/83.
15. *Financial Statement and Budget Report*, 1983/84.
16. Lawson, N., 'The Chancellor's Mansion House Speech', (H. M. Treasury, 20 October 1983).

17. Lawson, N., 'Chancellor of the Exchequer's Budget Statement', (H. M. Treasury, 19 March 1985).

18. Leigh-Pemberton, R., 'Financial Change and Broad Money', speech at Loughborough University, *Bank of England Quarterly Bulletin*, December 1986.

19. *Financial Statement and Budget Report*, 1987-88, paragraph 2.14.

2 Measures of Money in the UK

(i) A range of financial assets with varying degrees of 'moneyness'

There is a wide range of financial assets in the UK which possess, in varying degrees, the characteristics of money. The three functions of money are that it is a unit of account, a store of value and a means of payment. While all financial assets generally considered to be money satisfy the first two criteria, the extent to which they can be used as a means of payment varies. Notes and coin can be used for payment for many, although certainly not all, goods; for larger transactions payment by cheque may be required by the seller. Credit cards have become an increasingly common means of payment, although as they eventually entail the use of some other form of payment (typically a cheque drawn on a bank or building society deposit) their use is not explicitly regarded as a form of money.

A wide range of bank and building society deposits are now chequable, can thus easily be used for making transactions and may be regarded as money. Many of these chequable deposits are now interest bearing. Time deposits - requiring, say, seven days' notice of withdrawal - which were an important component of the broad money supply measures at the start of the 1980s are now much less important. It is such issues which form the subject matter of this chapter.

23

The authorities have long realised that given the range of financial instruments[1]

> ...no single statistical measure of the money supply can be expected fully to encapsulate monetary conditions, and so provide a uniquely correct basis for controlling the complex relationships between monetary growth and prices and nominal incomes.

This point has been well demonstrated by the changes in the monetary measures which have been targeted; and the changing definitions of the various monetary aggregates in response to the structural change and innovation in the financial system which has taken place over the last decade. Perhaps the most striking example of this change is that data for £M3, the measure of the money supply which was targeted between 1976 and 1986, are no longer published.

(ii) Relationships between the monetary aggregates and their components

Figure 2.1, 'Relationships among the monetary aggregates and their components', shows how different definitions of the UK money supply are built up. All measures of the money supply include notes and coin in circulation with the public, perhaps the most liquid financial asset. Wider definitions of money add various types of bank and building society deposits and other liquid financial assets. A distinction is generally made between narrow and broad measures of the money supply, although for the reasons discussed below the division is becoming increasingly difficult to maintain. Narrow measures of the money supply attempt to quantify the amount of money available for transactions purposes whereas the broader aggregates are designed to measure the overall growth of liquidity in the economy.

(iii) Narrow money

M0

M0, the authorities' targeted measure of narrow money, consists mainly of cash - that is, notes and coin in circulation with the general public. Cash is used only to a small extent as a means of saving and thus M0 consists, to a large extent, of money used for transactions purposes. But M0 also includes banks' holdings of cash (termed either 'vault cash' or 'till money') and

Figure 2.1 Relationships among the monetary aggregates and their components

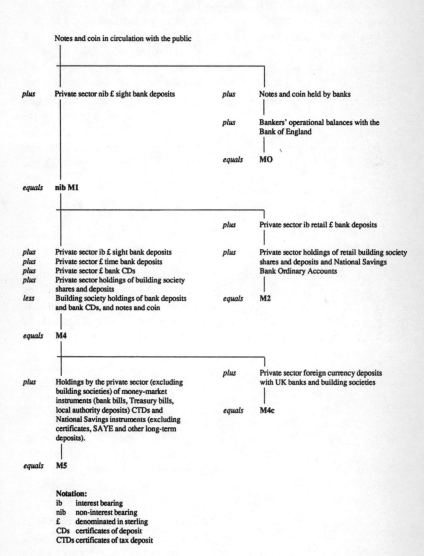

Notes and coin in circulation with the public

plus   Private sector nib £ sight bank deposits   *plus*   Notes and coin held by banks

plus   Bankers' operational balances with the Bank of England

equals   MO

equals   nib M1

plus   Private sector ib retail £ bank deposits

plus   Private sector ib £ sight bank deposits   *plus*   Private sector holdings of retail building society shares and deposits and National Savings Bank Ordinary Accounts
plus   Private sector £ time bank deposits
plus   Private sector £ bank CDs
plus   Private sector holdings of building society shares and deposits
less   Building society holdings of bank deposits and bank CDs, and notes and coin   *equals*   M2

equals   M4

plus   Private sector foreign currency deposits with UK banks and building societies

plus   Holdings by the private sector (excluding building societies) of money-market instruments (bank bills, Treasury bills, local authority deposits) CTDs and National Savings instruments (excluding certificates, SAYE and other long-term deposits).   *equals*   M4c

equals   M5

Notation:
ib   interest bearing
nib   non-interest bearing
£   denominated in sterling
CDs   certificates of deposit
CTDs   certificates of tax deposit

bankers' operational deposits with the Bank of England, two components which are not included in any of the other measures of the UK money supply. As discussed in detail in the next chapter, M0 was devised as a measure of the wide monetary base and it includes all of the possible components of such a measure; that is, it includes all of the monetary liabilities of the Bank of England. Although, when introduced, M0 was not specifically intended to be a measure of money used for transactions purposes, the latter is the role it has come to play in recent years. To understand why this is the case, it is important to be aware of the problems with other measures of narrow money, which are discussed below.

M1 and nib M1

Although M0 may be considered an appropriate measure of transactions balances as it comprises mainly cash, bank sight deposits are probably just as acceptable as a means of payment. Indeed, for large transactions, a cheque drawn on a bank or building society deposit may be more acceptable as a means of payment. Sight deposits can be split into those which bear interest and those which do not. Both types of sight deposit were included in the M1 measure of the money supply but when the Abbey National Building Society became a bank in July 1989, the break in the series for M1 was thought to be so large that the last data published for M1 were for June 1989. As the Abbey National had very few non-interest bearing sight deposits when it changed to being a bank, the break in the series for non-interest bearing M1 (nib M1) was negligible and consequently data for this measure of the money supply are still published.

As many interest bearing sight deposits can readily be used for making transactions, nib M1 cannot capture all of the monetary components used for transactions purposes. Indeed, the introduction of interest bearing current accounts by the large UK retail banks in 1989 has accelerated the shift away from non-interest bearing current accounts which was already under way. As this shift will probably continue in coming years, it is doubtful that nib M1 can play a useful role as a measure of money used for transactions. The particular behavioural difficulties associated with nib M1 and M1 as a result of these changes in the banking system are discussed in the next chapter.

M2

M2 was designed by the authorities as a measure of transactions balances; data were first published in 1982. When deciding on the types of deposit to include in M2, three factors were taken into account.[2] First, to be suitable for transactions, a deposit had to have a reasonably short maturity. Second, in an attempt to exclude deposits which were used primarily for investment rather than transactions purposes, a limit on the size of the deposits included in the aggregate was necessary. Third, the type of deposit should be taken into account. In particular, for a deposit to be suitable for transactions, it should be transferable to third parties on demand or at short notice. The balance of these considerations led to the following components being included in the M2 measure:

(a) notes and coin in circulation with the public (including holdings by building societies);
(b) non-interest bearing sight deposits held with banks by the UK private sector (including building societies' holdings);
(c) other deposits held with banks and building societies by the UK private sector of less than £100,000 having a residual maturity of less than one month, or for which less than one month's notice of withdrawal is required;
(d) deposits in National Savings Bank Ordinary Accounts.

Several problems have emerged with this definition of M2.[3] M2 is based on the principle that a transactions aggregate should not be restricted to the liabilities of any particular set of institutions but in practice the vast majority of transactions balances are held with banks and building societies. This raises the question of whether it might be best to make M2 a subset of M4. This would involve the exclusion of two types of deposit from M2: building societies' holdings of notes and coin and of non-interest bearing bank deposits, and National Savings Bank Ordinary Accounts. The exclusion of these two would make little material difference to the statistics for M2.

Another problem with M2 is that in terms of size it is closer to the broad measure M4 than the narrow measure M0 (see Table 2.1). More fundamentally, M2 has come to behave more like a measure of broad money than narrow money. It includes, for example, the high interest cheque accounts which have become increasingly popular with the personal sector. These were introduced by the banks in 1985 - well before the interest bearing current accounts discussed above. The accounts typically involve a minimum balance being maintained and there may also be a minimum withdrawal size. With such accounts, the cheque book provides the facility to make instant payments without notice of withdrawal; in this respect the deposits have the characteristic of money used for transactions purposes. But at the same time the deposits typically pay a rate of interest which is little lower than that paid on time deposits which are included only in broader measures of the money

supply such as M4. The result is that M2 includes deposits which are likely
to be for savings purposes even though the deposits can be easily used for
making transactions.

Table 2.1: Monetary aggregates, amounts outstanding
at the end of 1989

	£ billions
Narrow Measures	
Cash in circulation with the public	18.8
M0	19.0
nib M1	47.9
M2	238.5
Broad Measures	
M4	422.9
M4c	468.9
M5	439.8

The Bank of England is currently in the process of deciding whether, given
that transactions balances are becoming harder to define, there may be other
'narrow' measures of money that would be of interest. One, a Divisia
measure, is discussed later. The other two are a personal sector aggregate and
a 'retail' aggregate.

Although the definition of M2 makes no explicit reference to the sectoral
classification of the holders of the deposit the delineation of the account
facilities and the size limit ensure that the majority of deposits included in
M2 are personal sector deposits. This could be made explicit, with deposits
by companies - both industrial and commercial companies and financial
institutions other than banks and building societies - excluded from the
measure. In the light of evidence that the behaviour of deposits held by
companies does not bear a stable relationship with money GDP, such an
exclusion could be justified on economic grounds.[4] An alternative would be
to develop a 'retail' aggregate which would comprise small deposits, as
opposed to large deposits placed in the money markets. Such a distinction is
already made by the building societies because of the 1988 Building Society
Act's restriction on the raising of non-retail funds. Although a similar
distinction is made for bank deposits, the definition of 'retail' is not the same
as that made by the building societies.

It is most unlikely that either option would provide an accurate measure of money used for transactions purposes; indeed, it seems unlikely that it will ever be possible separately to identify such a class of assets. This does not mean that an aggregate based on either of these two considerations will not be useful. It may be that it is possible to construct a measure which does have a stable relationship with economic variables - specifically money GDP, interest rates and future inflation. Whether such a relationship, if found, would prove robust in a future which will undoubtedly be characterised by continued innovation in the financial system must be in question.

Explaining the demand for narrow money

Given these problems with M2, it is most likely that the authorities will continue to use M0 as their preferred measure of narrow money and the one for which a target range is set. M0 is as far away as possible from this blurring of the boundaries between money used for transactions purposes and money used as a store of liquid financial wealth and although it has been influenced by financial innovation this seems to have had a rather more predictable influence on M0 than other measures of narrow money. M0, or more specifically just the large part of it which is cash in circulation with the public, has another key feature. No attempt has been, or will be, made to influence the amount of cash in circulation from the supply side: the amount of cash in crculation is determined entirely by the demand for it. This means that, when estimating an equation for M0, one can be confident that one is identifying the demand for M0. Consequently, the analysis of the behaviour of M0 - which forms the subject of the next chapter - is quite different to the analysis of other measures of money.

(iv) Broad money

M4

M4 is currently the most widely used measure of the broad money supply. It comprises the following sterling denominated instruments held by the 'M4 private sector' (that is, all UK residents apart from the public sector, banks and building societies): notes and coin; bank deposits; and building society shares and deposits (including bank and building society sterling CDs and other issues of sterling paper up to five years' original maturity).

As M4 includes deposits with building societies it was unaffected by the conversion of the Abbey National Building Society to a bank in July 1989.

M5

M5 is the broadest measure of the money supply. It comprises all the components of M4 plus holdings by the M4 private sector of money market instruments (bank bills, Treasury bills, local authority deposits), CTDs and National Savings instruments (excluding certificates, SAYE and other long-term deposits).

Although M4 and M5 include a wide variety of deposits, they must be considered vulnerable to further change in the financial system. Indeed, this very point was made by the Bank of England at the time the M4 and M5 measures were introduced:[5]

> The institutional basis underlying M4 gives that aggregate the advantage - in comparison with M5 - of greater simplicity and comprehensibility, as well as enabling it to be subjected more easily to a counterpart analysis similar to that long applied to £M3. But M4 is vulnerable, as £M3 has been seen to be, to the switching of funds between assets included in the aggregate and close substitutes which lie outside it - whether they be of the sort included in M5, or other, possibly newer, ones which are not. M5, while unaffected by the former type of switch, is equally vulnerable to the latter. There is likely, given the current pace of innovation and change in the financial system, to be no shortage of new assets competing for attention. Sterling commercial paper is one such; various forms of packaged security, including those offered by new institutions entering the mortgage market to compete with both banks and building societies, could easily provide others. The inescapable conclusion is that there can be no unique definition of broad money. Any choice of dividing line between those financial assets included in, and those excluded from, broad money is to a degree arbitrary, and is likely over time to be invalidated by developments in the financial system.

M4c

M4c differs from the other measures of the UK money supply in that it adds to M4 deposits in currencies other than sterling placed with UK banks and building societies by the rest of the UK private sector. When exchange controls were in force it was known that the large bulk of such foreign currency deposits held by UK residents were related to transactions by the holders in other countries and therefore were not likely to be particularly closely related to economic activity in the UK. Since the removal of exchange controls, UK residents may have used such deposits for investment as well as transactions purposes and therefore there may be a stronger case for including them within the broad definitions of the UK money supply. Nevertheless, there still remain two reasons for exclusion. First, the sterling value of such foreign currency deposits is uncertain and, indeed, if there was a substantial switch out of foreign currency deposits into sterling an unfavourable exchange rate movement would be generated. Second, foreign currency deposits with banks abroad are not included in the UK monetary aggregates even though, to the holder, there may be little difference between such deposits and foreign currency deposits held with a UK bank.

This raises the broader issue of whether it is only sterling deposits held with UK banks which should be included in measures of the UK money supply. It may be that sterling deposits held by UK residents with banks overseas should also be included. The types of deposit which might be regarded as suitable for inclusion in a definition of the money supply can be characterised on the basis of: the currency of denomination; the residence of the depositor; and the location of the deposit taker. An eight fold classification of deposits can thus be set out, as in Figure 2.2.

On this basis, M4 consists of box (1) only; M4c adds together boxes (1) and (5). A worldwide sterling aggregate would comprise boxes (1), (2), (3) and (4). An aggregate consisting of UK residents' holdings worldwide and in any currency would comprise boxes (1), (2), (5) and (6). It may also be desirable to construct European Community based aggregates. In this case a

Figure 2.2: Classification of bank deposits

Currency	Sterling				Foreign currency			
Depositor's residence	UK		Overseas		UK		Overseas	
Deposit-taker's location	UK (1)	O'seas (2)	UK (3)	O'seas (4)	UK (5)	O'seas (6)	UK (7)	O'seas (8)

three-way distinction would have to be made between UK, other EC and non-EC for currency, residence and location.

The supply of, and demand for, broad money

Attempts to identify the demand for broad money, in a way similar to that described above for M0, consistently failed during the 1970s and 1980s. This can be explained by two factors. First, with the broad measures of the money supply one can never be sure that one is identifying the demand for broad money: broad money has been affected to an important degree by changes in conditions affecting the supply of money. Second, the demand for credit was, for most of this period, the dominant influence on the size of banks' and building societies' balance sheets.

M4 consists of notes and coin in circulation with the public and sterling deposits of the UK private sector with the banks and the building societies. These deposits form part of the total liabilities of the banks and the building societies. By definition, total assets must equal total liabilities: assets consist mainly of loans to other sectors of the economy. As banks' and building societies' balance sheets must balance, the level of deposits included within M4 can be expressed as the difference between the banks' and building societies' total assets and those liabilities in the balance sheet which are not included in the measurement of M4. Both sides of the banks' and building societies' balance sheets are subject to change by other sectors of the economy. For example, banks may receive new deposits, increasing the size of their liabilities or customers may draw down their overdraft facilities, thus increasing bank lending and the assets side of the banks' balance sheet. Banks will adjust their balance sheet in order to accommodate such changes.

The process whereby the banks adjust their deposit rates in order to bring their liabilities into line with their assets is known as liability management. The process whereby they adjust their lending rates and conditions in order to keep their assets side in line with their liabilities is known as asset management. Clearly, asset and liability management can, and do, occur simultaneously. However, at least since the late 1960s, and particularly since the inauguration of competition and credit control in 1971, liability management appears to have dominated asset management. In particular, deposit creation by the banks appears to have been primarily determined by the demand for credit, rather than the supply of credit being determined by the private sector's willingness to make deposits with the banks. The ability of the banks to attract deposits to fund their lending was facilitated in the 1970s by the creation of the certificate of deposit (CD) market.

The building societies typically asset managed during the 1970s, but since the start of the 1980s they too have been able to liability manage. The move of the banks into the market for residential mortgages in the early 1980s and the associated break up of the building societies' cartel which set interest rates for the industry marked the start of a shift to liability management. Building societies now have the facility to bid for wholesale deposits (again largely in the form of CDs) and mortgage queues and rationing (typical of the asset management era) have largely disappeared.

With banks and building societies' balance sheets now largely driven from the liabilities side, the analysis of broad money developments in the UK has centred not so much on the behaviour of the deposits included in the measurement of M4 but rather on its credit counterparts. The way in which these are constructed is relatively straightforward: the combined balance sheet of the banks and building societies can be viewed as consisting of the M4 deposits plus other liabilities of the banks and building societies on the one side which must equal total assets on the other. M4 can thus be viewed as the simple difference between total assets and non-M4 liabilities. Expressing the combined balance sheet in this way and then expressing the public sector's demand for credit from the banks and building societies as the residual of its borrowing requirement and other sources of finance gives the so-called 'counterparts to M4'. M4 is expressed as the PSBR *minus* sales of government debt to the UK private sector and overseas *plus* the change in the foreign exchange reserves *plus* the private sector's demand for credit from the banks and the building societies *plus* external and foreign currency flows and changes in non-deposit liabilities (the counterparts to broad money are explained in detail in Chapter 4).

Although the counterparts identity is just a statistical artefact based on these relationships, it has come to be of central importance in the analysis of developments in the broad money supply. It provides a framework in which fiscal policy (the size of the public sector borrowing requirement or debt repayment), the extent to which government borrowing is financed outside the monetary sector (i.e. funding policy), the expansion of the private sector's demand for credit and the change in the foreign exchange reserves (reflecting foreign exchange policy) can be brought together in one summary statistic (the growth of M4).

Some of the difficulties encountered with this counterparts approach to broad money are investigated in Chapter 6 whilst funding policy is discussed in Chapter 5.

(v) Divisia money

All measures of the money supply published by the Bank of England are constructed as simple sums of their various components. As has been demonstrated, however, this gives rise to considerable difficulty in deciding on an appropriate dividing line between narrow money used for transactions purposes and broad money, which also includes financial assets more likely to be used as a means of saving.

One approach to this issue which has been put forward is to add together the different monetary components, but with 'weights' attached to each component depending on how 'money-like' it is. For example, notes and coin in circulation with the public could be given a weight of one; non-interest bearing sight deposits a weight of 0.9; interest bearing sight deposits 0.7; and so on, so that assets least likely to be used for transactions purposes (for example, some types of National Savings included in M5) could be given only a small weight.

Three different methods have been put forward for assessing the weights. First, on the basis of the estimated 'user cost' measured, at its simplest, by the interest rate differential between that on the monetary component in question and that on an illiquid savings instrument: this gives an estimate of the lost return involved in holding that particular asset. Second, weights can be assessed on the basis of the turnover of the individual components, thus giving an indication of the extent to which they are used for transactions purposes. Third, weights can be assessed on a judgemental basis, taking into account whatever information is available from the first two sources.

In theory such Divisia based measures of the money supply are capable of providing a better reflection of the behaviour of liquidity in the economy, but there are five practical objections. First, the weights attached to each component may have to be changed regularly. Second, new components, with new weights, may have to be added if the Divisia measure is not to suffer the same drawbacks associated with simple sum measures. Third, the Divisia money supply measures would not be as easily understood, complicating the presentation of monetary policy. Fourth, such measures would not lend themselves easily to analysis within a counterparts framework. Fifth, if weights were based on the user cost method then a rise in interest rates will immediately increase the user cost of holding non-interest bearing monetary components. If, as seems likely, the shift out of such deposits is relatively slow then the Divisia money supply measure would give an immediate impression of a monetary tightening.

Notes and References

1. 'Monetary Control', Command 7858, (London: HMSO, 1980), piii.
2. 'Transactions Balances - A New Monetary Aggregate', *Bank of England Quarterly Bulletin*, June 1982, pp. 224-5.
3. Much of the discussion of the problems with the current definitions of the monetary aggregates is based on 'Monetary Aggregates in a Changing Environment', *Bank of England Discussion Paper*, Number 47 (March 1990).
4. See 'Financial Change and Broad Money', *Bank of England Quarterly Bulletin*, December 1986, pp. 499-507 for a discussion of the sectoral behaviour of deposits.
5. 'Measures of Broad Money', *Bank of England Quarterly Bulletin*, May 1987, p. 219.

3 Analysing Narrow Money

When monetary targets were first introduced in the UK they were formulated in terms of the growth of broad money. The Medium Term Financial Strategy (MTFS) at first continued to give broad money a central role, but by 1982 the presentation of the MTFS was modified to include a specific role for a narrow money target. Between 1982 and 1984 the same target ranges were applied to three monetary measures: narrow money (M1); broad money (£M3); and a broad measure of liquidity (PSL2). Furthermore, the authorities came to stress more strongly the importance of the examination of a range of financial and economic variables when judging the stance of monetary policy. These included such variables as the exchange rate, asset prices and the behaviour of inflation itself.

When Nigel Lawson was appointed Chancellor of the Exchequer in the summer of 1983, immediately after the return of the Conservative party to a second term of office, he embarked upon a review of the MTFS. The result of Lawson's review seemed to produce a movement back from this more pragmatic approach to one which placed primary reliance on the behaviour of monetary aggregates. The aim of policy remained, of course, to continue reducing inflation so as to create the conditions for a sustainable growth of output in the medium term. Lawson aimed to draw a clear distinction between the uses of both 'broad' and 'narrow' measures of money in the assessment of policy. Thus, Lawson stated in his Mansion House speech on 20 October 1983:[1]

... policy decisions have to be taken with an eye to both the
growth of liquidity in the economy - as shown by the broader
measures of money - and to the amount of money immediately
available for current transactions - as shown by the narrower
aggregates.

Formal recognition of this came in the 1984 Budget when two different
target ranges were set: one for broad money (£M3) of 6-10% and one for
narrow money (M0) of 4-8%. During the course of 1984 it became
increasingly clear that the behaviour of these two monetary aggregates was
of paramount importance in the authorities' thinking - especially in their
attitude to the appropriate level of short-term interest rates. In particular, the
authorities resisted rises in interest rates at times of exchange rate weakness
(especially in July and October 1984) on the basis that the behaviour of
domestic monetary indicators was satisfactory. Commenting in his Mansion
House speech on 18 October 1984 on the determination of short-term interest
rates, Lawson said:[2]

> ... [the markets] have come to recognise that it is the monetary
> aggregates that are of central relevance to judging monetary
> conditions and determining interest rates. That has always
> been our policy, and it remains so. We take the exchange rate
> into account when its behaviour suggests that the domestic
> monetary indicators are giving a false reading, which they are
> not.

Furthermore, it was the narrower measures of money (particularly M0)
which appeared to be the most useful in giving signals for setting short-term
interest rates (a subject which Lawson had discussed in his Mansion House
speech in the previous year).

When deciding on the switch from M1 to M0 as the target measure of
narrow money, it was thought that M0 possessed four key attributes:

(a) it was not distorted by changes in the banking system, which rendered
     the interpretation of other monetary aggregates difficult. Although the
     behaviour of M0 was influenced by changes in the usage of cash, these
     changes appeared to be reasonably stable and predictable. In the cir-
     cumstances of the early 1980s it appeared the most appropriate defini-
     tion of transactions balances to use;

(b) it appeared to provide leading information about the behaviour of
     inflation;

(c) its behaviour was readily explicable by the behaviour of a number of
     other economic and financial variables - its 'demand was stable';
(d) it appeared controllable by acceptable variations in short-term interest
     rates.

Each of these points is examined in turn in the following four sections,
followed by a discussion of the counterparts to M0 and the issue of monetary
base control.

(i) M0 as a measure of transactions balances

When deciding on the switch to M0 as the target measure of the narrow
money supply, the aim of the authorities was to obtain as reliable a measure
as possible of money used for transactions purposes. As discussed in Chapter
2, M0 (as it includes only cash in circulation with the public and that held by
banks as well as bankers' operational deposits at the Bank of England which
are readily convertible into cash) is at the narrowest end of the range of
monetary measures. It certainly does not include all money which is used for
transactions purposes but, equally, it is only used to a small extent for savings
purposes. When the choice was made as to the most appropriate measure for
targeting, there were thought to be particular difficulties with the interest
bearing element of M1 which rendered it largely unsuitable for inclusion in
a measure of transactions balances. Up until the early 1980s, interest bearing
sight deposits accounted for a fairly constant proportion of M1. These were
considered to be primarily large overnight balances belonging to companies
or financial institutions. In many cases these balances were likely to be
awaiting investment in other instruments (for example, gilt edged stock). It
is arguable that, as such, they ought to have been excluded from a transactions
measure of money.

In the early 1980s the problems of interpreting this interest bearing
element were further compounded by a rapid rise in its share of total sight
deposits. According to Johnston[3], the increase came from two sources:
wholesale deposits; and retail interest earning sight deposits (until the early
1980s thought to have been only a very small proportion of the total). In both
cases a transfer of deposits both from non-interest bearing sight deposits and
from more illiquid interest bearing deposits was likely to have taken place.
To the extent that the first type of shift occurred, M1 would not be distorted.
The shift from non-interest bearing to interest bearing deposits within the
total raises the average rate of interest paid on such deposits and this makes
the total less sensitive to movements in the absolute level of interest rates. In
these circumstances of structural change, the overall effect of a change in

interest rates on the demand for M1 becomes indeterminate. To the extent that the second type of shift occurred (i.e. a shift into sight deposits from interest bearing deposits) the broader measures of money may also have been affected. If funds were attracted into bank deposits and out of other assets, the overall growth of M4 would have been faster (although some of the shift would have reflected a shift between deposits within M4).

These problems with M1 and nib M1 were thought seriously to undermine their suitability for targeting. Moreover, Treasury research showed the demand for nib M1 was quite unstable, consistent with the view that nib M1 was being distorted by the growth of interest bearing M1. With the limited amount of data available for M2, the only narrow monetary aggregate suitable for targeting in early 1984 was M0. There was, however, some discussion of the possibility of using just notes and coin in circulation with the public rather than M0. Although the levels of bankers' operational deposits and banks' till money were small, their changes over the course of a month could be very large and greatly increase the volatility of monthly M0 data compared with notes and coin in circulation with the public. Even though the measurement of M0 was changed in order to dampen this volatility (by calculating the monthly data for M0 as the average of the weekly data within the month) the question still remained of why these additional elements were included in the authorities' measure of narrow money. This was reinforced by the fact that the econometric properties of notes and coin seemed to be rather more reliable than those of M0. One reason which was advanced was that the inclusion of bankers' operational deposits would ease the path towards a system of monetary base control. Under such a system, these deposits would have an important role to play. (Monetary base control is discussed in more detail in section (iii)). A second reason was the purely presentational one that M0 actually sounded like a monetary aggregate whereas notes and coin in circulation did not.

Since the choice of M0 as the targeted measure of narrow money in 1983/84, there has been little to encourage a switch to targeting another measure of narrow money. As discussed in Chapter 2, data for M1 are no longer published, nib M1 continues to be seriously affected by innovation in the financial system (especially the recent introduction of interest bearing cheque accounts) and M2 has come to behave more like a measure of broad money than of narrow money.

(ii) M0 and inflation

Commenting in his 1983 Mansion House speech, Lawson said:[4]

... it was the surge in the narrow aggregates in 1977 which was followed by the surge in inflation in 1979. And the deceleration in the growth of narrow money in 1979 and 1980 preceded the recent decline in inflation.

This relationship is shown in Figure 3.1. For some time in the UK, the extent to which developments in money provide leading information about the behaviour of inflation has been a subject of heated debate. In part, the original choice of M3 in 1976 was influenced by the fact that in the early 1970s it appeared to give leading information about the behaviour of inflation. As Figure 1.2 shows, there is a close correlation between M3 in 1972-73 and the subsequent surge in inflation in 1974-75. The rise in inflation was, of course, to a large extent due to the rise in oil prices and for this reason the correlation may be spurious. Perhaps largely because of this correlation, studies examining the relation between monetary aggregates and inflation in the 1960s and 1970s generally came up with the conclusion that broader measures of money were better predictors of future inflation.[5]

Figure 3.1: M0 and inflation, 1976 to 1983
The experience of the late 1970s and early 1980s provided contrary indications. As noted above, the narrow aggregates now appeared to give the best information about subsequent inflation. But just as the £M3/inflation relationship in the early 1970s may have been largely spurious, so might this

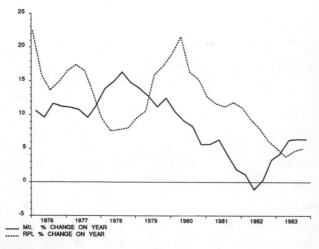

MO, % CHANGE ON YEAR
RPI, % CHANGE ON YEAR

SOURCE : DATASTREAM

relationship between the narrow aggregates and inflation in the later period. Examining the relationship between narrow money and inflation over a longer time period (Figure 3.2) shows little sign of a correlation in earlier periods. Indeed, narrow money growth appeared to be most closely correlated with inflation in the same time period: it was a coincident rather than a leading indicator of inflation. Furthermore, the surge in inflation in 1979 referred to by Lawson, was, to a large extent, the result of the switch from direct to indirect taxation in the 1979 Budget and the second oil price shock. Mills and Stephenson[6] found that, after allowing for these two effects, M0's behaviour actually gave misleading information about future inflation. Nevertheless, the Treasury did feel confident in the role of M0.

Figure 3.2: M0 and inflation, 1970 to 1990

Since the introduction of targets for M0, the relationship between its behaviour and that of future inflation has not been particularly close. One common criticism is that the behaviour of M0 gave no leading indication of the rise in inflation which took place in 1988 and 1989. As can be seen from Figure 3.3, M0 was well within its target for the first four years (with the one

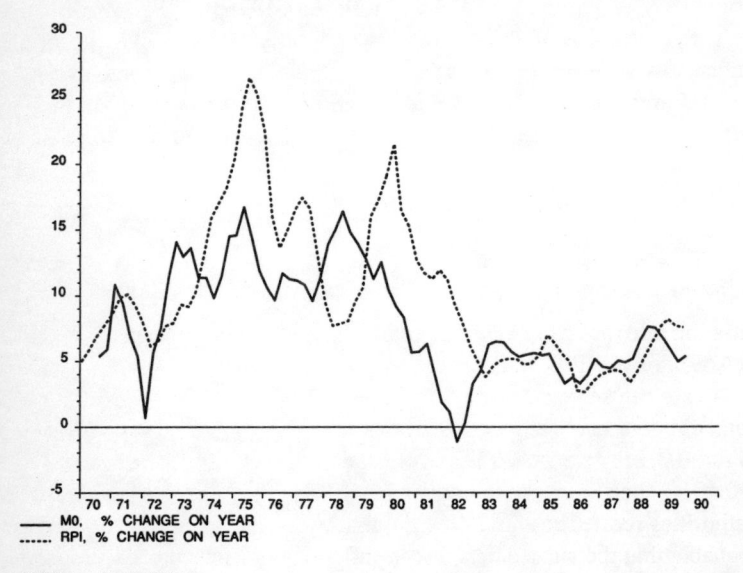

MO, % CHANGE ON YEAR
...... RPI, % CHANGE ON YEAR

SOURCE : DATASTREAM

exception of November 1985 when growth temporarily dropped below the 3% lower limit). M0 first exceeded target in April 1988 when its growth rate rose to 6.3% compared with its 1-5% target range: it then stayed above target (with the one exception of September 1989).[7]

Figure 3.3: M0 and target range

By the time M0 exceeded its target range, however, inflation had already risen. The year-on-year increase in the retail prices index rose from a low point of 2.4% in July and August 1986 to 3.9% in April 1988 and then to 8.3% in May and June 1989; excluding mortgage interest payments the

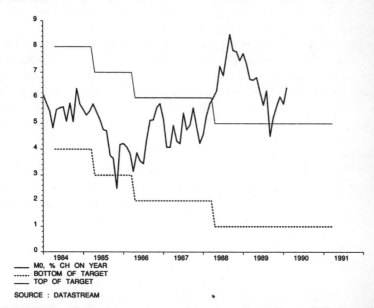

MO, % CH ON YEAR
BOTTOM OF TARGET
TOP OF TARGET

SOURCE : DATASTREAM

inflation rate rose from a low point of 3.1% (also in July and August 1986) to 4.3% in April 1988 and to over 6% in early 1990.

A case can be made for saying that the behaviour of M0 within its target band did give advance warning of this rise in inflation. Again, referring to Figure 3.3, M0 rose above the mid-point of its target range in September 1986 - that is, shortly after the low point in inflation was reached. Had the authorities reacted to this faster growth by raising interest rates then it is arguable that the subsequent rise in inflation could have been moderated, even avoided. Moreover, other indicators also suggested that monetary conditions had become looser (see Chapter 10). The growth rate of M4 rose from 13.3% year-on-year in September 1985 to 15.4% by September 1986;

the exchange rate fell from 102 to 85.5 (index measure) and from DM3.76/£ to DM2.93/£ over the same period; and base rates had been cut from 11.5% to 10% even though inflationary expectations had worsened. There was a one percentage point increase in base rates in October 1986 but that was reversed by March 1987 and base rates fell to 9% in May of that year.

(iii) Explaining the behaviour of M0

If there was some doubt about M0's ability to predict future inflation, concern about the extent to which its behaviour could be explained was even more acute. Shortly before the Chancellor began to comment on the merits of M0, the Bank of England had published an article which had concluded that 'structural changes imply that movements in cash are unlikely to be helpful as a guide to general economic or financial conditions'.[8] As cash comprises the largest part of M0 (98½%, on average, in 1989/90), the inference that targeting M0 would make little sense was easy to draw. The Bank found that the demand for cash could not be easily explained by reference to other economic variables; indeed, its forecasts had consistently overestimated the demand for cash for a number of years. Johnston's Treasury working paper[9] came to the different conclusion that a satisfactory explanation of M0's behaviour could be achieved by reference to a few key economic variables. Moreover, in contrast to the Bank of England's study, the Treasury found that M0 was sensitive to interest rate movements. We summarise below the arguments concerning M0's behaviour.

Bank of England explanations of M0 behaviour

The Bank work on changes in the use of cash started with the observation that there appeared to be a break in the trend of the ratio of consumers' expenditure to cash in 1978. Between 1963 and the end of 1978 the value of consumers' expenditure rose at an average annual rate of 11½% while cash increased by about 9½%. In the three years after that date, however, the average rates of growth were 11% and 5% respectively. A number of possible explanations were considered. First, that high nominal interest rates had led to economisation of cash balances. Second, that rising unemployment might have been important. 'Those becoming unemployed might have previously used cash to a greater extent than average and the lower level of unemployment benefits might thus have reduced the demand for cash'.[10] Third, the exchange rate might influence cash demand. 'In some small part this may be because of speculative demand, with exchange rate expectations playing a role. In addition, a large migrant population making transfer payments abroad and the increasing popularity of foreign travel may help to explain this effect'.[11] Fourth, was the increased use of banking services. In the late 1970s and early 1980s, the movement away from cash as a method of paying wages and salaries and as a medium for making consumer payments seemed to gain momentum.

These four factors influencing cash demand were considered in some detail in the Bank study. The factor which seemed to have the most important role to play in explaining the reduction in the demand for cash from 1978 onwards was the latter one - the increase in the use of banking services. Although this appeared to be the most important factor, data on the change in the use of banking services were severely limited; and in the Bank's econometric equations for the demand for cash, the variables which were used to try to measure this effect did not prove to have a significant explanatory power. In the Bank's equations the unemployment rate proved to be the only additional variable of the four mentioned above which provided any significant amount of extra information about the behaviour of cash. However, even allowing for this, cash holdings could not be forecast particularly accurately.

The Treasury's study of M0's behaviour

The Treasury paper by Johnston developed the Bank work, aiming to obtain rather more satisfactory measures of the changes in the use of banking services. In Johnston's equations for the demand for cash and M0, four variables were constructed in an attempt to measure the increasing spread of the 'banking habit':

(a) the number of current accounts relative to the total population;
(b) the number of building society share accounts relative to the total population;
(c) the total number of cash dispensers;
(d) the total number of credit card account holders.

Johnston found that trends in the velocity of cash and M0 were, in fact, closely related to the trends in financial innovation as measured by these variables (in particular, the per capita number of current accounts and building society accounts). Moreover, econometric equations including these terms proved capable of providing reasonable forecasts (in contrast to the Bank's equations). Johnston's equations for M0 included interest rate terms and he found that 'the response of both notes and coin to changes in interest rates is modest, significant, and reasonably stable in equations fitted to recent time periods'. A new equation, based on Johnston's work, was introduced into the Treasury's macroeconomic model of the UK economy:[12] this had the property that the demand for cash fell by around 0.25% in the same quarter as the three month interbank rate rose by one percentage point, with the effect rising to a 1% reduction in cash demand after one year and a 2% reduction in the long run. The maximum size of the long run effect detected in the Bank study had been just less than 1%, but they had found that in many periods the effect was close to zero and not statistically significant.

Subsequent work on the Treasury model has resulted in an equation which has the following (long run) properties:

(a) a 1% rise in real consumers' expenditure produces a 1% rise in the amount of cash in circulation. The measure of consumers' expenditure chosen excludes both expenditure on durable goods and on services - this is sensible given that purchases of the latter are unlikely to be paid for with cash;

(b) a 1% rise in prices leads to a 1% rise in the amount of cash in circulation. The price measure used is the consumers' expenditure deflator. Properties (a) and (b) together imply that a 1% rise in nominal consumers' expenditure produces a 1% rise in cash in circulation;

(c) an increased number of cash dispensers increases, by a very small amount, the amount of cash in circulation. The small coefficient is not surprising given that it is not clear, *a priori*, whether cash dispensers increase the amount of cash in circulation (by encouraging the use of cash rather than other means of payment) or reduce it (because it allows lower inventories of cash to be held);

(d) a decrease in the number of manual workers in relation to the total working population reduces the amount of cash in circulation as manual workers are more likely to be paid in cash;

(e) a one percentage point rise in post-tax short-term interest rates reduces the amount of cash in circulation by 1%.

The interest rate effect on the demand for M0 is thus smaller than in Johnston's original equation.

(iv) Controlling M0 by interest rate changes

The question of whether or not econometric methods are capable of providing a sufficiently accurate explanation of M0 becomes crucial when the question of controllability is considered.

Cash is supplied passively on demand by the Bank of England to the banks and, similarly, by the banks to the general public. No attempt is made to control the supply of cash. Such a method of control would involve major changes in the way in which the Bank of England operates and would, to say the least, undermine confidence in the currency. Thus, control of cash depends on the ability to control the demand for cash and thus the explanations of cash demand (discussed in the previous section) take on particular importance. Specifically, it is the interest rate effect which is the most significant for policy purposes. The long run properties of the latest Treasury equation imply that if M0 is growing at, say 7%, then in order to bring it back to the middle of a 1-5% target range by means of interest rate changes, a 400 basis point rise in post-tax short-term rates would be needed. To achieve such a rise in the post-tax short-term deposit rate would require a 530 basis point rise in base rates.

How does a rise in interest rates influence the demand for cash? The most direct effect likely is switching from cash to other monetary assets. Intuitively, however, it seems unlikely that any marked economisation of cash balances occurs in response to a rise in interest rates. Indirectly, of course, higher interest rates, through their depressing influence on overall economic activity, would be expected to lead to a reduction in the demand for cash. The combination of these two effects should be picked up by the parameters in both the Bank's and the Treasury's equations (in econometric terminology, these equations are 'reduced forms'). If we are correct in thinking that the direct 'asset switching' effect of a rise in interest rates on M0 is unlikely to be particularly strong, the conclusion is that an interest rate rise produces a slowdown in monetary growth by depressing economic activity. This seems a rather curious approach to using a monetary target.

(v) The counterparts to M0

An alternative is not to control M0 directly, but rather to control the counterparts to this aggregate. The approach would be similar to that used for analysing M4.

Expression of M0 in terms of its counterparts comes from the manipulation of the three following identities.

Definition of M0

M0 is the sum of notes and coin in circulation with the public including that held by banks (NAC) and bankers' operational balances held with the Bank of England (BB)

i.e. $\qquad$ M0 $\quad = \quad$ NAC + BB $\dots\dots\dots\dots\dots\dots\dots\dots$ (1a)

Furthermore, the change (Δ) in M0 must equal the change in its two components:

i.e. $\qquad$ ΔM0 $\quad = \quad$ ΔNAC + ΔBB $\dots\dots\dots\dots\dots\dots\dots$ (1b)

CGBR Financing Identity

The Central Government Borrowing Requirement (CGBR) can be financed by: (a) an increase in notes and coin in circulation (ΔNAC); (b) sales of central government debt to the banks, non-bank private sector or overseas sector net of Bank of England purchases of bills (CGD); (c) by a rundown of the foreign currency reserves (ΔRES) - selling foreign currency held in the Exchange Equalisation Account (EEA) and using the proceeds to repay outstanding government debt will reduce the amount of government debt sales needed to finance a given CGBR; or (d) other net sterling and foreign currency borrowing (CGOT)

i.e. $\qquad$ CGBR $\quad = \quad$ ΔNAC + CGD - ΔRES + CGOT $\dots\dots$ (2a)

or $\qquad$ ΔNAC $\quad = \quad$ CGBR - CGD + ΔRES - CGOT. $\dots\dots$ (2b)

Bank of England Banking Department's Balance Sheet

The liabilities of the Banking Department must equal its assets. For simplicity, we shall say that liabilities consist of bankers' operational deposits (BB), cash ratio deposits (CRD) and all other liabilities (OL). Total assets are referred to as BDA. So:

$\qquad\qquad$ BB + CRD + OL $\quad = \quad$ BDA $\dots\dots\dots\dots\dots\dots\dots$ (3a)

and $\qquad$ ΔBB + ΔCRD + ΔOL $\quad = \quad$ ΔBDA $\dots\dots\dots\dots\dots\dots$ (3b)

or $\qquad\qquad\qquad$ ΔBB $\quad = \quad$ ΔBDA - ΔCRD - ΔOL $\dots\dots\dots$ (3c)

Substituting expressions (2b) and (3c) into equation (1b) gives:

$$\Delta \text{MO} = \text{CGBR} - \text{CGD} + \Delta\text{RES} - \text{CGOT} + \Delta\text{BDA} - \Delta\text{CRD} - \Delta\text{OL}$$

That is, the increase in M0 is equal to the central government's borrowing requirement *minus* sales of central government debt to banks, non-banks and overseas (net of Bank purchases of bills) *plus* the change in foreign currency reserves (and the remaining counterparts which will, in practice, be less important).

Viewing M0 in this way highlights the fact that the change in M0 depends on the extent to which shortages in the money market - reflecting the CGBR minus sales of government debt and the change in the foreign currency reserves - are offset by Bank of England purchases of bills. The framework might be useful with a system designed to control banks' operational deposits: the Swiss, for example, use a similar type of approach when analysing the monetary base. We discuss such systems of monetary base control in the next section.

(vi) Monetary Base Control

The amount of cash in circulation is determined entirely by the public's demand for it and it would be unrealistic for the authorities to try to influence the amount of cash in circulation by restricting supply. There is, however, the possibility of controlling the level of bankers' balances from the supply side.

Two types of bankers' balances (or deposits) are kept at the Bank. The first type, cash ratio deposits, are non-interest bearing deposits which all institutions in the monetary sector must keep with the Bank. They are essentially a tax on the members of the monetary sector and are designed to provide income and resources for the Bank. They do not form any part of a system of monetary control. The level is adjusted twice a year and is at the rate of 0.45% of eligible liabilities (for details of the calculation of eligible liabilities, see the Glossary). This category of bankers' deposits is not included in the calculation of M0.

The second type of deposits, operational deposits, are deposits of the London Clearing Banks (LCBs) which are used for settling payments between themselves and the Bank of England. As is explained in more detail in Chapter 11, the Bank generally aims to offset flows in the money market on a daily basis. By providing assistance to the money market in times of shortage (normally by open market operations in bills but also by lending), or by absorbing surplus liquidity, the Bank aims to leave the LCBs' balances close to their target level. It could, however, by deliberately providing less assistance than necessary, produce a shortfall of bankers' deposits. This would provide a depressing influence on M0 growth. The authorities make no attempt at the moment to control M0 in this way.

As mentioned above, the inclusion of both bankers' operational balances at the Bank of England and banks' till money, as well as notes and coin in circulation with the public, in the target measure of narrow money gave rise to some speculation that this might be designed to ease the way to a system of monetary base control. Indeed, M0 has been termed the wide monetary base as it includes all three possible components of a measure of the monetary base. Narrower definitions would include just bankers' operational deposits at the Bank of England or these deposits plus banks' till money.

The concept of a monetary base scheme is that banks keep a certain proportion of their deposits as monetary base because there is a mandatory requirement on them to do so or because they can be relied on to do so over a period for prudential reasons. With a mandatory system the authorities could, by controlling the amount of monetary base in existence, control the total growth of the money supply (as this would be a specified multiple of the monetary base). Under a non-mandatory system, the authorities could use the signal provided by variations in the amount of monetary base as a leading indicator of developments in broader measures of money and, hence, as a trigger for changing interest rates. We discuss these two possibilities below.

Non-mandatory schemes

Since 1981, banks have been free to hold whatever level of operational deposits they think suitable. The Chancellor pointed out in his March 1981 Budget speech that this system could permit a gradual evolution to monetary base control as the authorities would be able to monitor the relationship between operational deposits and the monetary aggregates. It has become apparent, however, that banks' demand to hold such deposits is very low indeed. The average level of operational deposits in 1989 was £158m, only 0.04% of M4. Moreover, the relationship between the level of these deposits and changes in other monetary measures on a month-by-month basis has not been at all stable. This is not to say that the demand for operational deposits is not stable - it may be that such demand can be explained by reference to other factors apart from the size of a particular monetary aggregate. For example, the level of operational deposits may be higher during the main tax paying season due to uncertainty surrounding the magnitude of payments to the Exchequer and hence the extent of the drain on operational deposits (such influences are discussed in detail in Chapter 11).

The lack of evidence of stability concerning the relationship between operational deposits and other monetary measures casts doubt on the efficacy of a non-mandatory monetary base system designed to provide signals for changes in interest rates. In any case, the behaviour of operational deposits, even if it were related in a known fashion to changes in other measures of money, might not give much of a leading indication of developments in the monetary aggregates. Although the level of operational deposits can be observed daily by the Bank, it has weekly returns from a sample of banks which can be used to give an indication of developments in other monetary measures. The improvement in the timeliness of information would, therefore, be marginal. Furthermore, it is questionable whether the authorities would wish to react week-by-week, let along day-by-day, to changes in the monetary aggregates. Over such a short time scale, it is impossible to be certain about changes in deposits due purely to seasonal variations: the Bank would presumably react to seasonally adjusted developments.

Mandatory schemes

There also remain considerable doubts about the efficacy of a mandatory monetary base system. The essence of a mandatory scheme is that the authorities fix the amount of monetary base in existence. If the money supply grows at a faster rate than that consistent with the quantity of monetary base, there will be excess demand for monetary base. Although one individual bank can improve its base position by, say, selling bills and thus increasing its deposits at the Bank, the bank buying the bills from it will see a corresponding reduction in its deposits. If the banking system as a whole is aiming to be a net seller of bills, clearly sharp upward pressure on interest rates would result: only if the Bank buys bills (thus increasing the monetary base) would interest rate pressure be relieved. If the banking system as a whole aims to bring its balance sheet into line with the size determined by the fixed amount of monetary base supplied by the authorities, there are three possible adjustments which could take place. These have been identified as:[13]

(a) a reduction in banks' assets and liabilities;
(b) attraction of notes and coin from the public (which would clearly only be a method of relieving the pressure if the definition of monetary base was bankers' deposits at the Bank plus banks' till money. Even in this case, it would be difficult to accomplish);
(c) a shift between different types of deposit if different base requirements were attached to these.

The 'scramble' for monetary base, by raising interest rates may help to reduce the size of banks' balance sheets. Loan demand may be depressed (although, as discussed in Chapter 6, this appears largely insensitive to interest rate movements in the short run), but higher interest rates could have the perverse effect of attracting deposits to the banks. The payment of interest on cash lodged with the banks would presumably be the principal way in which adjustment (b) took place. Similarly, encouraging customers to shift deposits from, say, sight to time deposits (if, as in the USA, the latter had lower base requirements) would require higher interest rates on time deposits. All responses to a shortfall of monetary base thus seem likely to stimulate sharp upward pressure on interest rates. Similarly, in circumstances of excess supply of monetary base, interest rates could drop to very low levels indeed.

One response to such strict control is likely to be disintermediation of banking business (similar to the type which occurred in response to the 'corset'), with the banks developing mechanisms for channelling business off balance sheet in times of base pressure.

Actual experience with systems of monetary base control similar to that described above has, indeed, shown that greater interest rate volatility can be expected. In October 1979, the USA moved to a type of base control from a system which had been designed primarily to keep very short-term interest rates within a certain range (i.e. a system similar to that currently operated by the UK authorities). Much greater volatility of interest rates resulted, even though the type of system allowed some reserve flexibility by permitting banks to borrow from the central bank.

The possibility of such greater volatility in interest rates remains the authorities' main objection to this form of monetary control.

Notes and References

1. Lawson, N., 'The Chancellor's Mansion House Speech', (H.M. Treasury, 20 October 1983).
2. Lawson, N., 'The Chancellor's Mansion House Speech', (H.M.Treasury, 18 October 1984).
3. Johnston, R. B., 'The demand for non-interest bearing money in the United Kingdom', Treasury Working Paper Number 28, (February 1984).
4. Lawson, N., 'The Chancellor's Mansion House Speech', (H.M. Treasury, 20 October 1983).
5. See, for example, T.C. Mills, 'The Information Content of Monetary Aggregates', Bulletin of Economic Research, May 1983, pp25-46.
6. Mills, T. C. and M.J. Stephenson, 'The Information Content of M0', University of Leeds mimeo.
7.

The postal strike in September 1988 temporarily raised the level of M0 as more cash was held, especially at Post Office counters. In September 1989, the comparison with this period led to a temporary fall in M0's year-on-year growth rate.

8. 'Recent Changes in the Use of Cash', *Bank of England Quarterly Bulletin*, December 1982, pp519-529. The present author was part-author of this article.
9. Johnston, RB., op.cit.
10. *Bank of England Quarterly Bulletin*, op cit, p521.
11. *Bank of England Quarterly Bulletin*, op cit, p521.
12. H.M. Treasury, 'H.M. Treasury Macroeconomic Model: Supplement to the 1982 Technical Manual', (June 1984).
13. Goodhart, C.A.E., M.D.K.W. Foot and A.C. Hotson, 'Monetary Base Control', *Bank of England Quarterly Bulletin*, June 1979, pp149-159.

4 The Counterparts Approach to Analysing Broad Money

The counterparts analysis of developments in broad money has been a key feature of the interpretation of UK financial developments since the 1960s. It received renewed emphasis in the 1980s as the way in which the various aspects of fiscal, funding, exchange rate and monetary policy were integrated. In this chapter we explain how this approach to the analysis of broad money is developed. The problems faced by the U.K. authorities in implementing this approach in practice are left to Chapter 6.[1]

The expression of the growth of broad money in terms of its counterparts comes from the manipulation of three key relationships: the consolidated balance sheet of the banks and the building societies; the PSBR financing identity; and the definition of broad money.

(i) The balance sheet of the UK banks and building societies

The consolidated balance sheet of the banks and building societies is shown in Table 4.1.

For the balance sheet to balance, total liabilities must equal total assets:

$$G£D+G\$D+P£D+P\$D+O£D+O\$D+NNDL$$
$$= G£L+G\$L+P£L+P\$L+O£L+O\$L \ldots \ldots (1a)$$

and the change (Δ) in total liabilities must equal the change in total assets:

$$\Delta(G\pounds D+G\$D+P\pounds D+P\$D+O\pounds D+O\$D+NNDL)$$
$$= \Delta(G\pounds L+G\$L+P\pounds L+P\$L+O\pounds L+O\$L) \ldots (1b)$$

Table 4.1: Consolidated balance sheet of UK banks and building societies

Liabilities		Assets	
Public Sector Deposits		Lending to Public Sector	
- in sterling	G£D	- in sterling	G£L
- in other currencies	G$D	- in other currencies	G$L
Private Sector Deposits		Lending to Private Sector	
- in sterling	P£D	- in sterling	P£L
- in other currencies	P$D	- in other currencies	P$L
Overseas Sector Deposits		Lending to Overseas Sector	
- in sterling	O£D	- in sterling	O£L
- in other currencies	O$D	- in other currencies	O$L
Net Sterling Non-Deposit Liabilities	NNDL		

$$(G\pounds D + G\$D + P\pounds D + P\$D + O\pounds D + O\$D + NNDL)$$
$$= (G\pounds L + G\$L + P\pounds L + P\$L + O\pounds L + O\$L)$$

(ii) Financing the PSBR

The public sector finances its borrowing requirement by borrowing from the three other sectors of the economy: the private sector (excluding the banks and building societies, described by the Bank of England as the M4 private sector); the banks and building societies; and the overseas sector.

The M4 private sector finances the PSBR in two main ways. First, it can increase its holdings of cash (we represent this in the PSBR financing identity below as a change, Δ, in private sector cash holdings, PCASH). The authorities responds passively to any change in the demand for cash. If the M4 private sector increases its demand for cash, deposits at the banks and building societies are run down in exchange for cash and the banks' and building societies' cash holdings are reduced. The clearing banks then replenish their stocks of cash by running down their deposits at the Bank of England in exchange for cash. An increase in the issue of notes will further raise the liabilities of the Issue Department of the Bank of England, which in turn matches this increase in its liabilities by purchasing government securities. This will reduce the amount of debt which will need to be sold elsewhere to finance the PSBR.

Second, the M4 private sector can purchase government debt (ΔP£GD). This may be marketable debt (for example, Treasury bills or gilts) or non-marketable debt (National Savings of certificates of tax deposit). Against this, if the Issue Department of the Bank of England buys commercial bills in the process of providing assistance to the money market (see Chapter 12), the government needs to raise more from other sources. Thus Issue Department's net purchases of commercial bills (ΔIDCB) enter the PSBR financing identity with a negative sign.

The public sector may also borrow from the banks and building societies. This mainly takes the form of purchases of government debt (gilts or Treasury bills) by those institutions. The weekly purchase of Treasury bills by the discount houses (classified as banks) was traditionally the method by which the government financed that part of its borrowing requirement which could not be financed elsewhere. (As explained in Chapter 12, the use of the Treasury bill tender has changed several times during the 1970s and 1980s). Any increase in the banks' and building societies' holdings of cash also finances the PSBR. These forms of finance - purchases of government debt or an increase in cash holdings - are shown in the balance sheet above and are collectively referred to as lending by the banks and building societies to the public sector in sterling (G£L). The banks and building societies may also lend to the public sector in foreign currencies. This, again, appears on the assets side of the banks' and building societies' balance sheet as G$L. The public sector may also run down its deposits with the banks and building societies in either sterling or foreign currencies to finance its borrowing requirement: the levels of the public sector's deposits are shown on the liabilities side of the banks' and building societies' balance sheet (G£D and G$D for sterling and foreign currency deposits respectively).

In a similar manner, the overseas sector's purchases of government debt, as well as an increase in its holdings of cash, finance the PSBR (referred to as ΔO£G below).

Foreign exchange intervention by the Exchange Equalisation Account (EEA) has a public sector financing counterpart. The EEA holds international reserves (RES) and short-term claims (mostly Treasury bills) on the public sector. If the EEA purchases foreign currencies in exchange for sterling, the sterling is raised by selling government debt. In this instance, the EEA's international reserves rise and its sterling assets fall; as a result, the public sector is forced to finance more of its borrowing requirement by some other means. If reserves increase because of official foreign currency borrowing (for example, through the issue of ECU Treasury bills or a dollar floating rate note) or through a new allocation of Special Drawing Rights at the IMF (both of these forms of foreign currency borrowing are referred to as OF$ below) the EEA does not have to sell Treasury bills in order to raise the sterling to purchase foreign currencies. The change in the reserves (ΔRES) minus the change in official foreign currency borrowing (ΔOF$) and the change in banks' and building societies' foreign currency lending to the public sector (ΔG$L) is often referred to as the underlying change in the reserves.

We can bring together all these sources of financing the PSBR in the equation below:

$$\text{PSBR} = \Delta(\text{PCASH+P£GD-IDCB+G£L+G\$L-G£D-G\$D+O£G-RES+OF\$}) \ldots (2)$$

(iii) The definition of M4

The final relationship used in the construction of the counterparts to M4 is the definition of M4 itself. M4 is defined as cash in circulation with the M4 private sector (PCASH) plus sterling deposits of the M4 private sector with the banks and the building societies (P£D):

$$M4 = \text{PCASH} + \text{P£D} \ldots\ldots\ldots\ldots\ldots\ldots\ldots\ldots (3)$$

and $$\Delta M4 = \Delta\text{PCASH} + \Delta\text{P£D} \ldots\ldots\ldots\ldots\ldots\ldots (3a)$$

(iv) The counterparts to M4

Relationship (1b) can alternatively be expressed so that the change in the private sector's sterling deposits (ΔP£D) is related to all the other components of the balance sheet:

$$\Delta\text{P£D} = \Delta(\text{G£L+G\$L+P£L+P\$L+O£L+O\$L}) - \Delta(\text{G£D+G\$D+P\$D+O£D+O\$D+NNDL}) \ldots (1c)$$

Similarly, relationship (2) can be expressed as:

$$\Delta PCASH =$$
$$PSBR - \Delta(P£GD-IDCB+G£L+G\$L-G£D-G\$D+O£G-RES+OF\$) \dots (2a)$$

Substituting for $\Delta P£D$ and $\Delta PCASH$ from (1c) and (2a) respectively into equation (3a) gives:

$$\Delta M4 =$$
$$PSBR - \Delta(P£GD-IDCB+G£L+G\$L-G£D-G\$D+O£G-RES+OF\$)$$
$$+ \Delta(G£L+G\$L+P£L+P\$L+O£L+O\$L)$$
$$- \Delta(G£D+G\$D+P\$D+O£D+O\$D+NNDL) \dots (3b)$$

Simplifying and rearranging this equation gives:

$$\Delta M4 = \quad PSBR$$
$$- \Delta P£GD - \Delta O£G$$
$$+ \Delta RES - \Delta OF\$$$
$$+ \Delta P£L + \Delta IDCB$$
$$+ \Delta P\$L - \Delta P\$D$$
$$+ \Delta O\$L - \Delta O\$D$$
$$+ \Delta O£L - \Delta O£D$$
$$- \Delta NNDL \dots (3c)$$

That is, the change in M4 is equal to the public sector borrowing requirement (PSBR) *minus* sales of government debt to the M4 private sector ($\Delta P£GD$) *minus* sales of government debt to the overseas sector ($\Delta O£G$) *plus* the underlying change in the reserves ($\Delta RES-\Delta OF\$$) *plus* sterling lending to private sector including Issue Department's purchases of commercial bills ($\Delta P£L+\Delta IDCB$) *plus* the external and foreign currency counterparts ($\Delta P\$L-\Delta P\$D+\Delta O£L-\Delta O£D+\Delta O\$L-\Delta O\$D$) *minus* the increase in net non-deposit liabilities ($\Delta NNDL$).

(v) The counterparts to M4 in practice

Equation (3c) above corresponds to the way in which the counterparts to M4 are presented by the Bank of England in its *Quarterly Bulletin* and in the monthly *Monetary Statistics* Press Release.[2] The behaviour of these counterparts in each of the financial years from 1976/77 to 1989/90 is set out in Table 4.2: we show both the description of the counterparts used in the *Bank of England Quarterly Bulletin* and the corresponding notation used in developing the counterparts in this chapter.

Table 4.2: Counterparts to M4 growth

£billion	PSBR	Sales of public sector debt to M4 private sector:			External Finance:		Over(-)/under(+) funding	Lending to private sector	External and f.c. counterparts	NNDLs	M4
		Gilts	Other Central Govt. Debt	Other Public Sec Debt	Gilt sales to overseas	Other					
Notation used in this chapter:	PSBR		$\Delta P£GD$	$\Delta OPSD$	$\Delta O£G$	$\Delta RES-\Delta OFS$	$\Delta PEL+\Delta IDCB$	$\Delta PEL+\Delta IDCB$	$\Delta PSL-\Delta PSD +\Delta OEL-\Delta OED +\Delta OSL-\Delta OSD$	$\Delta NNDL$	$\Delta M4$
1976/77†	8.3		-7.3		-0.3	-0.8	-0.1	7.0	0.1	-1.0	6.0
1977/78†	5.4		-5.1		-0.8	5.2	4.6	8.3	-0.3	-0.5	12.2
1978/79†	9.2		-8.4		0.0	-0.5	0.4	11.4	0.0	-1.8	9.9
1979/80†	9.9		-8.4		-1.1	1.6	2.0	14.6	-2.7	-1.7	12.2
1980/81†	12.5		-9.5		-1.5	1.4	2.9	15.4	0.2	-1.1	17.4
1981/82†	8.6		-10.2		-0.2	-0.8	-2.6	20.9	-0.2	-1.8	16.4
1982/83	8.9	-3.8	-4.1	-0.1	-0.7	-1.7	-1.4	24.0	-0.8	-1.5	20.2
1983/84	9.8	-8.0	-3.1	0.5	-1.2	-0.2	-2.1	25.8	-1.3	-3.5	18.9
1984/85	10.2	-8.7	-3.6	-0.2	-1.3	-0.7	-4.3	32.5	0.3	-3.5	25.0
1985/86	5.7	-3.5	-2.1	1.4	-2.3	0.4	-0.3	34.9	-0.7	-3.9	29.9
1986/87	3.4	-3.6	-2.8	1.1	-2.6	1.1	-3.3	46.7	-1.5	-8.6	33.3
1987/88	-3.5	-3.4	-2.5	0.5	-4.3	11.8	-1.4	60.8	-8.0	-6.1	45.3
1988/89	-14.4	9.4	-0.3	0.8	-0.1	2.3	-2.3	85.4	-13.1	-12.8	57.1
1989/90	-8.0	8.3	0.8	-0.1	3.0	-5.1	-1.2	89.3	-10.8	-12.1	65.2

Note:

For years marked † a breakdown of public sector debt sales between the three components normally identified is not available and the amount in the 'other central government debt' column represents total sales.

Two points emerge from an examination of Table 4.2. First, the net funding position of the public sector, the external and foreign currency counterparts and net non-deposit labilities all generally acted to reduce M4 growth in the 1980s. Therefore, second, more than all the increase in M4 in each year can be explained by the behaviour of lending to the private sector. Thus, although M4 growth can be presented in this way and related to key aspects of policy, the main expansionary impulse has come from just one source - the private sector's credit demand.

Chapter 5 discusses the way in which the authorities' funding policy has developed during the 1980s. Chapter 6 examines the problems which have been experienced with this analysis of the counterparts to M4, in particular the fact that the demand for credit has been the predominant influence on broad money growth. In the remainder of this chapter we therefore concentrate on the two counterparts which are not dealt with in detail elsewhere, namely, the external and foreign currency counterparts and net non-deposit liabilities.

(vi) External and foreign currency counterparts

The external and foreign currency counterparts can be related to the size of the current account balance. Broadly, a current account deficit will tend to produce a contractionary effect of the external and foreign currency counterparts on M4. In this way, a current account deficit may be 'helpful' in reducing broad money growth. This could, at times lead to an incorrect assessment of the stance of policy. For example, if the emphasis is on controlling the growth of broad money and this is being reduced by a current account deficit which is itself an indication of too strong growth of domestic credit and domestic demand, it would be more appropriate to focus attention on the domestic counterparts (the funding position and the growth of lending to the private sector) than on broad money. This was the main reason why in the 1960s the IMF placed more emphasis on domestic credit expansion (DCE) than on broad money.

The way in which the external and foreign currency counterparts (XFCC) are related to the current account balance is explained below.

The external and foreign currency counterparts are, using the notation set out above:

$$XFCC = \Delta P\$L - \Delta P\$D$$
$$+\Delta O£L - \Delta O£D$$
$$+\Delta O\$L - \Delta O\$D \dots\dots\dots\dots\dots (4)$$

The balance of payments identity states that a balance of payments current and capital account imbalance must be equal to, and of opposite sign to, its financing counterparts. This is set out in equation (5) below:

$$CB+ETP+ETG-\Delta O\pounds L+\Delta O\pounds D-\Delta O\$L+\Delta O\$D+\Delta O\pounds G+\Delta OF\$-\Delta RES=0 \ . \ . \ (5)$$

where: CB is the current account balance;
ETP is the balance on the private sector's external capital transactions;
ETG is the balance on the public sector's external capital transactions contributing to, as distinct from financing, the PSBR; and the other terms are as set out above.

Thus, for example, if there is a deficit on the public and private sector's current and capital account transactions, this must be financed by the combination of a rise in overseas residents' net sterling or foreign currency deposits; a rise in overseas residents' holdings of gilts; or a rundown in the government's foreign exchange reserves (net of official foreign currency borrowing). Four of the financing components are included within the external and foreign currency counterparts. Thus, rearranging equation (5) and substituting into equation (4) gives:

$$XFCC = CB+ETP+ETG+\Delta O\pounds G+\Delta OF\$-\Delta RES+\Delta P\$L-\Delta P\$D.$$

The relationship makes clear the link between a current account deficit and a contractionary influence of the external and foreign currency counterparts on M4 growth mentioned above. In 1988 and 1989 as the UK moved into substantial current account deficit, the external and foreign currency counterparts became an increasingly large contractionary influence on M4 growth. This is demonstrated in Figure 4.1.[3]

(vii) Net non-deposit liabilities

Banks' and building societies' non-deposit liabilities consist mainly of their capital and reserves. When various assets - predominantly plant, equipment and leased assets - are deducted, we arrive at the total for net non-deposit liabilities (NNDLs).

Since 1985, the distinction has been made between sterling and foreign currency NNDLs, with foreign currency NNDLs being included with the other external and foreign currency counterparts. This is because foreign

**Figure 4.1: External and foreign currency counterparts to M4
and the current account**

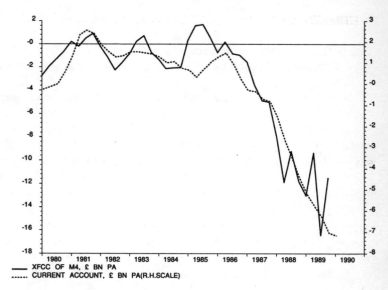

XFCC OF M4, £ BN PA
...... CURRENT ACCOUNT, £ BN PA(R.H.SCALE)

SOURCE : DATASTREAM

currency capital issues by banks are unlikely to be financed to a large extent
by a rundown in UK residents' sterling deposits, so the impact on M4 is likely
to be small. Such issues are more likely to be financed by a rundown of
foreign currency deposits. Thus, if foreign currency capital issues are
classified along with sterling issues in NNDLs, an issue of foreign currency
capital would be likely to involve a rise in NNDLs (reducing M4 growth)
and a fall in foreign currency deposits (raising the external influences on M4
growth). The approach adopted since 1985 of grouping foreign currency
NNDLs with the other external and foreign currency counterparts avoids
such movements in the counterparts.

NNDLs are defined as the residual item in banks' and building societies'
balance sheets, being the difference between the total balance sheet size and
deposits. When drawing up the consolidated balance sheet of the banks and
building societies, any error is included in NNDLs.

Retention of profits and issue of equity or bonds are the main ways in
which the banks and building societies can strengthen their capital base. An
increase in undistributed profits will expand the liabilities side of the bank's

balance sheet: in this way an increase in profits can act as the counterpart to an increase in lending and a substitute for deposit creation.

Notes and references

1. A more detailed analysis of the counterparts can be found in Temperton, P., 'A Guide to UK Monetary Policy', Chapter 3, Macmillan (London 1986).
2. See, for example, Table 12.1 in the February 1990 *Bank of England Quarterly Bulletin*.
3. The empirical linkage between the balance of payments and the external and foreign currency counterparts is, however, obscured by the particularly large balancing item in the UK balance of payments statistics.

5 Funding Policy

(i) The full funding rule

'Full funding' has always been stated as the general aim of the authorities' funding policy. This policy relates to the way in which the government finances its borrowing requirement or debt repayment. The current objective of funding policy is that the public sector borrowing requirement (PSBR, or debt repayment, PSDR) should be equal to sales of public sector debt to (or repurchases of public sector debt from) the private sector and overseas plus any external flows to the public sector (chiefly changes in the foreign exchange reserves). This is termed the full funding rule. The government does not necessarily aim to achieve a 'full fund' during the course of a particular financial year and has argued that, in some cases, this may not be possible. If the full funding objective is achieved then the public sector neither adds to nor reduces broad money growth. In this chapter we assess precisely what the full funding rule means; how funding policy developed to meet the changing requirements of the 1980s; and how policy might develop during the 1990s.

(ii) The funding rule in practice

In Table 5.1 we show data for the PSBR/PSDR and a breakdown of the way in which it was financed by the private and overseas sectors between 1976/77 and 1989/90. Five distinct phases to the government's funding policy

Table 5.1: Funding of the PSBR

£ billion	PSBR	Sales of public sector debt to the UK private sector:[1]					External Finance:		Over (-) or under (+) funding:	
		Gilts	National Savings	Treasury bills	CTDs & other	Other pub sector debt	Gilts to overseas	Other	Narrow definition	Broad definition
1976/77	8.3	-5.8	-0.9	0.3	0.0	-0.8	-0.3	-0.8	1.1	0.0
1977/78	5.4	-4.9	-1.1	-0.3	-0.4	0.0	-0.8	5.2	-1.3	3.1
1978/79	9.2	-6.2	-1.6	0.7	-1.1	-0.5	0.0	-0.5	0.5	0.0
1979/80	9.9	-8.3	-1.0	0.0	0.9	-1.1	-1.1	1.5	0.4	0.8
1980/81	12.5	-8.9	-2.2	-0.1	-0.3	0.6	-1.5	1.4	1.6	1.5
1981/82	8.6	-7.1	-4.2	-0.1	-0.4	0.5	-0.2	-0.8	-2.8	-3.8
1982/83	8.9	-4.6	-3.0	-0.2	-0.9	0.3	-0.7	-1.7	0.5	-1.9
1983/84	9.8	-9.8	-3.3	0.0	0.2	0.3	-1.2	-0.2	-2.8	-4.2
1984/85	10.2	-9.3	-3.1	0.2	-0.8	0.5	-1.3	-0.7	-2.3	-4.3
1985/86	5.7	-2.8	-2.1	0.0	-0.2	1.6	-2.3	0.4	2.2	0.3
1986/87	3.4	-1.5	-3.4	-0.2	1.0	2.8	-2.8	1.1	2.1	0.4
1987/88	-3.5	-3.1	-2.3	-0.2	0.1	1.3	-4.3	11.8	-7.6	-0.1
1988/89	-14.4	9.4	-0.6	0.0	0.3	0.8	-0.2	2.3	-4.5	-2.3
1989/90[2]	-8.0	8.3	1.7	-0.7	-0.2	-0.1	3.0	-5.1	0.9	-1.2

Notes:
[1] The UK private sector excludes banks, and from 1988/89 onwards, building societies as well.
[2] The definition of full funding was changed in October 1989 to exclude Treasury bill purchases from the calculation. Net purchases of Treasury bills in 1989/90 by the UK private sector and the overseas sector were £0.7 billion and £0.9 billion respectively. Excluding such purchases, underfunding of £0.4 billion (on the broad definition) took place.

can be discerned during this period and by way of back-ground we discuss each of these in turn.

1976/77 to 1980/81: 'full funding'

In the five years between 1976/77 (when the first targets for broad money were published) and 1980/81 full funding was broadly achieved. Until 1984/85 the extent of under or overfunding was assessed in relation to sales of public sector debt to the UK non-bank private sector only: external finance of the PSBR was not included. This definition of funding is commonly referred to as the 'narrow' definition and the measure on this basis is shown in Table 5.1 alongside the 'broad' definition which includes external finance of the public sector (see below). Of course, there are other sources of financing the PSBR apart from debt sales to the UK non-bank private sector and external finance. The two other primary methods are through the take-up of notes and coin by the private sector and by sales of government debt to the monetary sector. These two methods of financing are, however, not regarded as financing the PSBR in a non-inflationary way and so are disregarded from the full funding calculation. (This much should be clear from an examination of the way in which the counterparts to broad money growth were derived in Chapter 4).

During this period the government's preferred measure of broad money was £M3, not M4 as at present. This meant that sales of public sector debt to the building societies were regarded as debt sales to the private sector (see below).

1981/82 to 1984/85: overfunding

In the early 1980s the authorities began to overfund the PSBR (i.e. sell more government debt than was needed to fund the PSBR). This policy was intended, initially, to reduce month-to-month volatility in the growth of the broad money supply. With short-term changes in £M3 carefully watched in financial markets the authorities were keen to moderate any large month-to-month fluctuations: strong growth of £M3 could be expected to lead to a more substantial level of gilt sales, but this expectation could, in itself, lead to temporary problems with selling gilts. Generally strong growth of the private sector's demand for credit from the banking sector meant that overfunding became necessary on a more or less permanent basis. As can be seen from Table 5.1, the PSBR was overfunded by an average of almost £2 billion per year between 1981/82 and 1984/85.

1985/86 to 1986/87: overfunding abandoned, full funding on the broad definition

Overfunding was abandoned as a policy in the October 1985.[1] The principal reason was that continued overfunding had led to persistent shortages in the money market. In order to relieve these shortages the Bank of England bought commercial bills from the private sector, but these accumulated to such an extent that it was thought distortions were being introduced into the determination of short-term interest rates. Moreover, wider questions about the relationship between the Bank of England and the corporate sector were raised as the Bank accumulated, at one stage, almost £15 billion of bills. (The relationship between funding policy and money market shortages is discussed in detail in Chapter 11).

At the same time as overfunding was formally dropped, the full funding rule was restated. External finance of the PSBR was to be considered an equally valid form of funding the PSBR as sales of government debt to the UK non-bank private sector. That is, the full funding definition was changed from the narrow definition in Table 5.1 to the broad definition. It was intended that this funding objective should be met over the course of a financial year as a whole.

It can be seen that in 1985/86, the first year for which the new approach to funding was operational, the full funding objective was, broadly, achieved with the PSBR underfunded by £0.3 billion. Again, in 1986/87, there was a similar sized underfund. On the old, narrow definition, the PSBR was underfunded by around £2 billion per annum. The discrepancy arose because external finance was 'helpful' to the extent of around £2 billion per annum in reaching the funding objective. The policy change added around £4.5 billion per annum to M3 growth compared with what would have happened had overfunding continued at the rate seen in 1983/84 and 1984/85.

1987/88: relaxation of the timing of the full funding requirement

Although the change in the definition of funding meant that the government had to sell less debt to the UK non-bank private sector in 1985/86 and 1986/87 than would have been the case had the narrow definition been employed, the situation changed dramatically in 1987/88. The authorities successfully kept the value of sterling below DM3.00/£ up until close to the end of that financial year. This entailed heavy intervention in the foreign exchange market to keep sterling's value down and the foreign exchange reserves showed a substantial increase. In Table 5.1, the underlying increase in the foreign exchange reserves (that is, the increase in the reserves after allowing for changes in official foreign currency borrowing and lending) is shown as 'other' external finance. The £11.8 billion increase in this component of the funding calculation in 1987/88 reflects the increase in the reserves which took place.

This increase in reserves raised the possibility that the full funding objective would not be met, as the government would not be able to sell enough government debt to offset the expansionary effects of the foreign exchange intervention. The fear that the full funding objective would not be achieved within the financial year prompted the relaxation of the timing of the full funding objective in October 1987[2]. Up until that time it had generally been interpreted as referring to just one financial year, but now it was decided that it would be sufficient to achieve this over a longer period.

In the event, however, a modest overfund resulted as the public sector's finances underwent a dramatic transformation. At the time of the March 1987 Budget the government planned for a public sector borrowing requirement of £4 billion in the 1987/88 financial year. But by the end of the year a surplus amounting to £3.5 billion had been achieved. The term 'public sector debt repayment' or PSDR was used to describe such a negative PSBR.

The unexpectedly strong increase in the reserves and the similarly unexpected strength of the government's financial position resulted in an almost 'full fund' for the financial year on the broad definition.

1988/89 to 1989/90: unfunding the PSDR

Although the first PSDR was achieved unintentionally, in the years since 1987/88 the government has planned for a PSDR. The same principle of full funding on the broad definition has been used. The objective is now better described as matching the PSDR by purchases of government debt from the UK private sector and overseas and any change in the foreign exchange reserves. This was, rather inelegantly, described by Nigel Lawson as 'fully unfunding the PSDR'.[3]

1988/89 saw one other important change in the conduct of funding policy. In March 1988, M4 replaced M3 as the authorities' preferred measure of the broad money supply. As M4 includes deposits with both banks and building societies, debt sales to the non-bank, non-building society private sector replaced debt sales to the non-bank private sector in the full funding calculation. In Table 5.1, this change in the definition applies to the data from 1988/89 onwards.[4]

The March 1988 Budget forecast for the PSDR in 1988/89 was £3 billion, but once again government finances were much stronger than expected with an eventual PSDR of £14.4 billion. This raised the prospect of the government not being able to buy back enough debt from the private and overseas sectors to achieve the full funding objective. The eventual outcome was a relatively small overfund of £2.3 billion.

One further change to the funding calculation was made in October 1989:[5] purchases of Treasury bills by the UK private sector were excluded from the funding calculation. This point is discussed in more detail in the description of the individual funding instruments in the next section.

(iii) The different funding instruments

The extent to which new sales, or repurchases, of different types of government debt have been used to fund the PSBR (or unfund the PSDR) is shown in Table 5.1. Table 5.2 shows the outstanding amounts of each type of debt at the end of March 1989. The total outstanding amount of government debt in market hands (that is, excluding the official holdings of the Bank of England, government departments, the Northern Ireland government and the National Debt Commissioners) is commonly referred to as the National Debt. At the end of March 1989 it amounted to £167.2 billion, representing around one third of GDP. In the next section we discuss each of these funding instruments in detail with reference to both tables.

Gilts

In the period from 1976/77 to 1986/87, a period in which the public sector had a borrowing requirement in each year, sales of gilts to the UK non-bank private sector accounted for three quarters of all the funding of the PSBR (on the broad definition). From 1987/88 to 1989/90, when the public sector repaid its debt in each year, a similar proportion of debt repayment was accounted for by repayment of gilts outstanding.

In Table 5.2, it can be seen that three quarters of the outstanding stock of the national debt is accounted for by gilts. Within this, the largest proportion is in the form of 'conventional' gilts, that is gilts with a coupon and redemption payments denominated in money terms. The proportion of gilts in index-linked form - that is, having their coupon and redemption payments linked to the UK retail prices index - rose during the 1980s.

National Savings

National Saving's contribution to funding the PSBR up until 1986/87 was also important, regularly contributing around £3 billion per year. Indeed, a 'National Savings Initiative' was taken by the government in September

1980, with various measures introduced to increase the importance of
National Savings as a funding instrument. It was thought that by tapping the
market for personal savings in this way, pressure on gilt funding and hence
on long-term interest rates could be relieved.

Table 5.2 Composition of the National Debt

£ billion, nominal value, end-March 1989
Percentage of total in italic

Sterling Non-Marketable Debt:		
National Savings: index-linked	2.8	*1.7*
other	27.1	*16.2*
Certificates of Tax Deposit	2.3	*1.4*
Other	4.3	*2.6*
Sterling Marketable Debt:		
Treasury Bills	3.3	*2.0*
Gilts: index-linked	16.7	*10.0*
other	105.5	*63.1*
Foreign Currency Debt	5.3	*3.2*
National Debt	167.2	*100.0*

Source: *Bank of England Quarterly Bulletin,* November 1989.

National Savings attracted a net inflow of over £2 billion in 1987/88, and
of £0.6 billion in 1988/89, even though the government ran a PSDR in both
of those years. One obstacle to reducing sales of National Savings
instruments was that they were the only (onshore) savings vehicle paying
interest without the deduction of income tax at source. It was difficult for the
government, especially when it was attempting to encourage personal saving,
to make National Savings instruments less attractive. With the UK banks and
building societies able to pay interest gross from April 1991, and with Tax
Exempt Special Savings Accounts (TESSAs) available from January 1991,
the special role of National Savings will be removed in the early 1990s
facilitating a reduction in the amount of such debt outstanding if the
government continues to run a PSDR.

Treasury bills

Treasury bills are normally of three months maturity. They are sold at a discount, the rise in price bringing a return to the holder as no coupon is paid. They are allotted by tender each Friday and issued on each working day by the Bank of England. The discount houses have a traditional undertaking to underwrite the whole of the Treasury bill tender. Historically, this arrangement provided a residual form of financing for the government - meeting any financing requirement not satisfied by sales of other forms of debt. When the Bank of England receives the proceeds of the Treasury bill tender a shortage in the money market is created. Indeed, in the 1960s and 1970s, deliberate over-issuance of Treasury bills was the way in which the Bank of England enforced Bank Rate: the discount houses, in the face of the shortage which was created in the money market were forced to borrow from the Bank of England's discount window at Bank Rate.

From the mid-1970s onwards greater reliance was placed on control of broad money and sales of gilts replaced the need for the government to finance its borrowing requirement through the issue of Treasury bills. Indeed, the money market shortages created by greater reliance on sales of gilts were initially relieved by buying back Treasury bills from the market. In the early 1980s the process went one stage further with the Bank buying commercial bills as a means of providing assistance in the money market; the need for this was exacerbated by the policy of overfunding the PSBR to reduce broad money growth. Issuance of Treasury bills therefore amounted to only £100m per week, with the largest part of this taken up by the banking sector. In the early and mid-1980s purchases of Treasury bills by the UK private sector contributed only a modest amount to funding the PSBR (see Table 5.1).

The end of the 1980s, however, saw a return to surpluses in the money market, a reduction in the Bank of England's outstanding holdings of commercial bills and, in 1989, an enlargement of the Treasury bill issue. In May 1989 the size of the weekly three month Treasury bill tender was increased from the customary £100 million to £500 million, and for the first time a weekly six month Treasury bill tender of £100 million was introduced. In September 1989, nine week bills were also offered. Although the banking sector continued to be the largest purchaser of these Treasury bills, some were purchased by the M4 private sector (see Table 5.3). In the first half of the 1989/90 financial year purchases by that sector amounted to £1.5 billion at an annual rate. Given that the government was buying in gilts with the purpose of unfunding the PSDR, such purchases meant that an even larger amount of gilts had to be repurchased from the M4 private sector.

Table 5.3: Treasury bills

£ millions, net purchases by the public +/sales -

	Total Treasury bills	Overseas sector: CMIs[1]	Other Overseas	Banks	Discount Houses	Building Societies[2]	Other Public Sector	Private Sector[3]
1975/76	2,166	-517	1	1,404	471	--	0	807
1976/77	-1,192	-399	4	-697	179	--	70	-349
1977/78	-572	-387	-3	-547	35	--	0	330
1978/79	-840	93	2	100	-300	--	-59	-676
1979/80	56	285	18	237	-500	--	9	7
1980/81	-1,025	-318	-14	-531	-163	--	-73	74
1981/82	-111	-113	12	-19	-68	--	-25	102
1982/83	195	101	42	-120	-22	--	2	192
1983/84	126	-31	37	-38	57	--	74	27
1984/85	-185	58	46	-84	-23	--	-7	-175
1985/86	124	-61	5	128	14	--	51	-13
1986/87	670	262	-17	72	205	--	-51	198
1987/88	789	683	96	-58	-232	--	133	167
1988/89	460	163	38	-182	-87	103	443	-18
1989/90[4]	12,026	1,594	-234	7,106	600	2,612	-1,146	1,494

Notes:
1. Central Monetary Institutions and international organisations (for example, the IMF).
2. Up to and including 1987/88, building society purchases are included in purchases by the private sector.
3. The UK private sector excludes banks and discount houses and, from 1988/89, building societies as well.
4. 1989/90 data are for first half at an annual rate.

These purchases themselves further increased the surplus in the money market and hence the requirement for issuance of Treasury bills. The Chancellor of the Exchequer thus announced in October 1989 that 'it has become increasingly anomalous to chase our own tails in this way. Accordingly, we have decided to treat Treasury bill sales as outside the definition of funding irrespective of who buys them'.[6] The interaction between funding, money market assistance and Treasury bill sales is discussed in detail in Chapter 11.

Certificates of Tax Deposit (CTDs)

CTDs were introduced in October 1975: they are available to taxpayers generally and earn market related interest rates. The interest rate depends on the time for which the CTD is held, and is higher for larger deposits (over £100,000). CTDs can be withdrawn for cash (at a penal rate of interest) although they are normally used in the settlement of tax liabilities: they can be used in the settlement of all such liabilities apart from PAYE. UK industrial and commercial companies hold by far the largest proportion of CTDs outstanding.

Holdings follow a very seasonal pattern throughout the financial year and generally make a relatively small contribution to funding over the course of twelve months.

Other Public Sector debt

From 1980/81 the 'other public sector' (that is, the local authorities and public corporations) has been a net repayer of debt to the private sector. The local authorities have found it more attractive to replace market borrowings by borrowing from the Public Works Loan Board (PWLB), a central government department. The public corporations have more recently, like the central government, had a negative borrowing requirement.

In the mid-1980s, central government, encouraged the other public sector to borrow from the PWLB. This raises the level of the central government borrowing requirement, but leaves the overall PSBR unchanged. From the central government's viewpoint, this was useful as it reduced the daily cash shortage in the money market and so reduced the need for the Bank of England to purchase bills from the discount houses in its daily money market operations. More recently, the money market position has been much easier and measures have been taken to restrict borrowing from the PWLB.

External finance

There are two main forms of 'external finance' of the public sector: sales of gilts to overseas and 'other external finance'.

(a) Sales of gilts to the overseas sector

Sales of gilts to the overseas sector accounted for a relatively small and stable form of financing up until the mid-1980s. Overseas involvement in the gilt market has developed since then: the overseas sector purchased around £1¼ billion per year in both 1983/84 and 1984/85, but this rose to over £4 billion in 1987/88. Overseas purchases of gilts were stimulated both by the 'Big Bang' reforms in the gilt market in October 1986 (when the market changed over to a system similar to that in the USA and hence one which was more easily understood by overseas investors) and by the Bank of England issuing a growing proportion of new gilts in a form which paid coupons free of tax to residents abroad ('FOTRA' gilts).

Strong overseas purchases of gilts in 1987/88 meant that the reduction in gilt holdings which was required by the UK non-bank private sector was even larger than would otherwise have been the case.

(b) 'Other external finance'

Although having the unfortunately dull label of 'other external finance' this component of the funding equation has been perhaps the most interesting in recent years. The main influence on 'other external finance' of the PSBR is the underlying change in the UK's foreign exchange reserves, that is, the change in the reserves after taking account of foreign currency borrowing and repayments. Also included within the total are a number of other minor financing items.

In both 1977/78 and 1987/88, when the authorities attempted to keep sterling's value below a certain level, a substantial increase in the foreign exchange reserves resulted. In 1977/78 this meant that the contribution from 'other external finance' was expansionary by £5.2 billion, and on the broad definition of funding there was an underfund of £3 billion; in 1987/88 the increase was £11.8 billion, but a 'full fund' was broadly achieved as the public sector unexpectedly ran a debt repayment.

(iv) The gilt market in decline

The first few years of the 1990s are likely to see the public sector continue to have a debt repayment rather than a borrowing requirement. Although the latest MTFS projections see the PSDR falling to zero in 1992/93, it could be that a debt repayment continues for much longer than planned at the moment.[7]

Assuming that the PSDR averages 1% of money GDP during the 1990s and into the next century, the cumulative PSDR between 1990/91 and 2002/03 will be £120 billion (on the basis of money GDP growth running at 8% over the period). This £120 billion is equivalent to the stock of conventional gilts outstanding in the market with redemption dates after March 1990 plus the estimated redemption proceeds of all the index-linked gilts maturing in the period up until 2002/03 (see Table 5.4 on the profile of gilt maturities in the coming financial years). If the accumulated PSDR was used to repay gilts in this way then all that would be left of the gilt market in 2003 would be the seven index-linked gilts with maturity dates between 2006 and 2024.

Two techniques are likely to be used for bringing about this reduction in the size of the gilt market. First, purchases of gilts by the Bank of England in the open market; second, 'reverse auctions' for gilts. The latter technique was first used in January 1989: holders of certain gilts are invited to offer gilts to the Bank for sale.

(v) Possible changes to the full funding rule

Although such calculations imply the phasing out of the gilt market during the course of the next decade, there are notable risks to such a forecast. First, the government may no longer run a public sector debt repayment, choosing rather to run a public sector borrowing requirement. Second, the government may choose, even if they continue to run a PSDR, to revert to overfunding. This would mean that they did not buy in from the market enough gilts to offset the contractionary influence on M4 growth of the PSDR plus any underlying fall in the reserves. Some commentators[8] have argued for a return to this practice, claiming that the abandonment of overfunding in October 1985 was behind the sharp acceleration in broad money after that time and the subsequent sharp rise in inflation and deterioration in the current account of the balance of payments. Although a policy of overfunding could be recommended in terms of reducing M4 growth, such a policy would have the following disadvantages:

(a)

Table 5.4 Profile of gilt maturities
(£ billion)

Financial Year	Conven-tionals	Index-linked	Total
1990/91	6.7	0.7	7.4
1991/92	6.8	0.0	6.8
1992/93	7.2	0.8	8.1
1993/94	6.5	0.0	6.5
1994/95	8.0	0.0	8.0
1995/96	5.0	0.5	5.5
1996/97	7.9	0.0	7.9
1997/98	7.5	2.3	9.7
1998/99	11.6	0.0	11.6
1999/00	5.6	0.0	5.6
2000/01	6.5	0.0	6.5
2001/02	0.8	0.0	0.8
2002/03	6.6	2.3	8.9
2003/04	4.5	0.0	4.5
2004/05	2.7	2.2	4.9
2005/06	2.9	0.0	2.9
2006/07	2.2	0.0	2.2
2007/08	1.4	4.0	5.4
2008/09	1.8	0.0	1.8
2009/10	1.0	0.0	1.0
2010/11	0.0	3.5	3.5
2011/12	0.4	0.0	0.4
2012/13	1.0	5.9	6.9
2013/14	1.0	0.0	1.0
2014/15	0.7	4.4	5.1
2015/16	0.0	0.0	0.0
2016/17	0.0	0.0	0.0
2017/18	0.0	8.1	8.1
2018/19	0.0	0.0	0.0
2019/20	0.0	0.0	0.0
2020/21	0.0	0.0	0.0
2021/22	0.0	8.3	8.3
2022/23	0.0	0.0	0.0
2023/24	0.0	0.0	0.0
2024/25	0.0	5.6	5.6
Irredeemable	3.2		3.2
Totals	109.4	48.5	157.9

the policy would raise long term gilt yields and thus act as a disincentive to corporate bond issuance. The reduction in the size of the PSBR was associated with a fall in the yield on long-dated gilts during the 1980s, see Figure 5.1. To the extent that companies switched back to the banks as a source of finance the long-term effect would be to raise lending to the private sector and hence M4 growth;

(b) higher long-term interest rates could be seen as a reflection of little credibility in the government's counter-inflation policy;

(c) yet another change in funding policy would undermine the credibility of the authorities' funding tactics;

(d) if overfunding were continued for a prolonged period of time - as in the early 1980s - it would give rise once again to the distortions in the money market which were instrumental in the policy being dropped in October 1985.

On balance, it seems likely that the full funding rule will be maintained in its present form during the 1990s. If, as expected, this continues within the context of the government running a public sector debt repayment, then the size of the National Debt by the start of the next decade will be very small indeed.

Figure 5.1: Public sector finances and the yield on long-dated gilts

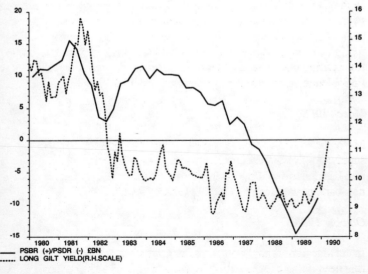

PSBR (+)/PSDR (-) £BN
LONG GILT YIELD(R.H.SCALE)

SOURCE : DATASTREAM

Appendix: Significant developments in UK funding policy, 1980 to 1989

1980/81-1984/85

Although full funding of the PSBR was the stated objective of the government, overfunding was in fact the normal situation. Over or underfunding was assessed in relation to the size of sales of government debt to the UK non-bank private sector only: external finance of the PSBR was not included.

October 1985

Overfunding was abandoned as a policy in the Chancellor's Mansion House Speech. The full funding rule was restated and re-emphasised. External finance of the PSBR was to be considered an equally valid form of funding the PSBR as sales of government debt to the UK non-bank private sector.

1985/86-1987/88

The full funding objective was broadly met in each of the financial years.

November 1987

In the Chancellor's Mansion House Speech the timing of the full funding objective was relaxed, so that full funding need not necessarily be achieved over the course of just one financial year. This was in response to the heavy foreign exchange intervention in the period, which threatened to make the full funding objective unattainable. In the event, the lower than expected PSBR led to an outturn very close to full funding.

March 1988

M4 replaced M3 as the authorities' preferred measure of the broad money supply. As M4 includes deposits with building societies, debt sales to the non-bank, non-building society private sector replaced debt sales to the non-bank private sector in the full funding calculation.

October 1988

In the Mansion House Speech the Chancellor reaffirmed that the full funding rule need not necessarily apply over the course of just one financial year.

Given the move from a PSBR, to a PSDR, the government's funding objective was now best described as 'unfunding the PSDR' rather than 'funding the PSBR'.

1988/89

Overfunding resulted from the fact that the authorities did not buy in enough debt from the UK private sector and overseas to match the size of the PSDR.

October 1989

The Chancellor announced in his Mansion House Speech that purchases of Treasury bills by all sectors would be excluded from the definition of full funding.

Notes and References

1. Lawson, N., 'The Chancellor's Mansion House Speech', (H.M. Treasury,October 1985).
2. Lawson, N., 'The Chancellor's Mansion House Speech', (H.M. Treasury, October 1987).
3. Lawson, N., 'The Chancellor's Mansion House Speech', (H.M. Treasury, October 1988).
4. It should be made clear that in Table 4.2, overfunding is assessed in each year on the basis of the counterparts to M4, whereas the data in Table 5.1 refer to M3 up until 1987/88 and to M4 from 1988/89 onwards.
5. Lawson, N., 'The Chancellor's Mansion House Speech', (H.M. Treasury, October 1989).
6. Lawson, N., 'The Chancellor's Mansion House Speech', (H.M. Treasury, October 1989).
7. Membership of the European Exchange Rate Mechanism, in particular, might lead to the government running larger PSDRs than expected at the moment. The arguments for this are set out in Chapter 9.
8. See for example, Congdon, T., 'Monetarism Lost and why it must be regained', Centre for Policy Studies Paper Number 106, 1989.

6 Problems with Broad Money

When monetary targets were introduced in the UK and then the importance of monetary control was re-emphasised in the Medium Term Financial Strategy (MTFS), £M3 was the measure of the money supply which was targeted. The choice of this broad measure of the money supply was based on the view that it possessed three key characteristics. First, it was thought that it gave a good indication of future developments in inflation. Its empirical behaviour in the early 1970s, in particular, had been encouraging. The peak rate of growth of £M3 reached in the fourth quarter of 1973 (27.4% year-on-year) bore an uncanny resemblance to the peak rate of inflation (26.9%) reached in August 1975. Second, broad money was related, through its credit counterparts, to other key aspects of government policy. This approach provided a coherent link between fiscal and monetary policy; it emphasised the need to finance a public sector borrowing requirement through sales of government debt to the private sector; and it made clear that foreign exchange intervention by the authorities had an effect on broad money growth. In this way the broad money supply encapsulated in one single measure all of the key dimensions of fiscal, funding and foreign exchange policy. Third, it was thought that broad money had a reasonably close relationship with money GDP. Control of broad money would, therefore, be associated with control of nominal incomes in the economy, the ultimate objective of policy.

During the 1980s, however, the behaviour of broad money changed markedly: it no longer gave a good leading indication of future developments in inflation; the counterparts framework proved to be of less value as the main expansionary impetus to broad money consistently came from one source - lending to the private sector; and its relationship with money GDP proved unreliable. The final problem, in particular, was put forward by the authorities as a reason for paying less attention to developments in broad money. The 5-9% target range set for £M3 in 1985/86 was suspended in October 1985; and although a new target range was set for 1986/87 at 11-15%, it became clear during the year that broad money was much less important in the authorities' assessment of monetary conditions. Targets for broad money were finally abandoned in the March 1987 Budget.

The more relaxed official attitude to broad money from 1985 onwards coincided with a rise in its growth rate and, in the late 1980s, inflation started to rise once again. This has led some commentators to claim that the abandonment of broad money targets was mistaken and that they should be reintroduced. In the next three sections we examine how the three key characteristics of broad money changed during the 1980s. The role of deregulation in the financial system is emphasised: it is argued that although such deregulation makes interpretation, leave alone control, of broad money more difficult, the forces of financial deregulation have had a very powerful effect on the real economy.

(i) Broad money and inflation

The first two years of the MTFS saw broad money grow well in excess of the targets which had been set; and of the six target ranges for broad money set between 1980 and 1986 only two were hit. This fast growth of broad money was, however, accompanied by considerable success in reducing inflation, as can be seen from Figure 6.1. The year-on-year growth rate of M4 remained between 11.5% and 14.5% from the end of 1981 to the start of 1986; but the year-on-year increase in the RPI fell from 12% (at the end of 1981) to a low-point of 3.7% (in May and June 1983) before rising again to a peak rate of 7.0% (in mid-1985) and then once again falling to 2.4% (in the summer of 1986). Broad money gave no indication at all of the future behaviour of inflation throughout this period.

The faster growth of broad money from 1985 onwards was, however, associated with a rise in inflation in the later 1980s. Given the breakdown of the relationship between broad money and inflation earlier in the decade, it was understandable that the authorities adopted a relatively relaxed approach to the faster growth of broad money during this period.

Figure 6.1: Broad money growth and inflation

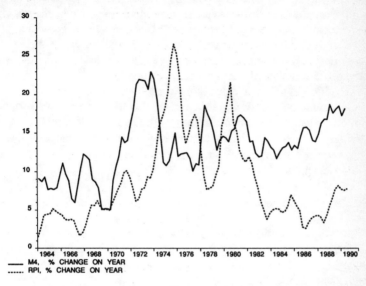

M4, % CHANGE ON YEAR
RPI, % CHANGE ON YEAR

SOURCE : DATASTREAM

(ii) Credit demand by the private sector - the most important counterpart to broad money growth

One key feature of the counterparts approach is that fiscal policy - the size of the government's borrowing requirement or debt repayment - is linked to broad money growth. Throughout the 1980s there was considerable success in reducing the size of the public sector borrowing requirement (see Table 1.4) and, indeed, from 1987/88 this was transformed into a public sector debt repayment. In most years in the 1980s the MTFS targets for the PSBR were at least met and, later in the 1980s, exceeded - a surplus resulted when the government was aiming for a borrowing requirement (as in 1987/88) or the surplus was even larger than expected (for example, in 1988/89). But this success in meeting fiscal objectives did little to help control of broad money: even when the government was overfunding the PSBR, the public sector contributed very little, in a statistical sense, towards broad money growth. In 1984/85, for example, when the PSBR was overfunded by £4.3 billion, lending to the private sector amounted to £32.5 billion and the overall growth of M4 was £25 billion. Developments in other counterparts - external and foreign currency finance and changes in net non-deposit liabilities - were generally a relatively stable (and contractionary) influence on the behaviour of broad money during the 1980s. This meant that it was one particular counterpart - lending to the private sector - which proved to be the principal expansionary force behind broad money. This consistently grew at a faster rate than that which was compatible with the targets for broad money. The authorities' approach to this was, first of all, to overfund the PSBR; when this approach led to distortions in the money market, they abandoned overfunding and tolerated faster monetary growth.

The counterparts approach thus came down to little more than concern with the private sector's demand for credit. Control of this was, however, frustrated by two factors: its apparent lack of sensitivity to changes in interest rates; and the effects of structural changes, deregulation and innovation in the financial system.

(iii) Relationship between broad money and money GDP

When explaining the reason for abandoning broad money targets the authorities did not emphasise that it was due to the breakdown of the link between broad money and future inflation, nor the less useful nature of the counterparts relationship. Rather, they pointed to a change in the relationship between broad money and money GDP. From the end of the war until 1979, with only a brief interruption in 1971-73, broad money grew less fast than money GDP (that is, its velocity rose steadily). In the first half of the 1980s, the velocity of broad money fell by an average of 4% per annum. The Governor of the Bank of England examined this change in the relationship between broad money and money GDP in his Loughborough lecture.[1] He claimed that the crucial question to ask when determining the appropriate attitude to these velocity changes, is whether the change is due to developments expanding the supply of money, or whether it is explicable in terms of changing influences on the demand for money with the enlarged stock willingly held at the prevailing level of interest rates.

The Governor's answer to the question rested to a large extent on a description of the changes in the nature of financial intermediation and the effects of this on different sectors of the economy. What were the changes in the nature of financial intermediation in the 1980s which led to the change in the relationship between broad money and money GDP?

(iv) Structural changes, deregulation and innovation in the financial system

The removal of exchange controls and the 'corset'

The process of financial deregulation started with the removal of exchange controls in 1979 and of the 'corset' in 1980. It is worthwhile, at this juncture, to examine the corset in some detail not only because the removal of the scheme was the antecedent to many of the changes in the financial system in the 1980s but also because the problems associated with the corset form the basis of the authorities' objection to the reintroduction of direct controls on the banking system.

The corset was a direct control on the growth of banks' interest bearing eligible liabilities (IBELs) - broadly their interest bearing sterling deposits. As liability management was thought to be predominant, the scheme worked by controlling the growth of IBELs which were created to finance credit expansion. Penalties (in the form of the banks having to hold supplementary non-interest bearing special deposits at the Bank of England) were levied on banks whose IBELs grew faster than a prescribed rate. The penalties were progressive, being greater the larger the extent of overshoot of the prescribed growth. The scheme was used on three separate occasions: from December 1973 to February 1975; from November 1976 to August 1977; and from June 1978 to June 1980. The scheme was largely successful in controlling the growth of IBELs.

The UK banking system responded to the controls, however, by diverting business through other channels. Specifically, two types of disintermediation occurred. First, the use of acceptance facilities became more popular: a bank would agree to accept (that is, guarantee) bills issued by a customer. These could then be sold to non-banks - the bank's guarantee making them highly marketable - and would not appear on the accepting bank's balance sheet: they were thus excluded from IBELs. The growth of holdings of such bank bills was well known and was referred to as the 'bill leak'. Second, after the removal of exchange controls in October 1979, UK residents were able freely to deposit with, and borrow from, banks overseas. This brought the possibility of channelling any excess growth of IBELs through offshore subsidiaries of UK banks (which were outside the controlled sector). In both cases, the UK banking sector no longer appeared as the intermediary but the effect was purely cosmetic in the sense that overall credit and liquidity in the economy were broadly unaffected: the term 'cosmetic disintermediation' was used to describe this process. Measures could have been taken to control either or

both problems - indeed, the Governor of the Bank of England requested that
the banks should not avoid the controls by using offshore subsidiaries - but
they risked further disintermediation which was less likely to be observed
and controlled by the authorities.

At that time the experience of the secondary banking crisis was still fresh
in the minds of the authorities. During the 1960s, when direct controls on
bank lending were in force, much of the frustrated business passed to a
'secondary' banking sector which was largely outside the supervision of the
authorities.[2] When these controls were removed in 1971, much of the diverted
business was channelled back through the primary banks, leading to a
collapse of confidence in the secondary banks and the launch of the Bank of
England's 'lifeboat'. A rerun of that episode was clearly not wanted.

Thus, in the light of the problems experienced after the removal of
exchange controls, the corset was removed in June 1980. The bill leak
contracted sharply as the banking sector reintermediated business and £M3
grew sharply as a result. Less predictable at the time was that this change
would lead to a more sustained period of competition in the banking industry,
the effects of which were felt throughout the 1980s. As can be seen from
Figure 6.2, the surge in lending to the private sector after the removal of the
corset was followed by a decade of persistently strong growth.

Figure 6.2: Growth of sterling lending to the UK private sector

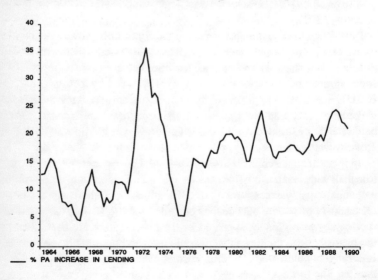

% PA INCREASE IN LENDING

SOURCE : DATASTREAM

Innovations in the mortgage market

With direct controls on their balance sheets removed the banks were free to enter the market for residential mortgages, which they did with gusto in 1981 and 1982. Two other factors gave an added impetus to the move into this area of business. First, the banks' position had been weakened by the less developed countries' debt crisis in 1982, which had reduced their credit worthiness relative to that of their own corporate customers. This both reduced the margins the banks could obtain on their traditional 'on balance sheet' activity and at the same time stimulated a new range of financial instruments issued by the corporate sector. Second, lending to the personal sector in the UK had traditionally been very low risk and relatively high margin business, previously dominated by the building societies.

Initially, at least, some of the business which the banks attracted in the mortgage market was at the expense of the building societies and the overall supply of credit to the personal sector may have been little affected. But the building societies then responded with their own wave of innovation. Their cartel arrangements for setting interest rates were abandoned; rationing of mortgages at times of high demand through the 'mortgage queue' disappeared; relatively high deposit requirements for house purchase were lowered; and the necessity to have been a customer of the lending institution for some time in order to qualify for a loan was often withdrawn.

The building societies were able to satisfy the increase in the demand for credit by becoming liability rather than asset managers. This was made possible by a series of major changes. The 1983 Finance Act gave building societies the power to pay interest gross on certificates of deposit of £50,000 or more. The first CD was issued in May 1983 and, from October 1983, societies were also allowed to pay interest gross on time deposits of over £50,000 with a maturity of less than one year. These techniques opened the way for building societies to attract wholesale funds in the same way as the banks had done in the late 1960s/early 1970s, when the bank CD market was first developed.

In September 1983, the Abbey National Building Society said it intended to withdraw from the Building Society Association's Interest Rate Cartel. In response to this, the Association replaced 'recommended' rates with advised rates and the requirement to give prior notice of a change in interest rates was replaced by a simple information agreement. The 1985 Finance Act removed the maturity limit on the instruments on which building societies could pay interest gross, thus enabling the societies to raise funds from the eurobond market. The first eurobond funds were raised in October 1985.

The 1985 Finance Act also extended the composite rate tax arrangement (previously only with the building societies) to the banks and other deposit taking institutions. Previously, the building societies had paid net rates of interest and were generally more attractive to taxpayers whereas the banks had paid interest gross and were generally more attractive to non-taxpayers. This extension of the composite rate tax scheme achieved broad fiscal neutrality between banks and building societies in the market for personal savings.

Further innovation in the market for residential mortgages came in 1986 with the appearance of the first centralised mortgage lending institutions, financing themselves primarily in the wholesale market. Lending by these institutions did not appear as a counterpart to any of the broad measures of the money supply, rendering even the broadest monetary measures inadequate guides to the amount of financial intermediation in the economy. 1988 saw a further wave of deregulation as the building societies obtained new powers under the Building Societies Act to offer unsecured lending to the personal sector.

These changes in the availability of credit to the personal sector were accompanied by changes in the types of deposit offered by banks and building societies. High interest bearing cheque accounts were first introduced by the banks in 1985; interest bearing current accounts were introduced by the building societies in 1988 and the banks followed shortly (these changes in the types of deposit are discussed fully in Chapter 2).

Innovations in the market for corporate finance

The pace of innovation in the market for corporate finance was also swift during the 1980s. Three broad groups of new financial instruments can be identified. First, those which allow the transfer of price or credit risk, for example futures and options. Second, those which enhance liquidity, such as the securitisation of existing debt. Third, those which broaden the access to financial markets. Swaps are perhaps the clearest example in this category as they allow a relatively good credit in one area of the market (for example, for fixed rate long-term finance) to be translated in to a relatively cheap borrowing in another market (for example, the market for floating rate short-term finance). Risk transferring developments (the first category) generally will not affect the growth of broad money whereas credit generating developments (in the second and third categories) will.

(v) Deregulation and financial innovation - how much of a concern?

There is no doubt that deregulation and innovation of the type described above was an important factor behind the strong growth of lending to the private sector and of broad money during the 1980s. Reviewing these developments in the financial system, the Governor's Loughborough lecture concluded that the 'demand for money is likely to have been increased by financial change' but it was emphasised that although a qualitative assessment could be made, the influences could not readily be quantified. No firm answer was given to the question of whether faster broad money growth in the 1980s was due to changes in supply or demand, although the Chancellor of the Exchequer (in his 1987 Budget speech) claimed that the Governor's lecture gave the reasons for the abandonment of broad money targets.

One earlier period of deregulation - the removal of direct controls on bank lending in September 1971 under the package of reforms called Competition and Credit Control - should have cautioned against too sanguine an interpretation of the financial deregulation which took place in the 1980s. This earlier period of deregulation led to strong growth of broad money and lending to the private sector which in turn fuelled a boom in the housing market, a sharp increase in consumer spending, a deterioration in the balance of payments and a surge in inflation. At that time, the authorities adopted a similarly relaxed approach (at least initially) to the strong growth of broad money and liquidity.

The change in the authorities' attitude to the relationship between broad money and money GDP attracted some criticism at the time. For example, Charles Goodhart (previously Chief Adviser to the Governor of the Bank of England on monetary matters) stated:[3]

> The capacity of the present Conservative Government, and of the Treasury, to move from an (invalid) viewpoint that the growth of broad money is an exact determinant of the growth of nominal incomes to the (invalid) viewpoint that the growth of broad money has no relationship at all with the growth of nominal incomes is staggering with respect both to its speed and the comprehensive nature of the intellectual somersault involved.

Although the Loughborough lecture laid the foundations for the authorities' more relaxed approach to broad money and credit, a later assessment of developments in the 1980s by the Governor of the Bank of

England produced a rather different interpretation.[4] Addressing the question of why inflation started to rise again in the late 1980s, the Governor commented that 'the root of the problem was a consumer boom', with consumer spending growing much faster than disposable income in the late 1980s. The reasons for this were twofold: a rebuilding of consumer confidence after the recovery from the 1981/82 recession, and 'a massive increase in the availability of credit, whose roots can be traced back to the lifting of a series of restrictions on lending institutions in the early 1980s'.

Thus, financial innovation was seen as an important factor behind the consumer boom and the rise in inflation in the late 1980s. In this later appraisal of developments it is changes in the supply of credit which are emphasised; in the Loughborough lecture it had been changes in the demand for money. Innovation and deregulation affecting both sides of the banks' and building societies' balance sheets went hand-in-hand during the 1980s. But it certainly seems that the banks continued to be predominantly liability managers - that is they met the demand for credit and then bid for deposits in order to match that demand; and building societies developed liability management techniques during the 1980s enabling them to act in the same way. If both banks and building societies typically behaved in this way in the 1980s - and that view is, of course, the reason why the authorities continued to analyse broad money in terms of its credit counterparts - then it would have been right to emphasise the extent to which innovation and deregulation affected the credit market. But the basis on which broad money targets were dropped was that financial innovation had changed the demand for money and, because of this, the inflationary consequences were unlikely to be too worrisome.

(vi) Financial innovation and real interest rates

Although financial innovation and deregulation was almost certainly the most important influence on the strong growth of broad money in the 1980s, the behaviour of real interest rates is often put forward as a supplementary explanation. The 1980s saw a move to higher real interest rates, as can be seen from Figure 6.3. Peter Lilley, Economic Secretary to the Treasury, pointed out that this may have explained the trend decline in the velocity of broad money in the 1980s:[5]

> ...one of the features of the 1980s has been the re-emergence of positive real interest rates, as inflation has fallen. That has meant that holding interest bearing money has become more attractive for any given level of income.

Figure 6.3: Real one year interest rate

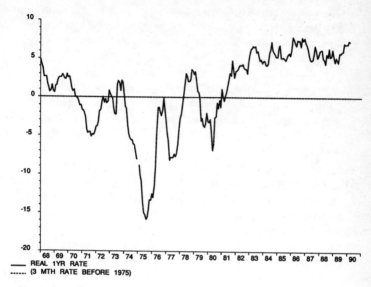

REAL 1YR RATE
(3 MTH RATE BEFORE 1975)

SOURCE : DATASTREAM

Although there is some validity to this argument, it is important once again to distinguish between the effects of real interest rates on the demand for money and the demand for credit. The demand to hold interest bearing deposits will increase as real interest rates rise. The demand for credit will tend to fall as real interest rates rise; and if the demand for credit has been the principal force behind strong broad money growth, then the influence of real interest rates could be quite the opposite of that postulated.

Indeed, the argument can be taken further. Financial innovation in itself may well make the demand for credit less sensitive to changes in interest rates: for example, mortgage lenders may extend repayment terms and offer 'low start' mortgages in response to high interest rates; short-term, relatively expensive credit can be refinanced with longer term cheaper credit; credit facilities denominated in low interest rate currencies (Yen, Swiss franc, ECU) can be obtained. If the authorities continue to regard interest rates as the principal tool for reducing credit demand, then very large movements in interest rates may be required.

(vii) The sensitivity of credit demand to changes in interest rates

The UK authorities, even before the wave of innovation and deregulation in
the 1980s, were rather sceptical both of their ability to explain the demand
for credit and their ability to control it by changing interest rates. Goodhart
has observed that:[6]

> ...we [the Bank of England] have not generally been able either
> to forecast in advance, or even to explain in retrospect, the
> fluctuations in bank lending to the private sector, the explosion
> in 1971-3, the period of quiescence 1974-7, the extended surge
> 1978-82.

Moreover, econometric studies of the demand for credit have generally
found that there is only a relatively weak effect of interest rates on demand:
thus control of credit demand may be difficult. Indeed, a number of studies
have found that there is no reduction in the demand for bank credit as interest
rates rise; in those studies where an influence has been found, the reduction
in demand has taken an appreciable time to come through.

Certainly it is unlikely that any appreciable effect will come through in
much less than one year. One reason is that a rise in interest rates, by raising
the 'interest bill', acts to raise the demand for credit in the short run.[7]

The conclusion for the authorities is that, with the private sector's demand
for credit the most important counterpart to broad money growth, and with
that counterpart largely insensitive to interest rates in the short (and maybe
even long) run, short-term control of broad money by changing interest rates
is not likely to be possible.

(viii) Could direct controls on the banking system work?

The apparent lack of sensitivity of credit demand to changes in interest rates
and the continued process of financial innovation have led to renewed calls
for direct controls on credit. No form of direct control is used at present and
it is most unlikely that any will be implemented in the near future. The
authorities are convinced that any form of direct control on the banks in the
financially sophisticated 1990s would face similar problems to those
experienced with the 'corset' scheme described above and calls for the
reimposition of such controls have been roundly dismissed. The Chancellor
in his 1989 Mansion House Speech said:[8]

...interest rates are the essential instrument of monetary policy. However, I have been urged by some to consider instead a return to some form of direct credit controls. Such a step would clearly be unattractive in itself, because of the distortions and inefficiencies it would create. But a more fundamental objection is that it is simply not a serious option in today's highly competitive and open financial markets, and in the absence of exchange controls. Nor, for precisely the same reasons, is it considered an option in other developed countries such as the US and Germany. Any attempt to impose restrictions on UK lending institutions would very soon be as full of holes as a colander, not least because of offshore flows.

The Governor of the Bank of England, in his Durham speech, added two more reasons.[9] First, credit controls would discriminate unfairly between borrowers - the financially sophisticated would have access to (possibly offshore) lines of credit whereas others would be excluded. Second, it would be extremely difficult to judge the timing of the lifting of controls, especially as this may well be associated with reintermediation of the type experienced after the removal of the corset.

(ix) Controlling credit demand without direct controls in a financially sophisticated world

Thus direct controls on the demand for credit are unlikely to be used and, even if they were, they would be largely ineffective; interest rates have only a limited effect on the demand for credit and financial innovation itself may further undermine the sensitivity of credit demand to higher interest rates; but strong growth of credit was undoubtedly behind the strength of consumer spending, the deterioration in the balance of payments and the rise in inflation in the late 1980s. This conundrum has raised the issues of whether targets for broad money should be set once again and whether other techniques for controlling broad money and credit growth should be used.

(x) A return to targets for broad money?

Congdon has argued that structural change and deregulation in the financial system does not invalidate the setting of broad money targets: rather the right approach is to calculate the probable effect of such changes on the demand for broad money and adjust the target accordingly.[10] Indeed, he goes so far as to say that, in trying to set a target in current circumstances, a safe starting assumption would be that the ratio of M4 to money GDP should be allowed to rise by two per cent each year, which would ensure the economy had neither grossly excessive nor seriously deficient liquidity. If the economy's trend growth is three per cent per annum and the target rate of inflation is five per cent, then the indicated target for M4 growth is ten per cent. Congdon's approach appears attractive in that it emphasises, rightly, that control over broad money and credit should be maintained, but there are two problems with the proposal.

First, there is no basis for stating that a 2% velocity trend in broad money is appropriate. The average change in velocity in the 1980s was 4% and there have been substantial variations from year to year. Second, Congdon has little constructive to offer in terms of the way in which the authorities would bring M4 into such a target range. He claims that the abandonment of overfunding in October 1985 was behind the sharp acceleration in broad money after that time and the subsequent sharp rise in inflation and deterioration in the current account of the balance of payments. In this light, he favours the return to a more active funding policy.

(xi) A return to overfunding?

In current circumstances this would mean that the authorities did not buy in from the market enough gilts to offset the contractionary influence on M4 growth of the PSDR plus any change in the reserves. We argued in Chapter 5 that such a policy would have serious disadvantages and is unlikely to be reintroduced. The more fundamental question, for which Congdon has no answer, is how to control the growth of lending to the private sector which has been behind the strong growth of broad money.

(xii) A reintroduction of the reserve assets ratio?

Another proposal for controlling broad money which has been put forward is to reintroduce some form of reserve assets ratio.[11] Such a scheme would involve the banks maintaining a certain proportion of their assets as reserve assets at the Bank of England. The Bank could then, the advocates claim, control the growth of banks' assets (and hence broad money) by controlling the supply of reserve assets. Such a 'money multiplier' approach to controlling the money supply is often described in introductory economics textbooks.[12]

A reserve assets ratio has been used in the UK in the past: one was introduced in September 1971 along with the 'Competition and Credit Control' measures and abolished in August 1981 when new techniques of monetary control were introduced. The scheme, however, did not operate in the money multiplier way described above. Rather, expansion of banks' balance sheets came first; banks then bid for reserve assets in order to meet the required reserve assets ratio.[13] The scheme was used by the Bank of England not as a method of controlling the growth of the money supply directly, but as a technique for controlling short-term interest rates. By reducing the quantity of reserve assets (principally by a call for Special Deposits) the Bank could reduce the liquidity in the money market and hence achieve greater control over interest rates. Similar reserve assets schemes, which are currently used in other countries, operate in the same way: that is, they increase the banking system's need for funds from the central bank and thus ensure that it has greater control over interest rates. As is discussed in Chapter 11, the Bank of England currently has other techniques for ensuring effective control over short-term interest rates, making the use of the reserve assets ratio unnecessary.[14]

(xiii) Control of the Bank of England's balance sheet

A variant on the reserve assets scheme has recently been put forward by Pepper.[15] He proposes that the Bank of England should limit the growth of its own balance sheet. This would, he claims, limit the growth of the money supply from the 'supply side'. The Bank would control the size of its balance sheet by deciding on the size of its daily transactions in the money and bill markets, rather than passively meet demand for money market assistance (as with the present system, discussed in Chapter 11). By controlling the size of its assets in this way, the Bank would also control the total of its liabilities. Its main liabilities are notes in circulation with the public, banks' vault cash and bankers' deposits, termed the monetary base or 'high-powered money'. Pepper claims that:

> If the Bank were to control the size of its balance sheet, it would control the supply of high-powered money. The control of high-powered money would in turn restrict the banks' ability to supply bank deposits, i.e., it would ultimately control the supply of money.

Pepper's proposal is similar, in many ways, to the non-mandatory monetary base schemes discussed in Chapter 3. Such schemes rely for their success on two factors: a stable relationship between the monetary base and the money supply, and on causality running from the monetary base to the money supply. These conditions are unlikely to be met by conventional measures of the monetary base, and are even less likely to be satisfied by Pepper's choice of monetary base measure. The conventional measures of the monetary base include some or all of the components of M0, that is, cash in circulation with the public, banks' vault cash and bankers' operational deposits with the Bank. M0 was chosen by the authorities as a measure of the broad monetary base as it includes all of the monetary liabilities of the Bank of England. The additional liabilities of the Bank include deposits by the Bank's non-bank customers (for example, Bank of England staff and overseas central banks) as well as banks' cash ratio deposits. Although these additional liabilities would be included in Pepper's proposal to control the total size of the Bank's balance sheet, neither would seem to have an appropriate role to play in a system of UK monetary control. It is most unlikely that the deposits of the Bank's customers bear a close relationship with the broad measures of the UK money supply or UK money GDP; and as cash ratio deposits are set by the Bank twice a year as a proportion of banks' eligible liabilities in the previous six months, they reflect changes in banks' balance sheets which have already taken place. Such deposits therefore give information about what has already happened to banks' balance sheets rather than what is likely to happen in the future.

The difficulties with including these two additional components of the monetary base in the measure which Pepper would target should not obscure the fact that the components of M0 are also most unlikely to satisfy the conditions set out above. As discussed fully in Chapter 3, the Bank does not attempt to control the demand for cash from the supply side, but passively meets the demand for notes and coin; and the level of operational deposits is kept at a very low level indeed and bears little relationship to banks' overall balance sheet size.

With the various components of the Bank of England's balance sheet determined in the way described above, it is most unlikely that its control could be useful as a means of controlling broad money and inflation.

(xiv) Conclusions

Strong growth of broad money and credit, fuelled by financial innovation and deregulation, is now seen to have had important effects on the real economy. In particular, it was an important influence behind the strong growth of consumer spending, the deterioration in the current account position and the rise in inflation in the late 1980s. The authorities have at their disposal only one instrument - interest rates - to control the demand for credit. Although not totally ineffective, the use of this instrument has been, and will continue to be, frustrated by financial innovation. Indeed, much larger changes in interest rates may be needed in the 1990s to influence the demand for credit. But if, as seems likely, the UK becomes a member of the Exchange Rate Mechanism (ERM) of the European Monetary System, short-term interest rates would be determined by the exchange rate (rather than domestic monetary conditions). This implies that fiscal policy will come to play a greater role in the management of the UK economy. The issues associated with the move to European Monetary Union and UK membership of the ERM are the subject of the next three chapters.

Notes and References

1. Loughborough University Banking Centre Lecture in Finance, 22 October 1986. See 'Financial change and broad money', *Bank of England Quarterly Bulletin*, December 1986.
2 Reid, M.I., 'The Secondary Banking Crisis, 1973-75,' Macmillan, London (1982), provides an excellent description of the problems of the period.
3. Goodhart, C.A.E., quoted in Congdon (see below).
4. Speech given by Robin Leigh-Pemberton on the occasion of the University of Durham and the Tyne and Wear Chamber of Commerce First International Celebrity Lecture at Durham Castle, Thursday 5 April 1990.
5. Lilley, P., speech a Centre for Policy Studies conference on Tuesday 18 July 1989, in response to Congdon, op. cit.
6. Goodhart, C.A.E., 'Monetary Theory and Practice: The UK experience', Macmillan, London (1984).
7. A comprehensive survey of econometric work on the demand for credit is presented as Appendix 2 to Chapter IV in Goodhart, op. cit.

8. Lawson, N., 'The Chancellor's Mansion House Speech', H. M. Treasury, 19 October 1989.
9. Leigh-Pemberton, op. cit., 1990.
10. Congdon, T., 'Monetarism Lost and why it must be regained', Centre for Policy Studies Number 106, 1989.
11. See, for example, Norman, P., 'The UK and minimum reserves', *Financial Times*, Tuesday 17 April 1990.
12. See, for example, Chapter 40 in Lipsey, R.G., 'An introduction to positive economics', Weidenfeld and Nicolson (5th edition, 1979).
13. The many drawbacks of the money multiplier approach are discussed in Goodhart, op. cit., Chapter VI.
14. Recent official criticism of the use of a reserve assets system can be found in Leigh-Pemberton, op. cit., 1990 and the *Financial Statement and Budget Report*, 1990/91, page 18.
15. Pepper, G., 'Money, credit and inflation', Institute of Economic Affairs Research Monograph Number 44, April 1990.

7 European Economic and Monetary Union

In a book entitled 'UK Monetary Policy - the challenge for the 1990s' a chapter on European Economic and Monetary Union (EMU) is probably the one which should attract the most attention. For, in a Europe with a free internal market in goods and services, no control on the free flow of capital between member countries and either rigidly locked exchange rates between countries or a single currency, then there would be no role for an independent monetary policy in the UK. Rather, the level of interest rates in the UK would be equal to the level in the rest of the European Community. In this light, the likely progress towards economic and monetary union in Europe is worthy of careful consideration. If monetary union were achieved during the 1990s, then it would ensure that the vast majority of this book would become redundant.

Although the start of the 1990s sees many calling for speedy progress towards EMU, such a state seems unlikely to be achieved in the next decade. After discussing economic and monetary union in this chapter we discuss the more practical issues of the experience the UK has had with using the exchange rate as a monetary indicator (in Chapter 8) and the issues raised by UK membership of the Exchange Rate Mechanism (in Chapter 9).

(i) What is meant by European Economic and Monetary Union?

'European Monetary Union' is generally understood to mean a European Community in which there are no margins of fluctuation between individual members' national currencies and exchange rate parities are irrevocably locked. In these circumstances, interest rates in individual countries would converge and there could be no independent national monetary policies. The adoption of a single currency would be a natural further development of monetary union (in fact the term 'monetary union' is sometimes defined more strictly as an area in which such a single currency is used).

'European Economic Union' is generally understood to be an unrestricted common market. There would be no internal barriers to the free movement of persons, goods, services and capital within the EC. The 1986 Single European Act and the package of reforms commonly referred to as the '1992' programme go some way towards achieving this state of economic union.

Economic and Monetary Union (EMU) covers both these aspects. The United States of America is often considered as an example of an area which enjoys the benefits of both economic and monetary union.

(ii) The Delors plan for Economic and Monetary Union

The Delors Committee, set up in 1988, had as its objective the analysis of the concrete stages needed to achieve Economic and Monetary Union within Europe. The Delors Report, published in April 1989 envisaged three stages towards EMU, described below.[1]

Stage One

The main aim of Stage One is to achieve greater coordination of economic and monetary policy within the existing institutional framework. It is during this stage that the dismantling of internal trade barriers would be completed (that is, the '1992' reforms). Programmes to solve long standing budget problems - for example, in Italy - would also be expected to take place during this stage; and there would be a strengthening of regional policies.

It is envisaged that all Community countries will join the Exchange Rate Mechanism (ERM) of the European Monetary System (EMS) during Stage One. Spain joined the ERM shortly after the publication of the Delors Report, leaving the UK, Portugal and Greece as the remaining EC member countries outside the mechanism.

During Stage One the powers of the existing Committee of Central Bank Governors and the Council of Economic and Finance Ministers would be increased. Their present functions of co-ordinating economic and monetary policy would be enhanced to include greater policy surveillance of individual member countries. The Committee of Central Bank Governors could express majority opinions, although they would be non-binding at this stage. This

Committee would set up three subcommittees which would be given research and advisory roles.

First, a monetary policy committee would define common surveillance indicators. It would also propose common instruments to achieve these objectives. It would attempt to bring about monetary policy co-ordination based more on an *ex-ante* approach than the current *ex-post* approach. Second, a foreign exchange policy committee would be expected to analyse exchange market trends and advise on intervention strategies. A third advisory committee would provide consultation on banking supervision policy.

Stage Two

During Stage Two, the transition would begin from the co-ordination of independent national monetary policies to the formulation and implementation of a common monetary policy. The margins of fluctuation within the ERM would be narrowed gradually from the common 2.25% bands in Stage One. But more importantly, the basic structure of economic and monetary union would be set up and the stage would provide a training period for collective decision-making. While final policy responsibility would still lie with national authorities, policy guidelines would be adopted by majority decision. These policy guidelines would cover two key areas. First, the setting of a medium-term framework for key economic objectives aimed at achieving stable growth. Procedures for monitoring performance and intervening when major deviations occurred would also be formulated. Second, the determination of precise rules regarding the size of annual budget deficits. However, these would not yet be binding.

During Stage Two the European System of Central Banks (ESCB) would be set up and would absorb the institutional monetary arrangements existing in Stage One. The ESCB would progressively assume the responsibility for a Community wide monetary policy scheduled for Stage Three. While the current ERM bands would still exist, realignments would take place only in exceptional circumstances. The ESCB would begin the transition from the co-ordination of independent monetary policies by the Committee of Central Bank Governors in Stage One to the formulation and implementation of common monetary policy that is scheduled to take effect during Stage Three.

In this stage, the ESCB would determine the general monetary orientation of the Community, with the understanding that national policies would be conducted according to these guidelines.

During Stage Two the ESCB would pool a certain amount of each country's exchange reserves which would be used to conduct foreign exchange market intervention. There would be increasing co-ordination of official foreign exchange operations involving non-member countries, leading eventually to a common Community approach. The ESCB would also harmonize regulations in the monetary and banking field such as reserve requirements and payment arrangements.

Stage Three

Stage Three would start with the move to irrevocably locked exchange rates and the national currencies would eventually be replaced by a single Community currency. This would require the transition to a single monetary policy to be completed. Community institutions would receive their full monetary and economic powers and their decisions in these fields as well as the budgetary field would become binding. The ESCB would be empowered to formulate and implement a single monetary policy for the Community and to decide on foreign exchange market intervention in accordance with a common exchange rate policy. The latter would be made effective by the pooling of all national foreign exchange reserves.

(iii) Controversial aspects of the Delors plan and the UK's attitude

The European Council agreed at its meeting in Madrid in June 1989 to launch Stage One of EMU on 1 July 1990. The UK is fully committed to Stage One and has agreed to join the ERM on the same terms as all other EC countries (that is, within the narrow 2.25% band) by the end of Stage One. No time scale has, however, been set for the end of Stage One.

Although UK membership of the ERM has been related to the progress towards full EMU in the Delors plan, Robin Leigh-Pemberton (Governor of the Bank of England) has pointed out that 'the issues raised by sterling membership of the ERM are of a different order of magnitude from those involved in Economic and Monetary Union'.[2] He pointed out that ERM membership would not require any significant institutional changes; that there would be no greater transfer of sovereignty than occurred through membership of the IMF during periods of fixed exchange rates; and that the effects of entry into the ERM would be within the realms of experience whereas the final form of EMU could not be known with any certainty. Accepting this argument, we consider in the remainder of this Chapter the question of the progress towards full EMU whereas the more immediate issue of UK membership of the ERM is dealt with separately in Chapter 9.

Although Stage One has not proved controversial as far as the UK government is concerned, the Delors Report's argument that 'the decision to enter upon the first stage should be a decision to embark on the entire process' has not been accepted[3]. One important reason is that Stages Two and Three require further amendments to the Treaty of Rome. The second controversial aspect is the linking (in the Delors plan) between economic and monetary union and the implicit assumption that monetary union is necessary for the completion of the internal market in Europe: it could be, instead, that economic union can proceed a good deal further without the need for monetary union. The third point of contention is that the Delors plan for EMU involves national governments surrendering control not only over monetary policy but also over fiscal policy. Loss of national sovereignty would be exacerbated by the envisaged greater need for regional transfers within the EC. These controversial aspects of the plan have led to alternative plans towards economic and monetary union being put forward. Before discussing these, we consider the three main controversial aspects of the Delors plan in detail.

(iv) Treaty changes in Stages Two and Three

Why does the Delors Report argue that 'the decision to enter upon the first stage should be a decision to embark on the entire process'? The alternative would be to examine progress during Stage One with future decisions towards economic and monetary union taken in the light of that experience. There are three reasons why the stages are linked. The first is that the mandate of the Delors Committee set out specifically that it should address the stages needed to achieve economic and monetary union. More fundamentally, Thygesen [4] has argued that there are two other reasons for regarding a more indefinite extension of Stage One as unsuitable for conditions in the 1990s and beyond.

First, the challenge to monetary policy co-ordination will grow significantly as capital restrictions are removed completely in those countries that still retain them and as membership of the ERM is extended to the UK, Greece and Portugal. Second, the scope for moving coordination forward towards a more genuine *ex ante* form of cooperation is extremely limited, and the first stage does not modify these limits.

In order to move forward through Stages Two and Three, however, amendments to the Treaty of Rome and consequent changes in national legislations would be required. The Delors Report sets out two options. First, make separate revisions of the Treaty of Rome as the second and third stages of the programme are implemented (a further revision would also be needed for the move to a single currency). Alternatively, a single, comprehensive

Treaty that addresses all the institutional arrangements of the union could be agreed at the outset, leaving to the European Council the authority to move by unanimous decision from one stage to the next. The first approach would provide more flexibility in drafting the Treaty for the following stages as modifications could be made with the benefit of experience. The second would have the advantage of dispensing with the necessarily complex and time consuming Treaty changes at the outset.

The UK government, however, has opposed any Treaty change, arguing that 'there can be no question of further Treaty amendments as proposed by the [Delors] Committee when the Treaty of Rome has been so recently amended by the Single European Act'.[5]

The Strasbourg Summit of EC leaders in December 1989 agreed to an inter-governmental conference in the Autumn of 1990 to discuss the required changes to the Treaty of Rome which would be necessary.

(v) The relationship between Economic and Monetary Union

The benefits of full monetary union are fairly obvious. The clearest is that, when prices are quoted in a common currency, uncertainties arising from exchange rate fluctuations are removed and the transactions costs associated with switching between currencies are eliminated. This would simplify business decisions and the cost reductions in themselves should further stimulate trade. The difficulties of having separate national currencies should, however, not be overstated - they discourage individuals, small businesses and firms new to cross-border trade more than larger firms or those used to buying and selling throughout Europe. Furthermore, the difficulties are being reduced all the time by developments in technology (such as the use of credit cards) and by developments in hedging instruments (such as currency options, futures and swaps).[6]

Monetary union would also entail equal access to financial instruments and services by all citizens and other borrowers and lenders within the Community. This greater competition should enable a more efficient allocation of resources, partly through the attainment of economies of scale in the provision of such instruments and services. But whether monetary union will be a sufficiently powerful force towards economic union, and moreover, whether the costs (in terms of loss of sovereignty) of such an activist strategy outweigh the benefits remains a moot point. The UK government's position is clear: that progress on economic union needs to go much further first of all, before monetary union becomes feasible. Indeed, Nigel Lawson has claimed that attempts to achieve monetary union are actually a diversion from the important task of completing the Single European market. In his view, economic union needs to be achieved - and sustained for some time - before monetary union becomes appropriate. Drawing on an earlier example of economic and monetary union in Europe he pointed out that:[7]

> ... the Customs Union or Zollverein which was formed in 1834 neither required, nor in itself led to, monetary union. It was only forty years later, after Bismarck had imposed political union under Prussian hegemony, that monetary union and a common currency followed.

(vi) Surrender of national sovereignty

The question of the extent to which economic and monetary union should develop together is intimately related to the third controversial aspect of the Delors plan, namely that of the loss of national sovereignty: the main drawback of monetary union is such a loss. Three types of loss of sovereignty can be identified: loss of nominal exchange rate changes as a means of promoting economic adjustment; the need for greater regional transfers; and loss of control over fiscal policy.

Loss of nominal exchange rate changes as a method of adjustment

Economic theory on the subject of monetary union can give some guidance on this issue. The theory of optimum currency areas concentrates on the problem of imperfect markets and, in particular, the problem of price rigidities in the market for goods or factors of production. Rigidities in these markets within a region may result in a failure to achieve economic equilibrium. One way to compensate partially for these rigidities is for the region to divide itself into a number of different areas, each with a separate currency that is allowed to vary in value against the others. But the theory of optimum currency areas suggests that the greater the mobility of goods and services within the region, the less is the need for the these separate currencies. Mobility in the factors of production compensates for price rigidities. In this light the question of whether monetary union is appropriate hinges on the degree of economic integration.

As 1992 approaches then clearly the mobility of factors of production will increase, but there must still be doubt about whether the European market will be sufficiently closely integrated. Currently, around one half of all the trade of the largest four EC countries (the UK, Germany, France and Italy) is with other European countries: this accounts for around 10% of each country's GDP. Robin Leigh-Pemberton has pointed out that this is far lower than the proportions which hold in other successful monetary unions - the United States, for example.[8] Furthermore, it is certainly the case that labour mobility in the Community will for a long time be hampered by cultural and language difficulties. On these grounds, economic integration needs to progress a good deal further before monetary union becomes appropriate.

An alternative view, however, sees monetary union itself as advancing the pace of economic union. The benefits of using a single currency, by reducing the costs of exchanging goods and services, should promote trade between countries within the union. This, the advocates of an activist approach to monetary union claim, would improve economic welfare.

The need for greater regional transfers

By ruling out nominal exchange rate changes as a source of adjustment, however, it is likely that regional differences will be enhanced. Specifically, relatively poor outlying areas in the community might find their prosperity further reduced. This would be particularly the case if, at the same time, uniform community standards on minimum pay and welfare were imposed. In order to rectify these expected disparities, greater regional transfers would be called for. Indeed, in February 1988 the Council of Ministers agreed to a doubling of the Community's structural funds up to 1992: under this programme transfers to the weak peripheral areas - Greece, Ireland and Portugal - will reach the level of 4-5% of their respective annual GNPs by 1993.[9]

The UK Treasury has argued that economic union in itself - i.e. without the simultaneous achievement of monetary union - may help to relieve regional disparities, as it 'will enable countries with the lowest per capita GNP to exploit market advantages, such as their low costs, and hence to maximise rates of return and profitable investment opportunities and attract the flows of private capital required to finance them'.[10]

Loss of national control over fiscal policy

As well as the certain loss of sovereignty over monetary policy and the (possible) need for greater regional transfers, monetary union is also likely to entail loss of sovereignty over fiscal policy. The Delors Report recognises this and calls for an increasing degree of supranational budget control during Stages Two and Three.

There are three arguments why such supranational budget control will be needed. First, the Community budget itself is likely to remain small in relation to the size of national budgets even if full economic and monetary union is achieved. This raises the prospect of an imbalance between monetary policy (determined at the Community level) and the overall stance of fiscal policy (determined as the sum of independent national policies) arising. Second, large budget deficits could be a threat to the fixed exchange rates within the monetary union. If some countries run large budget deficits, the effect could be to raise the overall level of interest rates in the Community as a whole; this could affect the exchange rate against other major currency areas (the US dollar and the Yen). Third, budget deficits may have monetary consequences. If the budget deficit is not fully funded by debt sales, but is rather allowed to raise monetary growth, it could raise overall monetary growth in the Community and once again affect the exchange rate against other major currency areas.

A counter-argument to the need for supranational budget control is that market discipline can be expected to exert a restraining influence on the size of deficits within the union. The UK Treasury believe that this is likely to be a sufficient constraint on national fiscal policy, although they do indicate that it may need to be buttressed by an agreement that the Community will not bail out governments which run excessive deficits. Others are not so convinced that market discipline will be effective. Indeed, the Delors Report itself states that 'market perceptions do not necessarily provide strong and compelling signals...the constraints imposed by market forces might either be too slow and weak or too sudden and disruptive'.[11] Thygesen has cited experience of the capital markets reacting too late and too abruptly to changes in the creditworthiness of individual borrowers within large federal states.[12]

(vii) UK alternatives to Stages Two and Three of the Delors plan

Nigel Lawson submitted to a meeting of European Community finance ministers in Antibes, France in September 1989 two principal alternatives to Stages Two and Three of the Delors plan. The first was to allow EC currencies to compete with each other, with the soundest EC currency eventually establishing itself as the dominant currency in Europe. The second plan was to link currencies to some form of gold or commodity standard. Both proposals would overcome the 'loss of national sovereignty' argument.

The first proposal was subsequently developed by the Treasury in a formal proposal for an evolutionary approach to EMU.[13] The Treasury argue that Stage One will bring about massive changes in the European economy and in particular point to three factors pushing in the direction of lower inflation and more stable exchange rates during Stage One. The first is the removal of exchange controls in the context of ERM membership by all Community currencies. This, the Treasury argue, will require quick action to tighten monetary policy in the face of downward pressure on the exchange rate. They argue that the pressures will be predominantly on the higher inflation economies to reduce their inflation rates. Not only do devaluations damage the credibility of national policy and hence raise inflationary expectations, but also foreign exchange reserves are finite so intervention to support a weak currency will be less effective than intervention to hold down a strong currency.[14]

Second, the Treasury argue, greater use will be made of the low inflation currencies at the expense of the high inflation ones in both transactions and deposits, mainly because the value of low inflation currencies is more predictable. Third, the greater mobility of labour and capital will mean that location decisions will be affected by relative stability of prices: the Treasury assert that 'governments will have an incentive to minimise inflation in order to attract economic activity'.

Given that these three forces operating during Stage One are considered to be powerful ones acting in the direction of reducing inflation in each Community member country towards the lowest in the Community, the Treasury advocate the further removal of barriers to competition between different currencies as a better alternative to Stages Two and Three of the Delors plan. Moreover, the Treasury claim that to decide on the appropriate path to EMU before Stage One has begun is both hazardous and unnecessary given that there will be many changes in the Community during Stage One which are currently impossible to ascertain.

In this light, the Treasury identifies two categories of measures which would assist and accelerate the beneficial trends towards economic and financial integration in Europe. First, remove unnecessary restrictions on the use of Community currencies. Even after Stage One has been completed, there will be many restrictions on the cross-border provision of financial services. For example, restrictions on the currency and location of long-term savings institutions' assets will remain. Second, barriers to the use of relatively cheap and convenient means of payment should be removed. The Treasury cite legal impediments to the simplification of cheque clearing systems, restrictive licensing of electronic value-added networks and anti-competitive practices by banks (for example, in their charging structures) as all needing investigation.

The Treasury's alternative amounts to an indefinite extension of Stage One of the Delors plan. There are likely to be several difficulties with the proposed plan.[15] The first drawback is that the Treasury apparently do not have any proposals for reforming the Legal Tender Laws. There will thus be no compulsion on the part of sellers to accept payment in currencies other than sterling; or, indeed, any on the part of buyers to pay in other currencies. To introduce such requirements could entail substantial costs: UK retailers, for example, would find the administrative burden of having to accept payment in any European currency quite burdensome. But without such a compulsion, is there any indication that certain currencies would come to be more acceptable as a means of payment and a store of value? The Treasury argues that the low inflation currencies (say, the Deutschemark) will be favoured. But, equally, the high interest rate paid on the high inflation currencies may make them more attractive as savings media. There will also continue to be a preference for holding assets in the same currency as that in which liabilities are denominated. The third, and most important, difficulty with the Treasury's idea is that it sees competition between currencies as leading to a 'convergence on the best', with inflation rates converging on the lowest and realignments in the ERM becoming less frequent. If that state is achieved, however, all currencies would have similar characteristics and there would be little to favour one over another.

The 'competing currencies' alternative to Stages Two and Three has received a lukewarm reception from other Community countries: the Bundesbank has been one notable exception, with President Pöhl supporting the plan.

(viii) Developing the use of the ECU

A third alternative path to monetary union is to develop the use of the ECU. This receives passing mention in the Treasury's competing currencies plan, the argument being that developing the use of the ECU could reduce transactions costs. The Delors Report did not support the development of the ECU as strongly as many had hoped.

The ECU has already become much more important in international banking and capital markets. At the end of March 1988, ECU bank lending amounted to ECU90 billion and the ECU ranked sixth amongst international currencies in terms of international bank lending.[16] In the capital markets, the ECU accounted for 4.5% of all new fixed and floating rate bond issues in 1985 (the fifth largest currency share in that year). Although the proportion of new bond issues denominated in ECU has fallen since then, ECU bonds still accounted for 3.9% of all international bonds outstanding at the end of June 1988. The short maturities of the ECU capital market were slower to develop but the Bank of England has recently been instrumental in promoting this area of the market with its programme of regular auctions of ECU Treasury bills.

Although ECU activity is still dominated by interbank business, there have been some indications of a growing use of the ECU in commercial transactions. The ECU has proved to be a particularly attractive currency in which to borrow for French and Italian companies, not only because the interest rate is lower in ECU than in their own national markets but also because exchange control restrictions in both countries have accorded the ECU a favourable position. Strong demand from non-banks for ECU loans has been important in explaining the growing net asset position of the banks in ECU: this expanded from ECU6 billion at the end of 1985 to ECU14 billion at the end of March 1988. Such growth can be taken as an example of the Treasury's competing currencies idea in operation: low cost ECU borrowing acting as a substitute for higher cost borrowing in the national currency.

The ECU is also being used to a greater extent in invoicing across Europe. Again, French and Italian companies have been the most active in this area, but the International Air Transport Association now offers the ECU as an alternative to the US dollar and sterling as a means of clearing payments between airlines. Some companies have also started to publish their accounts in ECU.

Development of the use of the ECU in retail transactions has been slow, to some extent hampered by the absence of ECU notes and coin. Luxembourg introduced an experimental scheme in November 1989 whereby all shops, hotels and restaurants quoted prices in ECU as well as Luxembourg francs, with settlement taking place either by cheque or credit card.[17]

Given these developments, it is not surprising that many think the ECU is already playing part of the role envisaged for a single European currency. But there are doubts about whether development of the ECU can advance the progress towards EMU: there is concern on three fronts.

First, a single currency could not be used until the required convergence of economic and monetary policies had been achieved: the development of the ECU, in itself, could do little to advance this process. In this light greater use of the ECU is not necessary for the attainment of EMU.

Second, some have argued that developing the use of the ECU could indeed be counterproductive to the process of EMU. It might distract attention from the important requirement of achieving greater convergence in economic policies and the development of the internal market.[18] Moreover, if the ECU were developed now without a central issuing authority, it would involve (potentially excessive) currency creation purely by the private sector. This could lead to serious instability within the European financial system. In this context, it would be dangerous to develop the use of the ECU as an alternative currency without an ECU central bank which could oversee and regulate the use of the ECU. Without such a central bank there could be no 'lender of last resort' in ECU.

A third problem is that, at the moment, two forms of the ECU coexist: the private sector ECU used in the banking and capital market business described above; and the official ECU which is used solely by central banks. The two are not fungible.

Against these objections it can be claimed that developing the use of the ECU would be more a replacement for, than an addition to, national money creation.[19] Indeed, there is a risk under the Treasury's competing currencies plan that one national currency - say, the Deutschemark - could become a *de facto* common currency without this being the intention of either the German or other national authorities. This would clearly frustrate the interpretation of German monetary conditions, a development which the Bundesbank is unlikely to welcome.

(ix) Other obstacles towards EMU

Although the UK has agreed to Stage One of the Delors plan and will most probably become a member of the ERM in the early 1990s, the problems faced by other EC countries in joining the ERM are at least as large as those faced by the UK. In particular, Italy, Spain, Portugal and Greece may all find it difficult to reduce their inflation rates quickly enough for exchange rate stability within the narrow 2.25% ERM bands to become feasible during the 1990s. One common problem for these countries is that high inflation brings the benefit of substantial seignorage to the government (i.e the profits accruing to it from the ability to issue non-interest bearing cash as a method of financing its budget deficit). Between 1976 and 1985 Dornbusch has estimated that seignorage was worth 2-3% of GNP per annum for Italy and Spain and 3.5% of GNP per annum for Portugal and Greece.[20] Efforts to reduce inflation through high interest rates would not only put pressure on the public sector debt position directly through higher interest payments but would also - to the extent that they were effective in reducing inflation - involve an erosion of seignorage.

Spain is currently a member of the ERM albeit with wider bands of fluctuation of +/-6% compared with the normal 2.25% bands; Portugal and Greece are not yet members. At the other extreme, the Netherlands has succeeded in keeping the fluctuation of the Dutch guilder/DM exchange rate within a narrower band than that permitted and France, with its 'franc fort' policy, has also stated its objective of revaluing the French franc along with the DM in any EMS realignment.

These observations have led some to expect a two tier ERM, with a core of countries following genuinely fixed exchange rate policies and attempting to make their currencies interchangeable; but with another group fixing their exchange rates in the system but allowing themselves periodic realignments.

Given these observations it seems likely that the completion of Stage One of the Delors proposals will itself take some considerable time. It is doubtful whether it can be completed during the 1990s. An independent UK monetary policy will survive for some time yet.

Notes and References

1. Committee for the Study of Economic and Monetary Union, *Report on economic and monetary union in the European Community*, Office for Official Publications of the European Communities (1989) (otherwise known as the Delors Report).
2. Leigh-Pemberton, R., 'Monetary Arrangements in Europe', *Bank of England Quarterly Bulletin*, August 1989.
3. Delors Report, Para. 39.
4. Thygesen, N., 'The Delors Report and European Economic and Monetary Union', LSE Financial Markets Group Special Paper, Number 22.
5. Treasury and Civil Service Committee, 'Fourth Report: The Delors Report', London HMSO, 1989.
6. Loehnis, A., 'European Currency and European central bank - a British view', *Bank of England Quarterly Bulletin*, August 1988.
7. Lawson, N., 'What sort of a European Financial Area?', speech at the Royal Institute for International Affairs, 25 January 1989.
8. Comments by Robin Leigh-Pemberton at a meeting of Central Bank Governors in Jackson Hole, Wyoming as reported in the *Financial Times* on Friday 1 September 1989.
9. Estimates taken from Thygesen, op. cit.
10. H. M. Treasury, *An Evolutionary Approach to Economic and Monetary Union*, November 1989.
11. *Delors Report*, op. cit.
12. Thygesen, op. cit.
13. H. M. Treasury, op. cit.

14. This argument is, itself, a controversial one. See the discussion of the 'Walters critique' in Chapter 9.
15. Davies, G., 'An empty plan, if only she knew', *The Sunday Correspondent*, 12 November 1989.
16. The data are taken from 'ECU Financial Activity', *Bank of England Quarterly Bulletin*, November 1988.
17. '"Pay in ECUs" scheme fails to take Grand Duchy by Storm', *Financial Times*, Tuesday 21 November 1989.
18. The argument is set out, for example, in Brittan, S. 'Variations on Delors', *Financial Times*, 7 September 1989.
19. This point is made in Thygesen, N., 'The role of the ECU in the process to economic and monetary union', ECU Banking Association newsletter Number 7, June 1989.
20. Estimates quoted by G. Holtham at a conference on 'European bonds : opportunities for investment', organised by Business Research International, London, 17 April 1989.

8 The Exchange Rate as a Monetary Indicator: the experience of the 1980s

(i) Early use of the exchange rate in the MTFS

The authorities have consistently stated throughout the period of the Medium Term Financial Strategy (MTFS) that they have no target level for the exchange rate. It has, however, always been one of the key factors taken into account in the assessment of monetary conditions and took on increasing importance during the 1980s. As early as 1980/81, the high and rising level of the exchange rate was taken into account when the authorities judged that monetary conditions were tight during that period, despite a substantial overshoot of the target range for broad money. Mainly due to the strength of the exchange rate, minimum lending rate was cut to 16% in July 1980, to 14% in November, and to 12% in March 1981: throughout the period £M3 grew above its target range.

From early 1981 to early 1985, however, sterling's exchange rate was on a declining trend. This period saw four occasions of acute exchange rate weakness, each of which led to a sharp rise in short-term interest rates. In the autumn of 1981, base rates rose in two stages from 12% to 16%; in the winter of 1982/83 from 9% to 11%; in July 1984 from 9¼% to 12%; and in January 1985 from 9½-¾ to 14%. This succession of crises has stimulated the comment that 'policy was determined more by the rate of change of the pound, in either direction, and action was taken to check too rapid an adjustment'.[1]

115

The exchange rate does, of course, reflect a large variety of factors and the authorities have attempted to isolate variations in the exchange rate due to domestic conditions from variations due to other factors. For example, the present author, with Charles Goodhart, undertook a study of the factors behind the sterling/dollar exchange rate's volatile behaviour in the period 1979-81, attempting to assess the extent to which the movement was due to changes in the domestic monetary environment, to changes in monetary conditions in the USA and to developments in the oil market.[2] The conclusion of that study was that the oil factor was rather less important in explaining changes in the exchange rate than were monetary factors. One of the clearest statements of the authorities' attempt to isolate the factors behind exchange rate movements was made by Nigel Lawson, Chancellor of the Exchequer, in October 1984:[3]

> ... we take the exchange rate into account when its behaviour suggests that the domestic monetary indicators are giving a false reading, which they are not.

At the time of his speech, M0 was growing at the centre of its target range, and £M3 towards the top of its range, but sterling had fallen by 10% against the US dollar and 5% on its exchange rate index over the previous two months. The authorities at the time considered that this weakness was due to two factors not under their control: the 'abnormal strength of the dollar' and the weakness of (dollar) oil prices.[4] Robin Leigh-Pemberton, Governor of the Bank of England, commented later that:[5]

> ... neither of those two factors are directly within our control... I think it is perfectly reasonable in those circumstances to accept a fall in the exchange rate without tightening domestic policy to counter it.

Perhaps because of the authorities' attempt in the Autumn of 1984 to discount the importance of the exchange rate and their willingness to see a quick reversal of the high interest rates of the summer, another crisis followed in January 1985. Indeed, with the authorities' attitude to the exchange rate appearing unclear, the rise in interest rates during January 1985 was the largest seen in any of the exchange rate crises of the 1980s. The Budget in March 1985 attempted to clarify the attitude to the exchange rate. In his Budget speech, Lawson claimed that 'benign neglect [of the exchange rate] is not an option'.[6] Moreover, it was stated that 'it will be necessary to judge the appropriate combination of monetary growth and the exchange rate needed to keep financial policy on track'.[7]

Some light on what this might mean in practice was given by Robin Leigh-Pemberton when he was asked whether he would want to see monetary growth well within target before he would envisage a reduction in short-term interest rates:[8]

> In circumstances of a weakening exchange rate, then I think it will be important to be convinced that monetary aggregates are working out preferably in the middle of the range or even lower.

The corollary is that monetary growth at the top of the range would be tolerated should the exchange rate be strengthening.

Although in theory a very elegant approach to reconciling monetary targets with the behaviour of the exchange rate, this 'dual targets' approach was not sufficiently robust to meet the developments of the mid to late 1980s. The growing frustration with the usefulness of the monetary aggregates to guide policy as well as increased attention internationally on the behaviour of key exchange rates culminated in a period during which capping the value of sterling at DM3.00/£ came to be the overwhelming objective of policy. This experience, which in many ways can be seen as a 'trial marriage' of sterling with the Exchange Rate Mechanism of the European Monetary System, is discussed in the next section.

(ii) Targeting the DM/£ rate

Although the authorities continued to deny any formal targeting of the exchange rate, the period between March 1987 and March 1988 saw the UK authorities attempting to keep sterling's value within a target band. More precisely, sterling's value was not allowed to move above DM3.00/£, a level which came to be regarded as a 'cap' on sterling.

Behind the evolution to this new approach to monetary policy was increased concern about the ability of the broad monetary aggregates to guide policy. £M3 growth was above target in each of the years 1984/85 and 1985/86. In October 1985, the target range for £M3 was suspended but a new target of 11-15% growth was set in the March 1986 Budget. This was well above the earlier Medium Term Financial Strategy target for that year of growth between 4-8%. However, this higher target range was itself suspended in the Chancellor's October 1986 Mansion House speech. The final abandonment of an explicit target range for £M3 in the 1987 Budget left M0 as the only monetary aggregate targeted by the authorities.

This demise of broad monetary targeting in the UK coincided with a growing movement internationally to place greater reliance on exchange rate movements in guiding monetary policy decisions. This started with the Plaza Accord of September 1985, the primary concern of which was to bring about a further decline in the value of the dollar. This Accord was superseded (in February 1987), once the required fall in the dollar's value had been achieved, by the Louvre Accord which aimed at broad stability of key exchange rates. As far as the UK was concerned, it was the latter agreement which was most influential in the formulation of policy.

Statements by the Chancellor of the Exchequer soon after the Louvre Accord gave the strong indication that the authorities were pursuing an unannounced exchange rate target. After the Paris G6 meeting on 21/22 February, Lawson said he did not want sterling 'to fall nor rise substantially' but with an indication that a fall in sterling's value would be a greater cause for concern than would a rise. Indeed, Funabashi reports that at a dinner on 21 February 1987, when the Louvre Accord was struck:[9]

> Lawson said that as far as the pound sterling was concerned, he reckoned that it was a bit weaker than it ought to have been because of declining oil prices, and therefore he wanted to operate within a slightly skewed range - that is, with sterling's midpoint a bit above where it was.

On the day after the March 1987 Budget, however, Lawson said that sterling's appreciation since the Louvre Accord meant the formulation had changed so that it was no longer as 'lopsided' as between downward and upward shifts. Immediately before the Louvre Accord sterling stood at DM2.82/£; on the day after the Budget at DM2.95/£.

At the time, however, it was far from clear how the exchange rate target was formulated. It could be that the government had an identified - although unannounced - target range for the DM/£ exchange rate (which, in retrospect would have been the correct interpretation). But the Bank of England, in particular, still attached more importance to fluctuations in sterling's exchange rate index and seemed to be basing its assessment on the appropriate level of the index on developments in other economic variables (in particular the oil price). In its September 1986 *Quarterly Bulletin*, the Bank of England drew attention to the combinations of the oil price and sterling's exchange rate index that would leave various macroeconomic prospects unchanged from the third quarter of 1985.[10] In particular, it pointed to the fact that, with a given percentage change in the oil price in sterling terms, a change in sterling's exchange rate index of around one quarter as much would leave inflation prospects unchanged.

In late 1986 and early 1987 such considerations seemed important in the Bank's thinking and were widely used in the City as a way of judging the 'appropriate' level of the exchange rate index. Certainly, immediately after the Louvre Accord there was doubt about whether 'Bank of England type' assessment of the appropriate level of the exchange rate index or some fixed target for the DM/£ rate was guiding policy. As 1987 passed, however, any uncertainty was removed as the authorities visibly acted to prevent any appreciation above the DM3.00/£ level.

The principal way in which the existence of the 'cap' was brought to general attention was the mounting intervention in the foreign exchange market which was needed to keep sterling below that level. In April and May 1987, the UK's foreign exchange reserves rose (in underlying terms, i.e. after allowing for the effect of changes in foreign currency borrowing and lending by the government) by US$7.7 billion; after little change in the June to September period, the reserves once again rose by US$6.7 billion in October and then by US$3.7 billion in December. The extent of this intervention is demonstrated in Figure 8.1

Figure 8.1: DM/£ exchange rate and official intervention

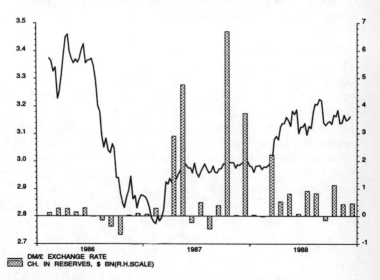

DM/£ EXCHANGE RATE
CH. IN RESERVES, $ BN(R.H.SCALE)

SOURCE : DATASTREAM

Throughout 1987 and into 1988 M0 remained within (albeit at the upper end of) its target range and did not give a clear signal that interest rates needed to be raised. The 1987 *Financial Statement and Budget Report* stated that:[11]

> ...if the underlying growth of M0 threatens to move significantly outside its target range in 1987-88 there is a presumption that the Government will take action on interest rates unless other indicators clearly suggest that monetary conditions remain satisfactory.

As M0 was not threatening to move outside its target and as the exchange rate remained firm (the most important 'other indicator') there was, for some time, no apparent conflict in terms of the messages from these two indicators of the stance of policy.

In October 1987 any potential conflict between the messages from the two indicators became relatively unimportant as the emphasis of the world's monetary authorities shifted to maintaining financial stability in the face of the global stock market crash. The world wide concern was that a global recession of the type that had been experienced after the stock market crash of 1929 might ensue if monetary policies generally did not become more accommodative. Interest rate reductions in the UK in November and December 1987 were due predominantly to the desire to avoid recession and the message from the domestic monetary aggregates was temporarily overridden.

(iii) Why the DM3.00/£ cap was abandoned

Perhaps because of such swift action by the world's central bankers, the threat of such a global recession had significantly receded by early 1988 and in March 1988 the DM3.00/£ cap on sterling's value was removed. The immediate reason for abandoning the cap was that the scale of foreign exchange intervention required to hold sterling down against the DM had became unacceptable to the authorities. After doubling in 1987 to US$44 billion, largely as a result of capping sterling against the DM but also because of general support of the US dollar, the foreign exchange reserves were little changed in the first two months of 1988. However, as upward pressure on sterling re-emerged in the first week of March the authorities quickly found themselves having to undertake sizeable intervention again to keep sterling below DM3.00/£. The authorities probably accumulated around US$2 billion in two or three days in the process and there seemed little prospect of the upward pressure on sterling slackening ahead of the Budget on 15 March.

An alternative way of offsetting the pressure on the exchange rate would have been to allow interest rates to fall again. This, however, would have conflicted with the desired stance of domestic policy. The UK economy grew strongly in 1987 (with GDP increasing by more than 5%) and towards the end of the year wages started to rise more quickly and the balance of payments deteriorated sharply. Concern about overheating of the economy, which temporarily abated after the stock market crash, resurfaced with a vengeance. The dilemma faced by the authorities at various times over the previous year became increasingly acute: domestic factors argued for a rise in interest rates but pressure from international capital flows was for lower rates. Finally, something had to give and ultimately the DM3.00/£ cap rather than the domestic objectives was sacrificed.

(iv) DM/£ exchange rate after the cap was removed

After the cap was removed, sterling appreciated strongly, moving up to a level of DM3.12/£ by the end of March 1988. After that, however, it settled down into a range of DM3.10-3.28/£ for the next twelve months. Compared with earlier fluctuations in the exchange rate, this represented a relatively stable performance. For example, during the five years 1983 to 1987, the rate fluctuated sharply in the range DM2.75/£ to DM4.10/£. This is demonstrated in Figures 8.2 and 8.3 which show, respectively, the actual behaviour of the DM/£ exchange rate and a measure of its volatility over the period from 1979 to 1990. The volatility of the exchange rate since the uncapping of sterling is much lower than that seen in 1986 but comparable with that seen in the early 1980s.

A closer look at the period between the Louvre Accord and the uncapping of sterling reveals that the volatility of the DM/£ rate in this period was indeed lower than that which would have been tolerated within the EMS. Figure 8.4 shows the behaviour of sterling in relation to the 'band' for the exchange rate which might have existed had sterling been a full member of the Exchange Rate Mechanism of the European Monetary System during the period. The band is derived from working back from the 'upper limit' of DM3.00/£ to obtain the conventional 2.25% fluctuation limits which would be imposed by membership of the Exchange Rate Mechanism. Figure 8.5 shows the behaviour of the French franc/DM exchange rate over the same period. As can be seen from the figure, and from the measures of the variability of each currency shown in Table 8.1, sterling was less volatile than the French franc during the period.

Figure 8.2: DM/£ exchange rate and one year moving average

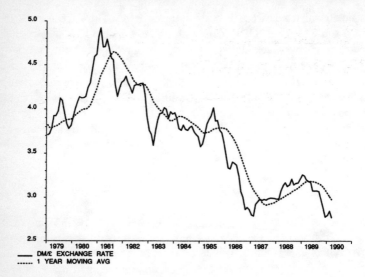

DM/£ EXCHANGE RATE
1 YEAR MOVING AVG

SOURCE : DATASTREAM

Figure 8.3: Volatility of the DM/£ exchange rate

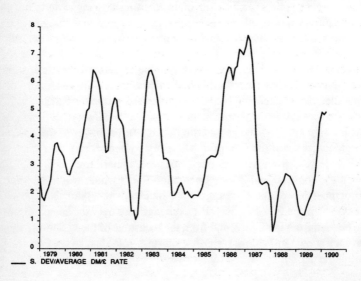

S. DEV/AVERAGE DM/£ RATE

SOURCE : DATASTREAM

Figure 8.4: DM/£ exchange rate, March 1987 to March 1988

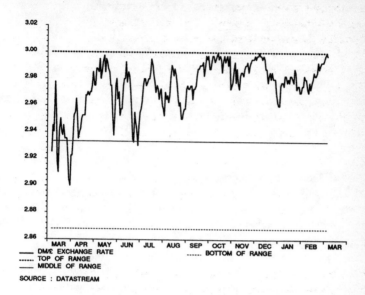

Figure 8.5: French franc/DM exchange rate, March 1987 to March 1988

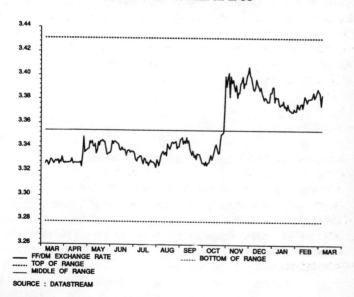

**Table 8.1 Behaviour of the DM/£ and FF/DM exchange rates
(20 March 1987 to 4 March 1988)**

	DM/£	FF/DM
Average	2.975	3.354
High	3.000	3.402
Low	2.921	3.324
Standard Deviation (SD)	0.019	0.026
SD/Average	0.006	0.008

In the light of these comparisons the period from March 1987 to March 1988 can be seen as one in which the UK authorities attempted to keep sterling within too narrow a band. Moreover, they attempted to do this by relying on foreign exchange intervention and changes in short-term interest rates. Other techniques for relieving pressure on the exchange rate were not used. These could have included foreign exchange controls and changes in fiscal policy. The former had been abandoned in 1980 and the free market Conservative government was most unlikely to consider their reintroduction. The latter - fiscal policy - was still cast within a medium-term framework and short-term changes in fiscal policy were thus ruled out as a technique for exchange rate management. Moreover, during 1987, the strength of government revenues and the consequent public sector debt repayment (rather than the public sector borrowing requirement which had been expected) indicated that fiscal policy was not loose. We return to the issue of policy adjustment within the context of ERM membership in the next chapter.

Notes and References

1. Riddell, P., 'The Thatcher Government', (Oxford: Martin Robertson, 1983) p.87.
2. Goodhart, C.A.E. and P.V. Temperton, 'The UK exchange rate, 1979-1981: a test of the overshooting hypothesis?', paper presented to the Oxford Money Study Group Conference in 1982.
3. Lawson, N., 'The Chancellor's Mansion House Speech', H. M. Treasury, 18 October 1984.
4. See the evidence of Robin Leigh-Pemberton to the House of Commons Select Committee on the 1985 Budget: Treasury and Civil Service

Committee of the House of Commons, Session 1984/85, Eighth Report, 'The 1985 Budget' (London: HMSO, 1985) p.27.
5. Robin Leigh-Pemberton's evidence to the House of Commons, op. cit., p.27.
6. Lawson, N., 'Chancellor of the Exchequer's Budget Statement', H. M. Treasury, 19 March 1985.
7. *Financial Statement and Budget Report,* 1985/86, paragraph 2.11.
8. Robin Leigh-Pemberton's evidence to the House of Commons, op. cit., p.34.
9. Funabashi, Yoichi, 'Managing the Dollar: from the Plaza to the Louvre', Institute for International Economics, Washington DC, 1988.
10. *Bank of England Quarterly Bulletin,* September 1986.
11. *Financial Statement and Budget Report,* 1987/88, paragraph 2.14.

9 UK Membership of the European Exchange Rate Mechanism

As discussed in Chapter 7, the Delors plan for Economic and Monetary Union sees all EC member countries becoming members of the Exchange Rate Mechanism (ERM) of the European Monetary System (EMS) during Stage One. The UK has agreed to Stage One, which starts on 1 July 1990. No date has been set for the completion of Stage One. In this chapter we discuss in detail the issues facing UK membership of the ERM which, as discussed in Chapter 7, can be seen as quite separate from those involved in full European Economic and Monetary Union (EMU). We examine first of all the benefits and costs of entry and follow this by an assessment of the factors influencing the timing of entry. The mechanics of entry - the choice of central rate and the width of the bands, in particular - is then examined. The final section deals with perhaps the most important aspect - the effects of ERM membership on the conduct of UK policy. We draw upon the experience of capping sterling at DM3.00/£, discussed in the previous chapter, and recent econometric evidence on the effects of entry.

(i) Benefits and costs of UK membership of the ERM

The influence of the UK in Europe

UK membership of the ERM would visibly confirm the UK's commitment to greater European economic integration and is likely, therefore, to enhance the UK's position within the Community. Conversely, if the UK were to remain outside the ERM then there is a real risk that its influence in the Community would diminish. Although sterling is not in the ERM, it is nevertheless a component currency of the European Currency Unit (ECU): it may be that continued UK opposition to joining the ERM will be met by a formal request to withdraw sterling from the ECU (the French authorities have already threatened such action). This would be highly embarrassing for the UK authorities who have recently attempted to develop further the use of the ECU by issuing a series of Treasury bills denominated in ECU.

Lower exchange rate volatility but higher interest rate volatility?

It seems highly likely that membership of the ERM would bring lower volatility in sterling's exchange rate with other members' currencies given that the mechanism itself is designed with this objective in mind. Experience with the ERM so far indicates that it has indeed brought greater currency stability to its member currencies. It may be argued that this has only been achieved at the expense of greater volatility in short-term interest rates, for example, as higher interest rates have been needed at times of exchange rate weakness in order to maintain the required stability within the ERM. Studies on the relationship between the two, for members of the system during the 1980s, indicate that this has not been the case; rather, ERM member countries have enjoyed both lower exchange rate volatility and lower interest rate volatility.[1] Nevertheless, it may be that this greater stability of exchange rates and interest rates owed something to controls over capital flows by France and Italy, and that exchange rate movements will be more volatile when all remaining exchange controls have been removed.

Stimulus to trade from lower exchange rate volatility

To the extent that exchange rate volatility is reduced in the ERM, this should facilitate trade within the EC. Econometric studies of the relationship between exchange rate volatility and trade have, however, generally found only limited effects. Moreover, any beneficial effect may be becoming even less important as the UK corporate sector finds itself able to use a wide array of financial instruments - forward transactions and options, for example - to hedge against the effects of exchange rate volatility.

 Furthermore, ERM membership would do nothing to reduce volatility with other currencies outside the ERM and it may well be that a greater overall benefit to trade would come from, say, targeting sterling's exchange rate index. Trade with countries outside the EC may be hampered if the EC develops into the 'fortress Europe' feared, in particular, by many in the United States.

Easier control of inflation?

It may be that inflation would be easier to control if sterling were a member of the ERM. Some ERM members have improved their inflation performance in recent years, France and Italy being the most notable examples. As can be seen from Figure 9.1, the inflation rates in those two countries fell relative to the rate in West Germany throughout the 1980s. The French and Italian authorities doubt that this narrowing of inflation rate differentials could have been achieved without ERM membership. Clearly there is no way in which ERM membership automatically brings a reduction in inflation. The advocates of ERM membership as a means to controlling inflation argue that a fixed exchange rate with the currency of a low inflation economy (such as West Germany) involves the need to run appropriately restrictive fiscal and monetary policies. This ensures that both countries, in the long run, have the same inflation rate.

**Figure 9.1: Italian-German and French-German
inflation differentials**

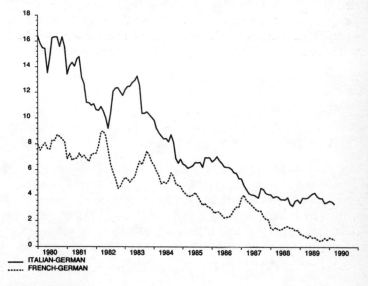

ITALIAN-GERMAN
FRENCH-GERMAN

SOURCE : DATASTREAM

There are four practical difficulties with using such an exchange rate link as the basis of counter-inflation policy. First, there are real doubts about whether this mechanism can work over the relatively short time scale dictated by the needs to maintain exchange rate stability within a system such as the ERM. The UK's experience with capping sterling's value between March 1987 and March 1988 (discussed in Chapter 8) should be seen in this light. Second, the operation of financial markets might actually mean that it is difficult to implement the appropriate monetary tightening (this point is discussed in full later in this chapter). Third, tying sterling's exchange rate to the Deutschemark would ensure long run equality of inflation only in the internationally traded goods sector. There is, for the UK, a large non-traded goods sector (for example, much of the service sector) which is relatively unresponsive to international competition. Fourth, it may be easier to reduce inflation whilst staying outside the ERM. We discuss this point more fully in (section ii).

A new framework for monetary policy

A related argument for entry to the ERM is that the need to achieve exchange rate stability would provide a new framework for policy similar to that envisaged when the Medium Term Financial Strategy (MTFS) was first announced. Just as with the MTFS, membership of the ERM would, the advocates say, be an important influence on the formation of inflationary expectations. Given that the direct effects of the MTFS itself on the formation of expectations were limited, there must be real doubt as to whether this process would be at all effective. There is little doubt, however, that ERM membership would prove to be an important constraint on the conduct of both monetary and fiscal policy. These issues are discussed in detail in the final section of this chapter.

Loss of sovereignty

The need to maintain exchange rate stability in the ERM would undoubtedly be a constraint on the conduct of policy and in this sense some loss of national sovereignty may be entailed. In the most extreme form this view has been described by some as 'handing over the conduct of UK monetary policy to the Bundesbank'. But with exchange rate stability a key aim of UK policy even outside the ERM (and with growing emphasis amongst the large industrialised nations on exchange rate management) the loss of sovereignty involved should not be exaggerated.

(ii) The timing of UK entry to the ERM

The Delors Report specified that Stage One should begin no later than 1 July 1990 and the Madrid Summit, shortly after the Delors Report was published, agreed that there will be full participation in the ERM on the same terms (that is, within the 2.25% narrow bands) for all members by the end of Stage One. No date has been set for the end of Stage One but Robin Leigh-Pemberton has said 'that means at the latest by the mid 1990s - and I would say, privately, the sooner the better'.[2] Within Stage One, three factors will influence the timing of UK entry to the ERM: the progress in removing exchange controls and other impediments to the free flow of capital in the rest of the Community; the relative growth of the UK and other European economies; and the inflation differential between the UK and other ERM members.

Removal of capital controls

One of the principal objections to UK membership of the ERM has been that foreign exchange controls are present in some ERM countries. The UK, which abolished exchange controls in 1979, would thus be more vulnerable to volatile capital flows than would other ERM countries as long as this were still the case. Restrictions on short-term capital flows are due to be dismantled in the early 1990s. Indeed, France abolished all remaining controls ahead of schedule on 1 January 1990; Belgium, which was due to remove its two-tier exchange market based on capital controls by the end of 1992 actually did so in May 1990; Italy removed all its remaining controls on 14 May 1990. Spain, Ireland, Greece and Portugal are due to remove their controls by the end of 1992. While Greece and Portugal may request a delay in the deadline set for them, the removal of the other controls looks likely to develop on schedule.

One view is that exchange controls have been crucial in holding the ERM together and that once they are abolished the mechanism may well collapse. In this light, the question of UK membership will not arise. It should be said that the experience of removing exchange controls in recent years does not support the view that these have been important in maintaining exchange rate stability. Rather, they have only been removed when underlying economic fundamentals have supported such a development.

As well as controls on short-term capital movements, the UK authorities have also cited controls on long-term funds' holdings of assets in foreign currencies as another form of exchange control. German life insurance companies, for example, hold only a very small proportion (around ½% at the end of 1988) of their assets in foreign securities, compared with around

10% in the UK.[3] The UK government is unlikely to insist that all restrictions on life insurance companies and pension funds holdings of foreign securities are removed before the UK will join the ERM: rather progress has to be made 'in the right direction'.

Assuming that the ERM does remain intact when remaining exchange controls are removed, it will be the behaviour of economic variables that will influence the timing of UK entry. Specifically, two conditions need to be met: a greater degree of 'conjunctural convergence' in demand conditions and a narrower inflation differential with other European countries.[4] We explore these two issues below.

Convergence of demand conditions

Greater 'conjunctural convergence' in demand conditions means that the behaviour of UK domestic demand should not be out of step with that in other ERM member countries. For example, UK domestic demand should not be strong when growth in Continental Europe is weak. If this were the case then divergent domestic monetary policies would be called for: the UK could be aiming to tighten policy at the same time as easier policies were being pursued elsewhere in Europe. In Figure 9.2 we show that, in the early years of the ERM, this condition was not met with growth of French and Italian domestic demand much stronger than in West Germany: it is no coincidence that the period saw the greatest strains within the ERM and frequent realignments. Since then, however, much greater convergence in conditions between the three major continental European economies has been achieved.

Throughout the 1980s, demand conditions in the UK were not particularly closely related to those in West Germany (see Figure 9.3). In 1990, this will probably remain the case with the tightening of UK policy from mid-1988 onwards leading to much slower growth of domestic demand at the same time as demand in West Germany is likely to grow quite strongly. On this basis, ERM membership during 1990 would be ruled out. Greater convergence is expected to be achieved in 1991 making membership more likely in that year.

Convergence of inflation performance

The same message comes from an examination of the behaviour of inflation differentials with other European countries, especially West Germany. The average inflation rate in the UK may well be around 4% higher than in West Germany in 1990, higher than the UK authorities would like to see on joining the ERM. The differential may well fall to a more acceptable 2-2.5% in 1991.

Figure 9.2: Domestic demand growth in Germany, France and Italy

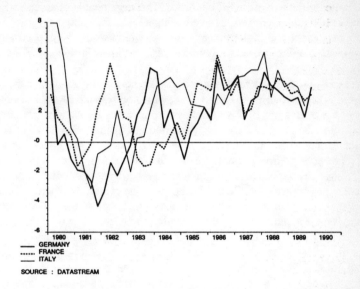

GERMANY
FRANCE
ITALY

SOURCE : DATASTREAM

Figure 9.3: Domestic demand growth in Germany and the UK

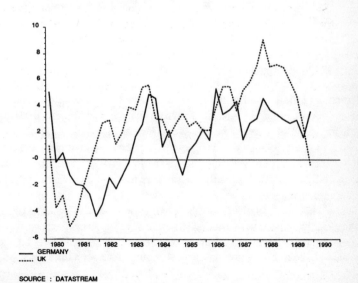

GERMANY
UK

SOURCE : DATASTREAM

It has been argued that rather than wait for the inflation differential to narrow, the UK should enter the ERM and this in itself would help to reduce inflation relative to other EC countries. This argument is often extended to make the point that the costs of achieving a lower inflation rate - in terms of the lost output and higher unemployment which would be expected from conducting a tight monetary policy - might be lower inside the ERM than outside.

The empirical work on this question suggests that the opposite is the case: that it is easier to bring inflation down whilst outside the ERM. Perhaps the most thorough study of this issue has been made by the National Institute of Economic and Social Research: it carried out a simulation of what would have happened during the period 1979-1988 if sterling had joined the ERM at its inception.[5] Specifically, it is assumed that sterling moved in line with a weighted average of the Deutschemark, French franc and Italian lira relative to non-EMS currencies. On this basis, the value of sterling would have been lower (in terms of its exchange rate index) for much of the period. Interest rates, on the assumption that these would have been in line with the average in other ERM countries, would have been much lower in 1979 and 1980 and again from 1985 to 1988. On the basis of these assumptions, it was found that inflation would have been higher at its peak in 1980 and slower to fall with ERM membership: the ability to allow the exchange rate to appreciate whilst outside the ERM gave the authorities the ability to bring inflation down faster than would otherwise have been the case.

This point is demonstrated in Figure 9.4 which shows the progress in reducing the UK inflation rate relative to that in West Germany during the 1980s. Progress between 1980 and 1983 was swift, with the average differential between the two inflation rates falling from 12.5% to 1.3%. When mortgage interest payments are excluded from the UK RPI, the fall in the differential is not quite so marked. In contrast, progress in reducing the French and Italian inflation rates was slower in the early 1980s. The Italian-West German differential fell from an average of 13% in 1980 to only 10% in 1983. But whereas the UK-West German differential started to widen out again after 1983, further progress was made in reducing the French and Italian rates relative to West Germany. The Italian-West German differential was still 3.7% in 1988, broadly the same as the UK-West German inflation differential in that year.

The National Institute study also examined the effects of ERM membership on output: membership would have modified the severity of the recession in 1980 and 1981, but the effects on GDP would never have been large and the trend in unemployment would have been little affected. The

Figure 9.4: UK-German inflation differential

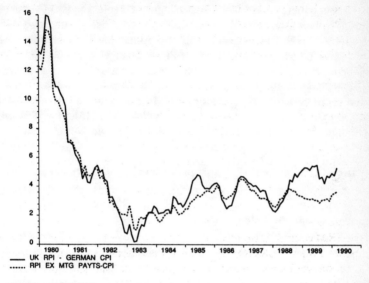

UK RPI - GERMAN CPI
RPI EX MTG PAYTS-CPI

SOURCE : DATASTREAM

current account surplus would have been larger with ERM membership in the early 1980s but the deterioration in 1987 and 1988 would have been more marked.

These findings are generally supportive of the view that inflation should be brought down before ERM membership, rather than enter with the hope that inflation would be brought down more quickly and painlessly.

(iii) The mechanics of ERM entry

There are a number of issues to be addressed as far as the mechanics of sterling's entry to the ERM is concerned. Most important, what would be the appropriate rate at which to join? We answer this by reference to estimates of the appropriate level for the DM/£ exchange rate. There is also the issue of how sterling's value would be tied to other ERM currencies, in particular how it would be related to the ECU and how it would fit into the 'parity grid'. Finally, how would the divergence indicator work? We discuss these issues below.

The appropriate exchange rate for ERM membership

Although there is no doubt that sterling would enter the ERM at the then current market rate, there is a good deal of divergence about views on the appropriate level. Assessment of this appropriate level is generally on the basis of purchasing power parity (PPP) exchange rates, but given that different price measures and base periods can be used there is certainly no agreement about the rate to choose. As an illustration we set out four estimates of the appropriate rate for the DM/£ exchange rate in Table 9.1. As the Deutschemark is the key currency within the ERM, it is this cross exchange rate which would be most closely watched as far as sterling's behaviour in the ERM were concerned.

Table 9.1: Estimates of appropriate level of DM/£ rate, end-1990

OECD method	PPP	3.45
Morgan Guaranty method	PPP	3.22
Simple regression	PPP	2.90
Williamson method	FEER	2.50

The OECD produce regular estimates of PPP exchange rates: their latest estimates suggest that the average rate for 1986 would have been DM4.35/£, compared to an actual rate of DM3.19/£, indicating a 27% undervaluation of sterling. Projecting this estimate forward to the end of 1990 on the basis of actual and forecast changes in consumer prices gives a rate of DM3.45/£ at that time. The OECD estimate, however, is based on prices of a basket of 'final demand' goods, including many goods which are not internationally traded and excluding many intermediate goods (the most important omission being oil) which are important in international trade.

An alternative way of assessing the PPP rate is to choose a base period in which exchange rates were judged to be in equilibrium and assess movements relative to this period: this approach is used by Morgan Guaranty.[6] The base period chosen is 1980-82, a complete cycle in the US economy. The choice of this period is, as far as the UK is concerned, unfortunate as it almost certainly covers a period during which sterling was overvalued.[7] An estimate of the PPP exchange rate on this basis - once again projected forward to the end of 1990 - is thus almost certainly too high.

The third PPP estimate is based on a simple regression of relative prices in the UK and West Germany between 1983 and 1989. This assumes that, on average over that period, PPP between the two countries was achieved (the price series chosen being consumer prices in West Germany and retail prices in the UK). 1983 is chosen as the starting period to exclude the 1980-82 period discussed above. The way in which the PPP estimate changed over the course of the period is shown in Figure 9.5. This emphasises that, given a faster inflation rate in the UK than in West Germany, a trend fall in the PPP exchange rate takes place. If, for example, UK inflation is 3% higher each year than in West Germany, a 3% decline in the PPP exchange rate takes place per annum. This estimate, once again projected forward to the end of 1990, suggests a DM2.90/£ level would be appropriate.

Figure 9.5: DM/£ purchasing power parity

SOURCE : DATASTREAM

A more sophisticated attempt at assessing the appropriate level of the exchange rate has been developed by Williamson.[8] He has put forward the concept of the 'fundamental equilibrium exchange rate' or FEER. This is the level of the real exchange rate index that produces an equilibrium level for the current account balance that is exactly matched by structural capital flows. If the current account balance is at this level then there will be no need to attract short-term, speculative capital inflows which may be more dependent on expectations of short-term exchange rate movements or short-term interest rate differentials. In the specific case of the UK, the FEER is defined as that level of the real exchange rate index which results in an appropriate level of the current account balance after taking into account three factors:

(a) the effect of the discovery of North Sea oil (it is assumed half of the net revenue should benefit the current account);
(b) the systematic under-recording of the UK's current account position. As the sum of the available data on world current account balances does not add up to zero, the UK is 'credited' with some of the 'missing' amount;
(c) the stimulus to economic activity which would be required to reduce UK unemployment to the OECD average.

On the basis of these considerations Williamson estimated the FEER as DM3.10/£ in the fourth quarter of 1984. The Public Policy Centre updated Williamson's estimates of FEERs, taking into account relative price movements and oil price changes and came to an estimate of a DM2.85/£ FEER for the fourth quarter of 1985.[9] Taking into account these considerations, the Public Policy Centre advocated ERM entry in 1987 at a central rate of DM2.80/£. Projecting this estimate forward to the end of 1990 on the basis of actual and expected inflation since 1987, a rate of DM2.50/£ is suggested.[10]

Clearly, there is a wide difference between views of the appropriate DM/£ exchange rate but the PPP framework does emphasise that as long as the UK inflation rate continues to be higher than that in West Germany, a continuous fall in the nominal value of sterling against the DM will be necessary if a real exchange rate level is to be preserved. On the basis of UK inflation at around 5-6% p.a. and West German inflation at around 3% p.a., devaluations of sterling within the ERM would probably be needed around once every year if sterling entered the system at the centre of a conventional 2.25% target band and if the aim was to keep sterling's real exchange rate stable. This approach to managing the target level of the exchange rate - i.e. making regular adjustments in the nominal rate to maintain a real rate - has been described by Charles Goodhart as the 'wet' approach to ERM entry.[11] The alternative 'dry' approach involves entering the ERM with the intention of making no adjustment in the nominal exchange rate - the UK government would therefore tolerate a rise in the real exchange rate. We return to the issue of the effect of ERM membership on the conduct of policy in the final section.

Sterling and the ECU

Although the DM/£ exchange rate would be the most closely observed rate for sterling inside the ERM, sterling's exchange rate parities against all the

ERM currencies would be derived from the 'central rate' of sterling against the ECU. Sterling is already a component currency of the ECU, which is defined as a basket of European currencies. The basket contains fixed amounts of each component currency. Currently, one ECU is equal to:

	0.6242	Deutschemarks
plus	1.332	French francs
plus	0.2198	Dutch florins
plus	151.8	Italian lira
plus	3.431	Belgian/Luxembourg francs
plus	0.1976	Danish krone
plus	0.008552	Irish punts
plus	6.885	Spanish pesetas
plus	1.393	Portuguese escudos
plus	1.44	Greek drachmas
plus	0.08784	Pounds sterling.

The ECU can thus be created by bundling together these quantities of each national currency. This is, in fact, how the private banking system creates ECUs.

For each currency in the ERM a central rate against the ECU is set. The current central rates - following the last realignment in January 1990 - are shown in the second column of Table 9.2. These are the amounts of each local currency equal to one ECU, for example, one ECU equals £0.72862. For sterling, the Portuguese escudo and the Greek drachma, which are not members of the ERM, these central rates are described as 'notional' central rates. The weight of each currency in the ECU is calculated as the quantity of that currency, divided by its central rate against the ECU, multiplied by 100, and is shown in the third column of the table.

By virtue of the fact that the number of units of each currency in the ECU is fixed, as currency values fluctuate against the ECU then the weight of each currency in the ECU changes. For example, if sterling appreciates against the other currencies in the ECU then its weight in the ECU will rise. This feature means that if, as has been the case in the past, the Deutschemark rises against other European currencies,then its weight will tend to rise in the ECU. Every five years, however, new weights in the ECU are assessed, with the appropriate weights being based on the relative size of national GDPs and the importance of each country within European trade. The amount of each currency in the ECU is then changed in order to give new weights which are considered appropriate. The last such reweighting occurred in September 1989.

Table 9.2: Composition of the ECU

	Amount of Currency in the ECU basket	Central Rate against the ECU	Weight in the ECU %
Deutschemark	0.6242	2.04446	30.53
French franc	1.332	6.85684	19.43
Dutch florin	0.2198	2.30358	9.54
Italian lira	151.8	1,529.7	9.92
Belg/Lux. fr	3.431	42.1679	8.14
Danish krone	0.1976	7.79845	2.53
Irish punt	0.008552	0.76316	1.12
Spanish peseta	6.885	132.889	5.18
Port. escudo	1.393	177.743	0.78
Greek drachma	1.44	187.934	0.77
£ sterling	0.08784	0.72862	12.06
			100.00

Width of band

On the basis of the central rates of each currency against the ECU, a system of central bilateral rates can be derived. Thus, the central rate of DM2.04446/ECU and the notional central rate of £0.72862/ECU give a notional central rate of DM2.80595/£. For each currency, fluctuations of +/- 2.25% around this central rate (+/- 6% at the moment for Spain) are allowed. If sterling were to enter the ERM with 2.25% bands of fluctuation, and the central rates and notional central rates were unchanged, then the new ERM 'parity grid' would be the one set out in Table 9.3. Fluctuations within such a band will be the most closely monitored aspect of UK exchange rate variations when sterling enters the ERM.

Divergence Indicator

Apart from this constraint on exchange rate fluctuations, a divergence indicator, designed to show the relative strength of each currency, is also used. The construction of this divergence indicator is explained in Table 9.4. In the top panel of the table we show the central rates of each currency in terms of the ECU (the same as the rates shown in Tables 9.2 and 9.3). From these we can derive the central rate for each currency against sterling.

		DM	Ffr	Dfl	Lira(1000)	Bfr	Dkr	I£	SP(100)	£
DM	+2.25%	—	3.43050	1.15235	0.76540	21.0950	3.90160	0.38125	0.69017	0.36450
	Central		3.35386	1.12674	0.74821	20.6255	3.81443	0.37328	0.65000	0.35639
	-2.25%		3.27920	1.10675	0.73157	20.1655	3.73000	0.36496	0.61217	0.34845
Ffr	+2.25%	0.30495	—	0.34360	0.22817	6.28970	1.16320	0.11383	0.20578	0.10868
	Central	0.29816		0.33595	0.22309	6.14977	1.13732	0.11130	0.19381	0.10626
	-2.25%	0.29150		0.32848	0.21813	6.01296	1.11200	0.10882	0.18253	0.10390
Dfl	+2.25%	0.90770	3.04400	—	0.67912	18.7215	3.46240	0.33887	0.61253	0.32350
	Central	0.88753	2.97660		0.66405	18.3054	3.38536	0.33129	0.57688	0.31630
	-2.25%	0.86780	2.91040		0.64928	17.8985	3.31020	0.32394	0.54331	0.30926
Lira (1000)	+2.25%	1.36700	4.45845	1.54000	—	28.1935	5.21400	0.51025	0.92241	0.48715
	Central	1.33651	4.48247	1.50590		27.5661	5.09803	0.49889	0.86873	0.47631
	-2.25%	1.30650	4.38300	1.47250		26.9527	4.98500	0.48779	0.81817	0.46571
Bfr	+2.25%	0.04959	0.16631	0.05587	0.03710	—	0.18915	0.01851	0.03347	0.01767
	Central	0.04848	0.16261	0.05463	0.03628		0.18494	0.01810	0.03151	0.01728
	-2.25%	0.04740	0.15899	0.05341	0.03547		0.18082	0.01770	0.02968	0.01689
Dkr	+2.25%	0.26813	0.89925	0.30210	0.20062	5.53000	—	0.10009	0.18094	0.09556
	Central	0.26216	0.87926	0.29539	0.19615	5.40722		0.09786	0.17040	0.09343
	-2.25%	0.25630	0.85970	0.28883	0.19179	5.28689		0.09568	0.16049	0.09352
I£	+6%	2.74000	9.1890	3.08700	2.05005	56.5115	10.4511	—	1.84892	0.97646
	Central	2.67894	8.9848	3.01848	2.00443	55.2544	10.2186		1.74130	0.95474
	-6%	2.61900	8.7850	2.95100	1.95983	54.0250	9.9913		1.63977	0.93349
SP (100)	+6%	1.63300	5.4785	1.84050	1.22230	33.69300	6.2310	0.60977	—	0.58224
	Central	1.53847	5.1598	1.73346	1.15111	31.73167	5.8684	0.57428		0.54829
	-6%	1.44900	4.8595	1.63250	1.08410	29.88500	5.5260	0.54086		0.51632
£	+2.25%	2.86981	9.62497	3.23354	2.14724	59.19120	10.94671	1.07125	1.93678	—
	Central	2.80595	9.41079	3.16159	2.09946	57.87405	10.70311	1.04741	1.82386	
	-2.25%	2.74351	9.20137	3.09123	2.05274	56.58621	10.46494	1.02410	1.71752	
Central Rate —Currency/ECU		2.04446	6.85684	2.30358	1.52970	42.16790	7.79845	0.76316	1.32889	0.72862

Given the quanity of each currency in the ECU, the value of one ECU in terms of sterling can be obtained.

Now suppose that sterling appreciates by 2.25% against each currency in the ECU. The new exchange rates in terms of national currency per ECU are shown in the lower panel of the table. Again, using the quantity of each currency in the ECU, the new value of sterling in terms of one ECU can be obtained: the increase in sterling's value is 1.98%. This is termed the 'maximum permitted divergence' of sterling. This is not the full 2.25% increase that might be expected as sterling itself has a weight of 12.06% in the ECU and its exchange rate cannot change. Expressed in a slightly different way, the maximum permitted divergence (MPD) is:

MPD = 2.25% multiplied by (1-weight of currency in the ECU).

Given the current weight of sterling:

MPD = 2.25% x (1-0.1206) = 1.98%

Thus, for a currency with a low weight in the ECU, the maximum permitted divergence is higher. Sterling's actual divergence at any one time can be measured as the percentage deviation of sterling from its central rate against the ECU. This actual divergence is expressed as a proportion of the maximum permitted divergence to give the divergence indicator. This theoretically can move from zero (when sterling is at its central rate against all other currencies) to plus or minus 100 when sterling is respectively at its strongest and weakest positions against all other currencies. Two complexities need, however, to be mentioned.

First, as long as sterling, the drachma and the escudo are outside the ERM, and as long as the peseta has a +/- 6% band of fluctuation, adjustments have to be made to the divergence indicator. These adjustments consist of deducting from the change in the value of a currency against the ECU the share of this movement which is due to the overstepping of the +/- 2.25% bands by either the non-ERM members or by the peseta. For example, if sterling is strong, this will push up the value of the ECU and lead to a weakening of ERM member currencies against the ECU. An adjustment is therefore made to subtract from the ERM member currencies' movements against the ECU that change which is due simply to movements in sterling.

Second the divergence indicator is not allowed to move to the +/-100 extremes. Rather, a divergence threshold is set at 75% of the maximum permitted divergence. At this level there is a 'presumption to act' on the part

Table 9.4: Calculating the effect of a 2.25% rise in sterling against all other currencies in the ECU

(i) sterling at its central rate against all other ECU currencies:

	Central rate, national currency per ECU	Central rate, national currency per £	Amount of currency in the ECU basket	Contribution to value of £ in terms of 1 ECU
Deutschemark	2.0446	0.35639	0.6242	0.2225
French franc	6.85684	0.10626	1.332	0.1415
Dutch florin	2.30358	0.31630	0.2198	0.0695
Italian lira	1,529.7	0.00048	151.8	0.0723
Belg/Lux franc	42.1679	0.01728	3.431	0.0593
Danish krone	7.79845	0.09343	0.1976	0.0185
Irish punt	0.76316	0.95474	0.008552	0.0082
Spanish peseta	132.889	0.00548	6.885	0.0377
Port. escudo	177.743	0.00410	1.393	0.0057
Greek drachma	187.934	0.00388	1.44	0.0056
£ sterling	0.72862	1.00000	0.08784	0.0878
			1ECU is worth:	£0.7286

(ii) sterling rises 2.25% against all other ECU currencies:

	Rate at 2.25% limit, national currency	Amount of currency in the ECU basket	Contribution to the value of £ in terms of 1 ECU
Deutschemark	0.36440	0.6242	0.2275
French franc	0.10865	1.332	0.1447
Dutch florin	0.32341	0.2198	0.0711
Italian lira	0.00049	151.8	0.0739
Belg/Lux franc	0.01767	3.431	0.0606
Danish krone	0.09553	0.1976	0.0189
Irish punt	0.97622	0.008552	0.0083
Spanish peseta	0.00561	6.885	0.0386
Port. escudo	0.00419	1.393	0.0058
Greek drachma	0.00396	1.44	0.0057
£ sterling	1.00000	0.08784	0.0878
		1 ECU is worth:	£0.7430

Increase in value of sterling against the ECU:	%	1.98

of the country concerned. This can take the form of either foreign exchange intervention or changes in domestic monetary and fiscal policy. In the final event, a change of central rate may be needed.

The Basle/Nyborg agreement of EC Finance Ministers in 1988 attempted to place more reliance on intra-marginal intervention, with the intention of ensuring that action was taken before the divergence threshold was reached. The relatively long period since the last general ERM realignment provides some testament to the efficacy of these measures.

In practice, however, it has normally been the position of a currency within its 2.25% bands rather than the divergence indicator which has been the more important determinant of policy action. This brings us on to the more important question of how the maintenance of sterling within the ERM would operate alongside domestic monetary objectives.

(iv) Effects on policy of joining the ERM

If the UK joined the ERM with the UK inflation rate still higher than that in the rest of Europe, how are policies expected to develop in order to ensure that sterling maintains its stability within the ERM? The conventional adjustment process is set out in Figure 9.6. First, the UK would be expected to have real interest rates higher than on average in the other ERM countries in order to maintain the (relatively) fixed value of sterling. Second, sterling would be expected to be under some pressure given the higher UK inflation rate, obliging the Bank of England to intervene in support of sterling. To the extent that this intervention was not sterilised it would lead to a contraction in relative monetary growth, augmenting the depressing effects of higher real interest rates. Both these 'monetary routes' would lead to relatively slower domestic demand in the UK and hence an improvement in relative inflation performance. Tight monetary policy could also be supplemented by tight fiscal policy.

Sir Alan Walters has argued that the adjustment process in the ERM may not operate along these lines at all but rather in the way set out in Figure 9.7.[12] He has argued that, with exchange rates perceived to be fixed, capital will flow from countries with low interest rates to those with higher interest rates. This will lead to downward pressure on nominal and real interest rates and also require the government to intervene to keep down the value of a 'high inflation' currency. Thus the thrust of monetary policy would be in totally the wrong direction to that which is appropriate. The experience of 'capping' sterling's value at DM3.00/£ from March 1987 to March 1988 (discussed in Chapter 8) shows that such a process did indeed operate in the UK at that time. If the monetary route to tightening domestic policy is thus

Figure 9.6: The convential adjustment process within the ERM

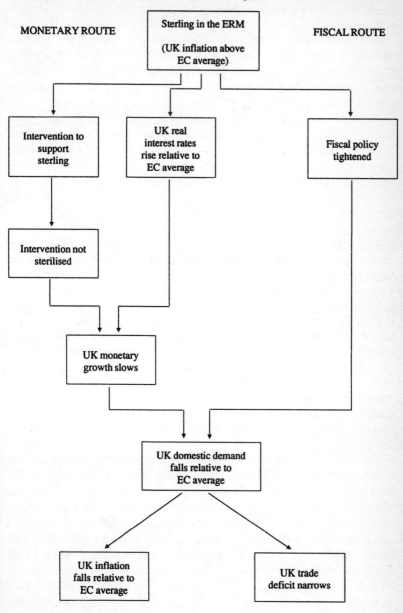

Figure 9.7: The Walters critique

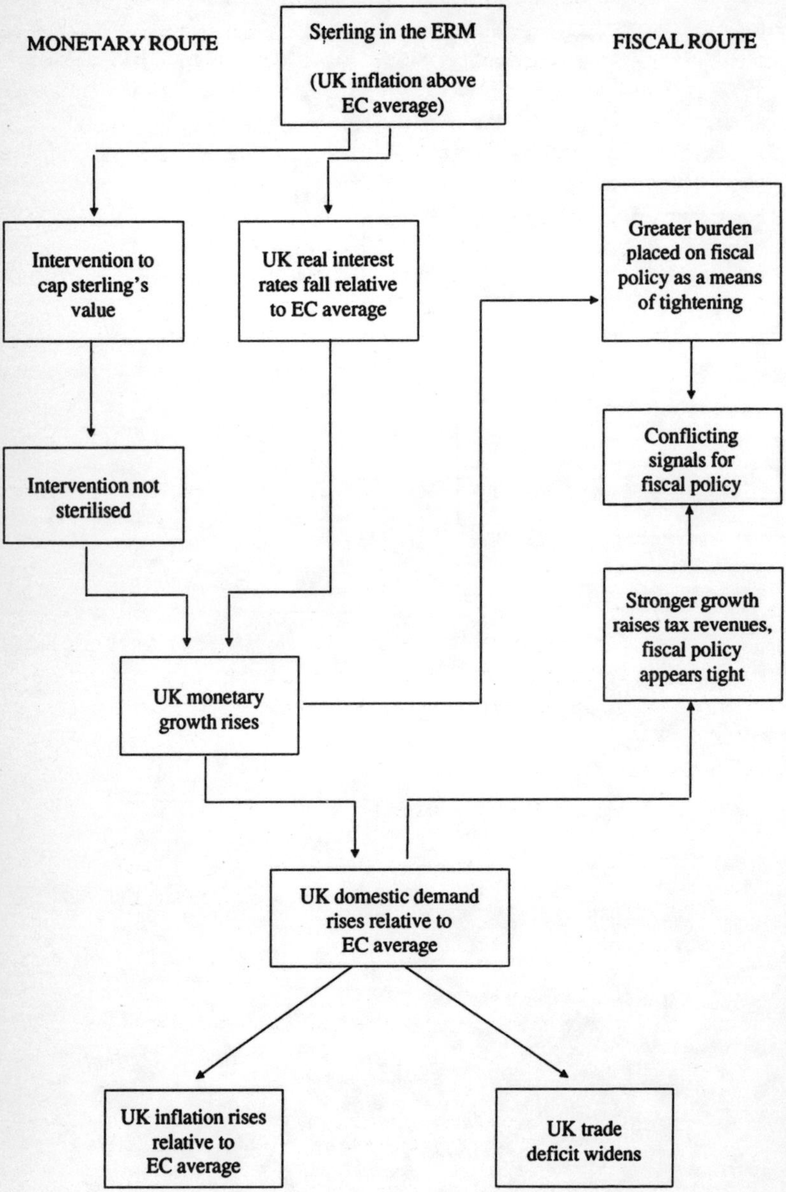

MONETARY ROUTE

Sterling in the ERM

(UK inflation above EC average)

FISCAL ROUTE

Intervention to cap sterling's value

UK real interest rates fall relative to EC average

Greater burden placed on fiscal policy as a means of tightening

Intervention not sterilised

Conflicting signals for fiscal policy

Stronger growth raises tax revenues, fiscal policy appears tight

UK monetary growth rises

UK domestic demand rises relative to EC average

UK inflation rises relative to EC average

UK trade deficit widens

not only ruled out but, indeed, leads to a looser monetary stance being adopted then much more of the burden of adjustment in domestic policy has to be taken by fiscal policy. One problem, however, is that strong growth, by raising tax revenues and reducing government expenditure may (as it did in 1987-88) give the impression that fiscal policy is tight, rendering the appropriate adjustment in fiscal policy less likely.

Estimates of the required tightening in fiscal policy in such circumstances have been produced by the National Institute of Economic and Social Research.[13] They simulated the effects of sterling being an ERM member in the early 1990s by assuming that sterling moved in line with a weighted average of the Deutschemark, French franc and Italian lira against non-EMS currencies. They explicitly accepted the 'Walters critique' in that they saw UK nominal short-term interest rates converging on the European average over the course of two years. The behaviour of the economy under these assumptions was compared with its path in the National Institute's 'base' forecast. Maintaining sterling's value in the ERM entails a loss of competitiveness and the lower level of short-term interest rates gives a boost to both consumer spending and investment. This combination leads to the current account deficit deteriorating sharply with no prospect of a return to an equilibrium level. The National Institute thus assumes that there is a tightening of fiscal policy, taking the form of an increase in income tax of £2 billion (equivalent to slightly more than one penny on the basic rate of income tax) each year and a cut in public authorities' consumption by ½% per annum. This represents a marked tightening of fiscal policy with the PSDR/GDP ratio stabilising at 6% (compared with 3% in the base case) in the mid-1990s. Having lost control of monetary policy by becoming full members of the ERM, the UK authorities must use their remaining fiscal instruments to hold back domestic demand and to restore external balance. Even with this fiscal tightening the current account deficit/GDP ratio would still be 2.8% in 1993 but would be heading for a position close to balance by 1997.

Inflation, instead of running at around 5-6.5% per year in the base case, falls by one percentage point a year, almost reaching zero by the mid-1990s. The inflation rate, as measured by the retail prices index, is actually negative in 1992 and 1993 because of the inclusion of mortgage interest payments (which follow short-term interest rates downwards) in that index. In the mid-1990s, the underlying rate of inflation stabilises at around 2% per annum, in line with the German rate.

The required tightening of fiscal policy, if the 'Walters critique' held, is certainly very large. In this light it is worth examining the behaviour of fiscal policy during the 1987/88 'trial marriage' of sterling in the ERM. The conduct of policy in that period did evolve along the lines described by Walters: short-term interest rates fell sharply; there was substantial official foreign exchange intervention to keep sterling's value down; and these two contributed to a sharp acceleration in the broad money supply. But the real errors in that period may well have been with fiscal policy, which did not compensate for the loosening of monetary policy. The OECD's estimates of the way in which the UK budget deficit developed in that period are shown in Table 9.5. These show that between 1986 and 1987, the ratio of the general government financial balance (a measure of the government's fiscal position preferred by the OECD as it excludes the financial surplus or deficit of the public corporations) to GNP narrowed from a deficit of 2.4% to a deficit of 1.5%. At face value, this narrowing of the budget deficit suggests that fiscal policy became tighter. However, of this 0.9% change in the ratio, more than all (1.0%) was due to cyclical factors - that is, to economic growth deviating from its trend level. Thus, the apparent tightening of fiscal policy can be more than fully explained by the strong economic growth in the year. 'Structural factors', that is, reflecting all other influences including deliberate policy actions and fiscal drag, actually contributed to a slight (0.1% of GNP) widening of the budget deficit, that is, a looser policy. In this light the errors of the March 1987 to March 1988 period in capping sterling can be put down to a failure to compensate for the looser monetary stance by tightening fiscal policy.

The conclusions as far as the conduct of policy in the event of UK ERM membership appear clear. By joining the ERM, the UK will abandon control of domestic monetary policy and a compensating tightening of fiscal policy will be needed. This would be unpalatable to the extent that it involved sacrificing the present government's objective of reducing the burden of taxation.

Table 9.5: OECD estimates of UK general government financial balances

	GGFB/GNP Ratio (%)	Change in ratio	Explanation of change in ratio: Cyclical Factors [1]	Structural Factors [2]
1979	-3.1			
1980	-3.3	-0.2	-2.1	1.9
1981	-2.5	0.8	-1.6	2.4
1982	-2.3	0.2	-0.2	-0.4
1983	-3.3	-1.0	0.5	-1.5
1984	-3.9	-0.6	-0.1	-0.4
1985	-2.7	1.2	0.6	0.6
1986	-2.4	0.3	0.4	-0.1
1987	-1.5	0.9	1.0	-0.1
1988	0.8	2.3	0.6	1.7
1989	1.6	0.8	0.1	0.7
1990	1.7	0.1	-0.1	0.2

[1] Due to economic growth deviating from its trend level.
[2] Reflecting all other factors including deliberate policy actions and fiscal drag.

Notes and References

1. Artis, M. J. and M. P. Taylor, 'The EMS: assessing the track record', in *The European Monetary System*, editors F. Giavazzi, S. Micossi and M. Miller, Cambridge University Press (1988).
2. Comments at a meeting of Central Bank Governors in Jackson Hole, Wyoming as reported in the *Financial Times* on Friday 1 September 1989.
3. Davis, E.P., 'International Investment of Life Insurance Companies', paper presented at the European Finance Symposium, Antwerp, 25 October 1989.
4. Leigh-Pemberton, R., 'Monetary Arrangements in Europe', *Bank of England Quarterly Bulletin*, August 1989.
5. National Institute of Economic and Social Research, 'National Institute Review', Number 129, August 1989, pp. 7-10.
6. Morgan Guaranty estimates of PPP exchange rates are reported regularly in their publication *World Financial Markets*.
7. Williamson, J., 'The Exchange Rate System', Institute for International Economics, June 1985.

8. Williamson, op. cit.
9. Public Policy Centre, 'Exchange Rate Policy for Sterling', 1987.
10. More recently, FEER estimates have been updated in a paper by Barrell and Wren-Lewis. These suggested that in mid-1988 sterling was overvalued by between zero and ten per cent on the basis of its FEER. This would suggest a rate of around DM3.10/£ to have been appropriate at that time. See Barrell, R. and S. Wren-Lewis, 'Fundamental Equilibrium Exchange Rates for the G7', Centre for Economic Policy Research, Discussion Paper Number 323.
11. Goodhart, C.A.E. in *The Times*, Monday 15 June 1987.
12. Walters, A., 'Britain's Economic Renaissance', Oxford University Press (1986) Chapter 7.
13. National Institute of Economic and Social Research, op. cit.

10 Bringing Together Information on Monetary Conditions

(i) Assessment of a range of factors

The assessment of the tightness or laxity of UK monetary policy by the authorities takes into account a range of factors. Different emphasis has been placed on each of the factors at different points in time but the range of indicators which is examined has not changed since the early 1980s. The most important indicators in the early 1990s are the behaviour of the exchange rate and the narrow measure of the money supply, M0. Other information includes: the behaviour of broad money; the level of real interest rates; and the behaviour of asset prices.

The purpose of this chapter is twofold: to discuss the supplementary evidence on monetary conditions which has not been examined elsewhere in the book; and to present a way of aggregating the information from all of these indicators in order to come to an overall judgement about the stance of policy. In this way we attempt to quantify the authorities' 'look at everything approach' to assessing monetary conditions.

(ii) The method used in aggregating the information

In aggregating the information, we start by creating, for each indicator, a measure of the extent to which it indicates that monetary conditions are 'tight' or 'loose': it is convenient to present this in an index form so that for each measure a value of 100 represents 'neutral' conditions, a value of above 100

represents 'tight' conditions and a value below 100 'loose' conditions. The
various indices can then conveniently be aggregated, by assigning
appropriate weights to each of the 'tightness' indicators. Weights are chosen
on the basis of an assessment of their relative importance in the authorities'
judgement of monetary conditions. The importance of different factors has,
and will continue to, change over time. The method can easily incorporate
this: for example, if the behaviour of broad money becomes a more reliable
indicator, a greater weight could be attached to that particular index. The next
sections discuss each of the individual components of the overall index of
monetary tightness.

(iii) The exchange rate

The exchange rate has come to be regarded as one of the most important
indicators of monetary policy as well as one of the most important channels
through which monetary policy works. Chapter 8 gives a full description of
the way in which the exchange rate was used as an indicator of monetary
conditions in the 1980s. It has always been recognised that the exchange rate
is influenced by a number of factors, some of which are unrelated to the stance
of policy. The most important of these external influences is the level of oil
prices. The Bank of England, in its September 1986 *Quarterly Bulletin*, drew
attention to the combinations of the oil price and sterling's exchange rate
index that would leave various macroeconomic prospects unchanged from
the third quarter of 1985. In particular, it pointed to the fact that, with a given
percentage change in the oil price in sterling terms, a change in sterling's
exchange rate index of around one quarter as much would leave inflation
prospects unchanged. We have used this relationship to assess, for the period
from 1980 onwards, the levels of the exchange rate index which would leave
inflation prospects unchanged from the third quarter of 1985, given the level
of the oil price. For example, the oil price at the end of December 1989 was
£12.65 per barrel; the level of sterling's exchange rate index that would have
left inflation prospects unchanged from the 1985, third quarter, benchmark
period would have been 92.3. The actual level of the exchange rate index at
that time was lower than that, at 86.6, indicating that inflation prospects were
worse than if the exchange rate had been at the 'inflation neutral' level. The
deviation of the actual from the 'inflation-neutral' level thus provides a
measure of monetary tightness. In order to simplify interpretation, and to
facilitate comparison with the other constructed index measures, the data
series is rebased so that 100 on the index measure indicates a neutral level of
the exchange rate. Furthermore, 110 represents a value one standard

deviation above the mean level; and 90 one standard deviation below the mean.

The calculated 'exchange rate tightness indicator' is shown in Figure 10.1. The index is 'neutral' at 100 in the third quarter of 1985, the benchmark period. The period 1980-81 is seen as one of aberrantly tight policy; February 1985 is the point of 'easiest' policy when the index fell as low as 75; at the end of 1988 the exchange rate was again indicating monetary tightness as sterling continued to rise after the DM3.00/£ 'cap' was removed; but from then onwards, the exchange rate tightness indicator showed progressively less tight conditions and by the end of the decade was standing at around 90.

Figure 10.1: Exchange rate tightness indicator

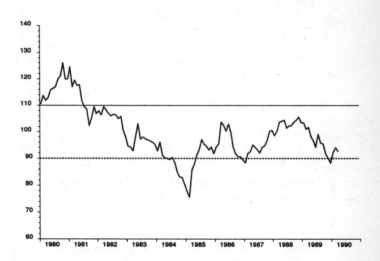

SOURCE : DATASTREAM

(iv) Narrow money

Assessment of the behaviour of M0 by the authorities hinges on its growth rate relative to its target range. Our index for this measure of monetary tightness is, therefore, based on the position of M0 relative to target, with a rate above the midpoint of its target range indicating monetary laxity (thus with an index number below 100); a rate below the midpoint, monetary tightness (i.e. an index number above 100). As targets for M0 growth have only been set since March 1984, this method can only be used since then.

Before that date an alternative method is used, described below for broad money. Both narrow money tightness indicators are shown in Figure 10.2.

Figure 10.2: Narrow money tightness indicator

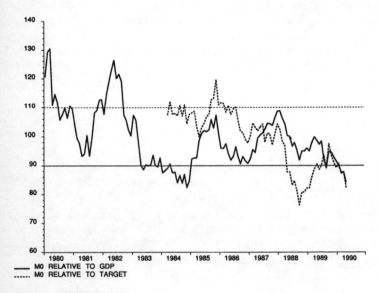

--- M0 RELATIVE TO GDP
...... M0 RELATIVE TO TARGET

SOURCE : DATASTREAM

(v) Broad money

The behaviour of broad money could also be assessed in the same way, as target ranges were set for most of the 1980s. But the view of the authorities is now, and has been for some time, that broad money has not proved to be a reliable indicator of monetary tightness for much of the period and that its behaviour relative to target has not always given a reliable indication of underlying monetary conditions. The reasons for the authorities' coming to attach less weight to the behaviour of broad money are thoroughly discussed in Chapter 6: the authorities have emphasised the importance of structural changes in the banking system; increased competition between banks and other financial institutions and between financial institutions themselves; and the high level of real interest rates in the 1980s. These factors have all made assessment of the behaviour of broad money, relative to its target ranges and to GDP, difficult to assess.

Throughout the 1980s the velocity of M4 fell by an average of 4% per annum (the average year-on-year growth rate of M4 was 14% and of money GDP 10%) reflecting these changes in the financial system. Our index of monetary tightness for M4 is based on deviations from this trend movement in velocity. A faster decline in velocity is taken as reflecting looser monetary conditions (so that the M4 monetary tightness indicator is below 100). On this basis the broad money tightness indicator shown in Figure 10.3 is produced. It indicates that conditions in 1989 became looser, with the constructed index measure moving down to a level of around 89 at the end of 1989. The reason for this was a slowing of growth of money GDP to below 10% year-on-year, coupled with little change in the growth of M4, which remained at around 17.5% year-on-year.

Figure 10.3: Broad money tightness indicator

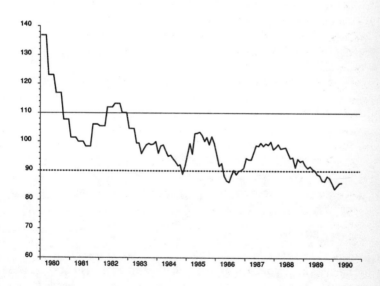

SOURCE : DATASTREAM

(vi) Asset prices

The behaviour of certain asset markets can also give an indication of the stance of monetary policy. For example, the behaviour of house prices may give an indication of the relative ease with which mortgage finance can be obtained and be an important influence on inflationary expectations. Indeed, house prices proved to be a reasonably good leading indicator of the behaviour of general inflation throughout the 1970s and 1980s: the sharp rise in house prices in 1971 and 1972 presaged the more general rise in inflation in 1974 and 1975 (see Figure 10.4). Similarly, a sharply rising equity market may give an indication of easier monetary conditions.

Figure 10.4: House price and retail price inflation

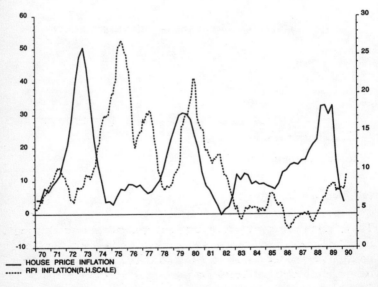

SOURCE : DATASTREAM

Tightness indicators are devised for both asset prices. For house prices the Department of the Environment's mix-adjusted series is used; for equity prices the *Financial Times* All Share index. In the case of asset prices, however, it is deviations of the growth from a long run moving average which is used to assess whether asset prices are indicating tight or loose policy. A rise in asset prices faster than trend indicates looser monetary conditions (giving a constructed index number below 100) and *vice versa*. Data for both indicators are shown in Figure 10.5.

Figure 10.5: Asset prices tightness indicator

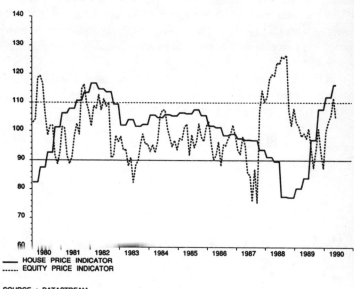

HOUSE PRICE INDICATOR
EQUITY PRICE INDICATOR

SOURCE : DATASTREAM

(vii) Real interest rates

The level of real interest rates, or even nominal interest rates when inflation is low and stable, can be used as an indicator of the tightness of monetary policy. The expected real interest rate is defined as the nominal interest rate minus the expected rate of inflation over the period. As mentioned in Chapter 1, at times of high and volatile inflation it may not be feasible to assess expectations about future inflation with any degree of certainty. Indeed, this problem of assessing real interest rates was one of the reasons for shifting emphasis from the behaviour of nominal interest rates to the behaviour of the monetary aggregates in the 1970s. When inflation is lower and more stable, it may be that real interest rates can be assessed with more certainty.

Assessing real interest rates is far from straightforward: three main factors have to be taken into consideration. First, the term of the interest rate: generally, the focus is on short-term interest rates as it is very difficult to assess expectations about future inflation over long time horizons. Assessing the expected real return to maturity on a twenty year gilt would, for example, involve the formation of expectations of inflation over such a twenty year period. Second, the question of the most relevant price index to use has to be addressed. Although the retail prices index is the most widely used this can, at times, give a misleading impression of underlying inflation (not least because it includes mortgage interest payments). Third, the tax status of the borrower or lender will be important. For example, an individual borrowing to finance the purchase of a house will be able to claim some tax relief on the interest paid.

The constructed real interest rate tightness indicator which is shown in Figure 10.6 is based on the nominal one year interbank rate minus expected inflation over the next twelve months.[1]

Figure 10.6: Real interest rates tightness indicator

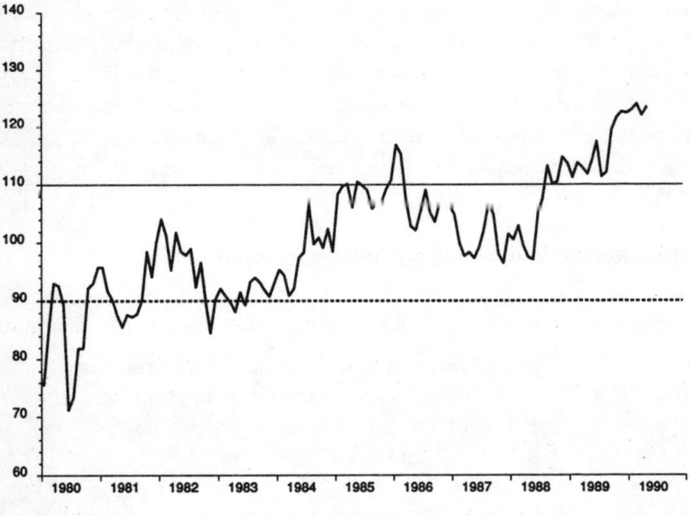

SOURCE : DATASTREAM

Again, deviations of real interest rates from a long run moving average are used to assess the tightness or laxity of policy; real interest rates above a long run moving average indicate tight conditions and *vice versa*.

(viii) Assigning weights to the different measures

The individual tightness indicators can now be weighted together to produce an index of the overall tightness of UK monetary policy, shown in Figure 10.7. The weights chosen, which are thought to reflect the weight attached to each indicator by the authorities in the early 1990s, are:

Exchange Rate	40%
M0	30%
M4	10%
Real interest rates	10%
House Prices	5%
Equity Prices	5%
Total	100%

Once again, the index is constructed in the same way as the individual indices: i.e. a value above 100 represents tight conditions, below 100 loose conditions. A value of 110 indicates a reading one standard deviation 'tighter' than the mean, a value of 90 one standard deviation 'looser' than the mean.

This measure indicates that UK monetary policy was very tight in the early 1980s, became relatively easy in the mid-1980s and, despite the rise in interest rates since mid-1988, remained relatively loose at the start of the 1990s.

(ix) Relationship between the index and inflation

The index of monetary tightness would become useful if it gave advance warning of changes in inflation, control of which is the ultimate objective of monetary policy. If it were a reliable measure of monetary conditions, for example, persistently high levels of the index, signalling tight conditions, would lead to an eventual reduction in inflation. Persistently low levels would lead to a rise in inflation. As can be seen from Figure 10.7, in the recent past trends in this index have proved to be a good leading indicator of movements in future inflation. This very pragmatic measure of the stance of monetary policy provides a better indication of future inflation than any one of the indicators taken in isolation.

(x) Conclusions

The framework developed here is helpful in aggregating the many sources of information taken into account by the authorities when judging monetary conditions and provides a convenient summary statistic. It gives support to the authorities' view that it is necessary to take a variety of factors into consideration when coming to an assessment of the stance of monetary policy as its behaviour has proved to be a reasonably good leading indicator of inflation.

Figure 10.7: Monetary tightness index and inflation

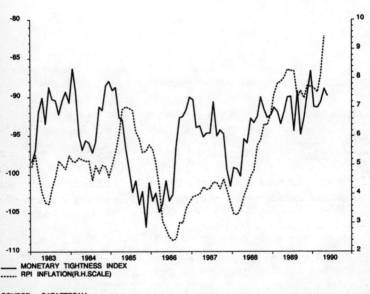

MONETARY TIGHTNESS INDEX
RPI INFLATION(R.H.SCALE)

SOURCE : DATASTREAM

Notes and references

1. The Treasury produces a regular survey of forecasts of RPI inflation by both independent and City forecasters; we use the City consensus forecast in the assessment of the real one year interest rate.

11 Bank of England Operations in the Money Market

This chapter discusses the mechanics of the money market and explains how the authorities act to set interest rates. A discussion of the change in the authorities' attitude to the relative merits of 'administered' and 'market related' interest rates is followed by a detailed discussion of present practices. The reasons for Bank of England intervention in the money market and its operational techniques are examined. The relationship between official money market actions and the determination of the clearing banks' interest rates is discussed in the final section.

(i) Administered versus market related interest rates

Up until the early 1970s, the Bank of England's Bank Rate was the pivotal interest rate in the money market. Bank Rate was the rate at which discount houses could borrow from the Bank in order to meet any shortage of liquidity. The Bank could, and did, make Bank Rate effective by open market operations. In particular, as the discount houses were obliged to take up the whole of the weekly offering of Treasury bills by the Bank, the Bank could, by deliberately overissuing Treasury bills, leave the discount houses short of cash balances and force them to borrow from the Bank. Bank Rate was the rate charged for such 'last resort' lending. Any rise in Bank Rate would induce the discount houses to raise their lending rates and this in turn would be reflected in the clearing banks' interest rates.

The importance of Bank Rate was recognised to the extent that this process became short-circuited. From the 1930s, the clearing banks directly linked their interest rates to Bank Rate. The rate became the central rate in a system of 'administered' rates.

In September 1971 a new system of Competition and Credit Control was introduced. Under the new system, the role of quantitative controls on bank lending was reduced and greater reliance was placed on the role of market determined interest rates in the allocation of credit. The role of Bank Rate as the pivotal interest rate was reduced. In particular, the clearing banks ceased to tie their deposit and lending rates to it. However, Bank Rate remained as the 'last resort' rate for lending to the discount houses and, furthermore, continued to have a high political profile. In order to make the rate more flexible, but still leave it as a penalty rate, a new system of determining the Bank's lending rate to the market was introduced. From 13 October 1972, Bank Rate was replaced by Minimum Lending Rate (MLR). MLR was set at ½% above the average rate of discount for Treasury bills at the most recent tender, rounded to the nearest ¼% above. The rate was automatically determined by this formula and announced each Friday afternoon with the results of the Treasury bill tender. The right to suspend the formula was, however, reserved. If the Bank decided, with the approval of the Chancellor, to make a special change of this kind, the announcement would normally be made on Thursday at midday.

Although the formula-related MLR was considered a more satisfactory system at the outset, the new system itself was found to be lacking when interest rates became much more volatile in the mid-1970s: high and variable inflation was accompanied by sharp changes in interest rate expectations and in the term structure of short-term rates. Lending to the discount houses at MLR was never for periods longer than seven days but that rate was tied to the three month Treasury bill rate. Such a firm link between interest rates for different periods proved inappropriate in such volatile conditions. Indeed, it was only a year after the formula was introduced that the first suspension took place (on 13 November 1973, when MLR was raised from 11¼% to 13%). On 7 October 1976 and on 3 February 1977 the formula was again suspended. On the fourth occasion of suspension, 11 April 1978, when MLR was raised from 6½% to 7½%, it was stated that the formula would remain suspended until it was capable of being applied without a change in the rate: that is, until market rates had risen to a level consistent with the administered rate. After two further administered rises in rates, it was announced on 25 May 1978 that from then onwards MLR would be a purely administered rate.

Disenchantment with this regime soon set in. Changes in the official interest rate once again took on a high political profile and this led to problems with the conduct of monetary policy. Specifically, as soon as market interest rates started to rise, expectations of an increase in MLR were generated and the government's funding programme became difficult. Because official sanctioning of a rise in interest rates could be slow, a 'funding pause' could result: this led to problems with controlling broad money, which in turn could reinforce expectations of a rise in interest rates.

These problems, coupled with the Conservative government's free market philosophy led to a move back towards more market related official rates in the early 1980s. On 20 August 1981, it was stated that MLR would no longer be announced continuously: greater reliance was to be placed on market forces in the determination of interest rates, although the Bank would still aim to keep 'very short-term' interest rates within an unpublished 'band'. The Bank said, however, that it 'might in some circumstances announce in advance the minimum rate for which, for a short period ahead, it would apply in any lending to the market'. The technique has been used and is discussed in section (iv) on operations for relieving a money market shortage.

The next sections discuss in detail the arrangements which have been in place - without significant change - since the early 1980s. We discuss the techniques the Bank uses in setting short-term rates and assess how the arrangements have worked in practice. In particular, we emphasise that the attitude of the authorities is, once again, more in favour of administered rather than market related interest rates.

(ii) The role of the Bank of England in the money market

There are certain key features of the UK financial system which must be made clear when discussing the way in which the Bank of England operates in the UK money markets. The most important is that the Bank acts as the main banker to central government. The government does not hold balances, other than working amounts, with other banks. As the rest of the banking system maintains the accounts of all other sectors of the economy, any net payment to central government will produce a net flow of cash from the banks to the Bank. The banks will typically seek to restore their liquidity by drawing down some of their funds which they keep in the form of call or short-term deposits with the discount houses. The clearing banks keep operational balances at the Bank which are used for settling the final position at the end

of the day between the Bank and the banking system, and their drawing down
of money from the discount houses will be designed to keep these balances
at a 'target' level considered appropriate given the uncertainty of the daily
cash flows to the Bank. The cash shortage in the money market is, in this
way, passed to the discount houses who in turn balance their position, if short
of funds, either by selling eligible bills to the Bank or by borrowing from the
Bank.

Figure 11.1: Money market structure and flows

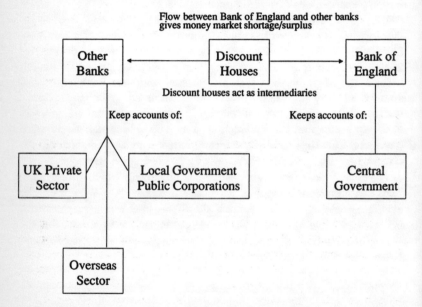

Payments to government are not the only flows affecting the net position
between the Bank and the rest of the banking system on a particular day. The
flows can be placed in the following six main categories.

Exchequer transactions

The Exchequer is broadly equivalent to central government and this category
comprises the main flows which are the result of the Bank of England acting
as the banker to central government. The category comprises: payments to
the Exchequer net of expenditure by it; the proceeds of net official sales of
government debt (gilts, National savings, treasury bills etc.); and net receipts
of sterling on the Exchange Equalisation Account (EEA). In all three cases
net sterling payments to the government's accounts at the Bank reduces

market liquidity. Thus, if the government receives tax payments from, or if it sells government debt to, the private sector the proceeds will act to produce a reduction in the money market's cash position. Conversely, government spending will increase the deposits of the banks and reduce those of the government at the Bank of England. If the EEA intervenes to support sterling (i.e. if it sells foreign currencies and buys sterling) then the receipt of sterling by the Bank will act to drain market liquidity.

Many elements of the Exchequer transactions total can be predicted with a reasonable degree of accuracy by the Bank of England on a day-to-day basis: the impact of foreign exchange transactions passing through the EEA is generally known since most such transactions are settled two days later; gilts transactions are generally settled on the next business day; and various government sources give information on both government expenditure and expected tax receipts. But the timing of some tax payments is not known with certainty and can lead to substantial changes in this component of the money market cash position during the course of the day. (These intra-day revisions to the cash position are very important to the discount houses and close observers of the Bank of England's operations and are discussed later in this chapter.)

The change in the note issue

If the demand for cash, in the form of notes issued by the Bank of England, rises, the clearing banks meet the rise in demand by obtaining notes from the Bank, at the same time running down their operational balances with it. Thus a rise in the note circulation leads to a money market shortage. Generally, the note circulation rises towards the end of the week (as the general public withdraws cash for the weekend and the banks anticipate the demand) and falls at the start of the week: thus on Mondays and Tuesdays the fluctuations in the note circulation generally raise money market liquidity and on Thursdays and Fridays generally reduce it. The note issue also follows a pronounced seasonal pattern throughout the year rising, in particular, at Easter and Christmas. The Bank has an estimate based on past experience of daily and seasonal patterns, and on the banks' declared requirements, of likely changes in the note circulation.

Bills maturing in official hands and the take-up of Treasury bills

If the Bank holds bills which then mature, repayment will come from the rest of the banking system so market liquidity falls. Similarly, as the discount houses take-up Treasury bills from the tender on the Friday of the previous week, net payment will be made to the Bank from the rest of the banking system. The Bank will know the extent of these influences on the market's cash position with certainty.

Unwinding of previous assistance

The Bank occasionally lends to the market or uses purchase and resale agreements, see section (iv). The unwinding of such assistance (repayment of loans given by the Bank to the market or resale to the market of bills bought from it by the Bank) will drain market liquidity and will, of course, be known by the Bank in advance.

Clearers' balances above or below target

If the clearing banks' balances are above target - that is, if the final clearing on the previous day left the clearers with balances at the Bank above those which they desire to keep in order to meet day-to-day requirements - then there will be a corresponding easing of the market's cash position. The clearers tell the Bank of England of their target balances so this influence on the money market cash position will be known with reasonable certainty.

Other flows

As well as acting as the government's banker, the Bank also acts as banker for other customers, for example, overseas central banks and international organisations. Flows due to the transactions of these customers influence the cash position of the money market but are not disclosed by the Bank. Such customers generally provide information to the Bank on flows across their accounts and hence help in the process of predicting the cash position in the money market.

(iii) The objective of money market operations

The objective of the Bank when operating in the money market is broadly to offset the cash flows between the Bank and the money markets and to leave the clearing banks within reach of their desired operational balances. The Bank thus provides whatever assistance is necessary to offset the daily cash position in the money market: the terms (that is, the interest rates at particular maturities) at which the cash position is offset are, of course, determined by the Bank. In order to help this process the Bank forecasts the daily position of the money markets and makes its forecast available to market participants via the various screen-based news services (for example, on Reuters pages RTCA through to RTCD). The Bank's initial forecast and the factors behind it are made available at 9.45 a.m. each day. Factors are normally grouped together under each of the first five headings given above (flows due to the behaviour of other Bank customers are never disclosed). Revisions to the overall shortage may be made during the course of the day, typically being announced at noon and 2 p.m. Revisions to the individual components of the shortage are not made, but generally it is the estimate for exchequer transactions which is subject to the greatest uncertainty. When deciding on the amount of intervention needed, however, the Bank also takes account of the reports of their positions from the discount houses and the major banks, and the behaviour of short-term interest rates. Different techniques are used depending on whether there is a shortage in the money market (section (iv) below) or a surplus (section (v) below).

(iv) Techniques for relieving money market shortages

The Bank of England uses three principal techniques to relieve money market shortages: outright purchases of bills from the discount houses; purchases of bills with associated resale agreements; and lending to the market. These are discussed below.

Outright purchases of bills

Under the arrangements first introduced in late 1980, emphasis is placed on bill dealings as a method of relieving money market shortages and the outright purchase of bills from the discount houses is the most common form of assistance provided. If the Bank informs the market that it is prepared to buy bills, the discount houses will generally offer bills to it, specifying a discount rate, for each combination of instrument and band - or, if they wish, different rates for separate amounts within each combination. Bills are classified as falling into one of four remaining (rather than original) maturity bands:

> band 1:   1-14 days
> band 2:   15-33 days
> band 3:   34-63 days
> band 4:   64-91 days.

Since May 1989, the Bank has normally purchased bills only in bands 1 and 2. The Bank decides which offers to accept: often the decision is the straightforward one of buying bills to relieve the estimated shortage, but purchases may fall short of the estimated shortage for three main reasons. First, because the discount rates are out of line with what the Bank considers the appropriate level: discount houses may then have the opportunity to submit revised offers. If these revised offers are still unacceptable, they may be forced to borrow from the Bank. Second, if Bank estimates of the shortage are unusually uncertain, it may decide to buy a relatively small amount of bills in the morning session leaving the final relief of the shortage until the afternoon. Third, the discount houses might think the shortage is smaller than that expected by the Bank and might thus offer a correspondingly lower amount of bills for sale.

The amount of bills bought in each band, the type of bill and the interest rate at which the deal was made are published after both the morning and afternoon sessions. Normally the Bank operates in the markets just before and just after lunch. Occasionally, on days of very large shortages, it may offer to buy bills earlier in the day (10.00 a.m.) as well as at the normal times. The Bank may also provide late assistance at around 3.30 p.m.

Purchase and resale (repo) agreements

Purchase and resale agreements are occasionally used as an alternative to outright purchases. In this case, the Bank buys bills but agrees to sell them back to the market at an agreed price some time in the future. The technique is used for three main reasons. First, to smooth out a known future market position (for example, arranging for the unwinding of the repo on a date of large central government spending). Second, to prevent a particular interest rate structure from becoming too entrenched. Third, it may be used when the market is reluctant to sell bills outright because of interest rate expectations. Thus, if interest rates are expected to fall, market participants will be unwilling to sell bills outright to the Bank. In particular, they will not wish to sell longer dated bills, the prices of which rise by a larger amount for a given change in interest rates. Another form of repo which has been used at times of particularly heavy tax receipts by the government is one undertaken directly with the banks. The repo is generally in gilts, although other instruments have also been acceptable.

Lending

Lending to the discount houses takes three principal forms. First, the Bank can lend to the discount houses as a method of providing further assistance if it has not provided adequate assistance earlier in the day. Discount houses have borrowing facilities at the Bank, with limits related to the capital base of each discount house. If a discount house finds itself short of funds after the Bank's main bill business has been concluded, it can request to borrow on a secured basis from the Bank. The Bank publishes the total amount of this so-called late assistance, although not the terms on which it has been granted.

Second, the Bank can, by refusing to relieve market shortages through bill operations, force the discount houses to borrow from it. This technique may be used when the Bank is keen to produce a change in interest rates faster than that which could be obtained by waiting for bill offers to respond to an initial rejection of bids by the Bank: it was used more frequently in 1988 and 1989, especially as a method of signalling the Bank's desire to see higher short-term interest rates. Typically, the Bank will announce that discount houses wishing to use their borrowing facilities are invited to do so at 2.30 p.m.: on such occasions the interest rate at which loans are made is usually published. The limits on the size of borrowing facilities are suspended for 2.30 p.m. lending. A variation on this technique is for the Bank to announce a Minimum Lending Rate which, for a short period ahead, it will apply in any lending to the discount houses. This technique was used on Monday 14 January 1985, when the Bank wished to take a decisive lead in raising short-term interest rates (in the face of substantial downward pressure on the exchange rate): an MLR was announced in the morning. The shortage in the money markets on that day was expected to be quite small and thus the Bank would probably have had to wait until the end of the day to force the discount houses to borrow from the discount window and hence enforce higher short-term rates. On that occasion, such a process was thought likely to be too slow.

Third, the Bank may lend to relieve 'technical shortages' due to, say, oversubscription to a privatisation issue (for example, on 30 October 1981, the Bank lent £121 million over the weekend through the discount window because of the heavy oversubscription for shares in Cable and Wireless). In such circumstances, lending will be at rates close to market rates and will be designed to avoid any distortion to bill rates.

(v) Techniques for absorbing a money market surplus

If there is a surplus, the Bank will normally only absorb it in the afternoon. Such operations are carried out in Treasury bills, of one or more specified (usually short) maturities. The clearing banks as well as the discount houses have the opportunity to buy Treasury bills on such occasions as otherwise they would be at a substantial disadvantage compared with the discount houses in finding an outlet for surplus funds.

Looking ahead, there is one other technique which could be used to offset a money market surplus: a call for special deposits. All monetary sector institutions with eligible liabilities of £10 million or more may be called upon to place special deposits with the Bank. Such deposits would normally earn a rate of interest close to the equivalent of the average rate of discount at the most recent Treasury bill tender and would be called in amounts set as a percentage of eligible liabilities. Although the scheme has not been activated since December 1979, it remains available as a method of withdrawing cash from the banking system. Since a call for, or a repayment of, special deposits requires a period of notice, the scheme is best suited to occasions when there is the prospect of a protracted period of surplus cash which the Bank wishes to offset. Once special deposits have been called, their release can be timed to match an expected money market shortage.

(vi) Relationship between money market flows and the government's funding policy

During the early and mid-1980s, there were persistent shortages in the money market and the Bank of England found itself regularly providing assistance to the market in the form of purchases of commercial bills. The Bank accumulated a substantial portfolio of commercial bills which came to be termed the 'bill mountain'. As these bills were of short maturity (up to three months) they 'rolled over' rather quickly. This factor, described as 'bills maturing in official hands' in section (ii) above, came to be an important influence on the daily cash position of the money market. Overall shortages often amounted to more than £1 billion per day in the mid-1980s.

The growth of the bill mountain in the first half of the 1980s was due largely to the policy of overfunding the PSBR - that is, selling more public sector debt to the non-bank private sector than was needed to match the size of the PSBR. There is not, however, a precise linkage between the extent of overfunding and the shortage in the money market.

First, as discussed above, it is only central government and not overall public sector transactions which impact on the money market's cash position. This is because the Bank of England acts as the banker for central government whereas the local authorities and public corporations have accounts with the commercial banking system (see Figure 11.1). Indeed, in order to reduce the size of money market shortages the government encouraged the local authorities and public corporations to borrow from the Public Works Loan

Board, which is part of central government. Such borrowing raises the size of the CGBR but leaves the PSBR unchanged. As it is only the central government's transactions which impact on money market liquidity, the higher CGBR tends to reduce the cash shortage in the market. This is demonstrated in Table 11.1 where we show the influences on the cash position of the money market in recent financial years. It can be seen that borrowing by central government for on-lending to local authorities and public corporations took on growing importance as a factor behind the cash position of the money market throughout the 1980s.

Second, sales of government debt to all sectors influence the cash position of the money market whereas the funding position is affected only by sales of debt to sectors other than the banks and building societies. Third, changes in the currency circulation and other factors can also exert an important influence on the cash position of the money market during the course of a financial year.

The combination of the abandonment of overfunding and continued heavy borrowing by central government for on-lending to the local authorities and public corporations led to a move to overall money market surpluses in the later 1980s. The replacement of persistent shortages in the money market with recurrent surpluses led to a fall in the amount of money market assistance outstanding. From a peak level of £17 billion in July 1985, the amount of assistance outstanding fell to £4.1 billion by the end of March 1989. The Bank's holdings of commercial bills - the 'bill mountain' - fell from a peak level of £14.3 billion in February 1985 to £2.4 billion at the end of June 1989.

(vii) Relationship between Bank of England interest rates and market interest rates

In offsetting the daily cash flows in the money market the Bank's intention is to keep 'very short-term' interest rates within an unpublished band. This is generally interpreted as a band for overnight money rates. The technique of enforcing the appropriate dealing rate is, as noted above, one of accepting only the offers for sale of bills which are considered to be at the appropriate interest rates or, if these are not forthcoming, forcing the discount houses to borrow from the Bank at a rate considered suitable by the authorities.

Although the discount market is the 'traditional' money market in London, in the last twenty years or so large 'parallel' markets have developed. The most significant of these from the standpoint of the determination of short-term interest rates is the interbank market. In this

Table 11.1: Influences on the cash position of the money market and official offsetting operations

£billion, increases in market's cash (+)	81/82	82/83	83/84	84/85	85/86	86/87	87/88	88/89	89/90[1]
Factors affecting the market's cash position									
CGBR(+)	+ 7.6	+12.7	+12.2	+10.2	+11.0	+10.5	+ 0.9	- 6.9	- 5.0
of which, on-lending to local authorities and public corporations	+ 1.0	+ 5.0	+ 4.1	+ 3.7	+ 6.7	+ 6.0	+ 4.2	+ 6.0	+ 4.5
Net sales (-) of central government debt[2]	-10.8	- 9.2	-14.7	-14.1	- 8.2	- 8.7	- 9.3	+13.3	+19.7
of which: Gilt edged	- 6.0	- 5.1	-11.7	-10.2	- 5.7	- 6.1	- 7.0	+13.3	+18.3
National Savings	- 4.3	- 3.0	- 3.3	- 3.1	- 2.1	- 3.3	- 2.3	- 0.6	+ 1.5
CTDs	- 0.6	- 1.0	+ 0.2	- 0.8	- 0.4	+ 0.7	0.0	+ 0.6	- 0.2
Currency circulation (increase-)	- 0.2	- 1.2	- 0.3	- 0.9	- 0.7	+ 0.3	- 1.9	- 0.8	- 1.2
Reserves etc	- 1.3	- 1.6	+ 0.1	- 0.5	+ 0.9	+ 1.5	+11.4	+ 1.5	- 6.7
Other	- 0.4	+ 0.1	- 0.3	- 0.3	+ 0.7	+ 0.9	- 0.6	- 0.8	- 0.8
Total factors affecting cash position	- 5.1	+ 0.8	- 3.0	- 5.7	+ 3.7	+ 4.4	+ 0.6	+ 6.2	+ 6.0
Official Offsetting Operations									
Net increase (+) in Bank's commercial bills[3]	+ 4.7	- 0.3	+ 3.8	+ 1.5	- 2.0	- 3.3	+ 2.5	- 5.7	- 3.0
Net increase (-) in Treasury bills in market	+ 0.1	- 0.2	+ 0.1	+ 0.2	- 0.1	- 0.7	- 0.8	- 0.5	- 3.1
Securities acquired (+) under sale and repurchase[4]	0.0	+ 0.6	- 0.6	+ 3.4	- 1.1	- 1.2	- 1.1	0.0	0.0
Other	+ 0.3	- 0.6	- 0.1	+ 0.7	- 0.4	+ 0.9	- 1.5	+ 0.1	0.0
Total Official Offsetting Operations	+ 5.1	- 0.5	+ 3.0	+ 5.8	- 3.7	- 4.2	- 0.9	- 6.1	- 6.0
Change in bankers' operational balances at the Bank	0.0	+ 0.3	0.0	+ 0.1	0.0	+ 0.1	- 0.3	+ 0.2	0.0

Notes:
[1] Twelve months to December 1989. [2] Other than Treasury bills. [3] By the Issue and Banking Departments of the Bank of England. [4] Gilt edged stocks and promissory notes related to guaranteed export credit and shipbuilding paper.

market, banks offer surplus deposits which they might have to other banks: banks who wish to acquire additional deposits in order to match their loan commitments bid for such deposits. These deposits are for a range of maturities from overnight to one year: generally, the shorter maturities are the most actively traded. Rates in this market have taken on particular importance in the recent past for two main reasons. First, the UK clearing banks have come to rely heavily on raising funds in the interbank market; second, many corporate customers now have loan facilities at rates linked to interbank rate. The London Interbank Offered Rate (LIBOR) has come to be widely used as a benchmark rate, deposit and loan rates being set on margins related to LIBOR. Many corporate customers now have access to both traditional base rate related loan facilities as well as LIBOR related facilities.

In the light of these two developments, the clearing banks have moved to a system whereby their base rates are now largely determined by the prevailing interbank rate. The three month interbank rate has become particularly important as the key reference rate which is watched by the clearers. Indeed, Barclays Bank took the step in March 1984 of announcing that it would aim to keep its base rate within 1/4 - 3/8% of the prevailing three month interbank rate. As Figure 11.2 shows, the relationship between the two rates in the recent past has been very close.

Figure 11.2: Base rates and three month interbank rate

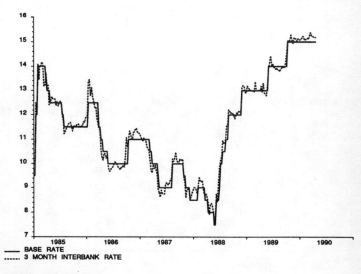

___ BASE RATE
...... 3 MONTH INTERBANK RATE

SOURCE : DATASTREAM

As well as taking into account the current level of the three month interbank rate, the clearers will also assess the likelihood of changes in the near future and will examine the term structure of interest rates. Thus, for example, if interbank rates have fallen ahead of the release of a set of money supply figures which are expected to be well received, the clearers might wait until the release of the data before changing their base rates.

The term structure of interbank rates can give an important indication of expected interest rates. If interbank rates are determined solely by expected future interest rates, then the current structure of rates can be 'unwound' in order to obtain expected future rates. As an example of how this can be done, refer to Table 11.2.

In this table we show interbank interest rates at maturities from one to twelve months. From one month and four month rates we can derive the three month interest rate which, if prevailing in one month's time, would lead to the same return being achieved from investing either in a combination of a one month deposit followed by a three month deposit, or in a four month deposit from the outset. Similarly, the two month and five month rates can be used to derive the expected three month rate in two months' time. In this way, we can build up a profile for expected three month interest rates, shown in the right hand column of Table 11.2. Given the close relationship between three month interbank rates and base rates, this provides a good guide to the money market's expectation of the path of base rates over the next twelve months.

Table 11.2 UK money market term structure

Interbank market				
Interbank rates (% pa):		Implied 3 month rates (% pa):		
One month	15.09			
Two months	15.09			
Three months	15.13			
Four months	15.13	in 1 month	Mar 90	14.95
Five months	15.13	in 2 months	Apr 90	14.78
Six months	15.13	in 3 months	May 90	14.58
Nine months	15.13	in 6 months	Aug 90	14.08
One year	15.09	in 9 months	Nov 90	13.49
LIFFE market				
Short sterling contract for:	Price:	Implied 3 month rates (% pa):		
Mar 90	84.94			15.06
Jun 90	85.36			14.64
Sep 90	86.06			13.94
Dec 90	86.59			13.41
Mar 91	87.03			12.97

Notes:
Data are for 8 February 1990
See Reuters pages FULB(interbank rates)/LIIA (futures)

Alternative information on expected interest rates is available more directly from the prices of the short sterling contract traded on the London International Financial Futures Exchange (LIFFE). This contract is deliverable on the first business day after the third Wednesday in the relevant month (that is, usually about the 19th). The contract is expressed as 100 minus the three month interest rate to be delivered. Thus an 8.5% expected rate gives a contract price of 91.50. The data for the LIFFE market are shown in the lower section of Table 11.2.

Notes and References

This chapter draws heavily on descriptions of the Bank of England's operations in the money market in various editions of the *Bank of England Quarterly Bulletin*. The most recent description was contained in 'Bank of England dealings in the sterling money market: operational arrangements', *Bank of England Quarterly Bulletin*, August 1988, pp. 403-409. This, in turn was an updated version of 'The role of the Bank of England in the money market' in the *Bank of England Quarterly Bulletin*, March 1982. See also A.L. Coleby, 'The Bank's operational procedures for meeting monetary objectives', *Bank of England Quarterly Bulletin*, June 1983.

The suspension of minimum lending rate was described in the *Bank of England Quarterly Bulletin*, September 1981, p.333. For the most recent developments in money market assistance see: 'Recent developments in money market assistance', *Bank of England Quarterly Bulletin*, May 1989, pp. 212-213; 'Recent developments in the commercial bill market', *Bank of England Quarterly Bulletin*, August 1989, p. 342; 'Recent developments in the Treasury bill market', *Bank of England Quarterly Bulletin*, November 1989, p. 505-506. The 'Operation of monetary policy' section of each *Bank of England Quarterly Bulletin* provides a regular update of developments in market assistance.

12 Conclusion

The challenge for UK monetary policy in the 1990s lies in maintaining control of domestic monetary conditions within the context of UK membership of Exchange Rate Mechanism (ERM) of the European Monetary System (EMS). ERM membership will almost certainly take place in the early 1990s as the UK fulfils the commitment made at the June 1989 Madrid Summit. Of the three factors influencing the timing of entry, the requirement for a lower inflation rate in the UK relative to that in existing ERM member countries will be the most difficult to achieve. After falling close to the German inflation rate in the mid-1980s, the UK rate rose sharply in the latter part of the decade and the first half of 1990: the differential should narrow sufficiently in 1991 and 1992 for ERM membership to be acceptable to the UK authorities. Arguments that the UK should join the ERM, even with a relatively high inflation rate, in the hope that membership would help to reduce inflation do not seem to be well founded. Econometric work suggests it is easier to bring down inflation whilst outside the ERM; and there is no reason why ERM membership *per se* would reduce it. The other two conditions the UK has attached to ERM membership will be easier to achieve. Substantial progress has already been made in removing exchange controls in other EC countries, with Belgium, France and Italy removing their controls ahead of the timetable set out in the Delors plan; and a greater degree of convergence between the cyclical positions of the UK and other EC countries should be achieved in the early 1990s.

ERM membership is, of course, only one method of expressing the commitment to a stable exchange rate. A target for the exchange rate index is another and, whatever the form of exchange rate objective, it need not be announced. With growing integration of the UK and other EC economies, the weight of EC currencies within sterling's exchange rate index will rise further in the 1990s, so that targeting the exchange rate index will, in practice, become almost equivalent to ERM membership. Furthermore, an announced exchange rate target does seem to have merit. It would provide a framework in which to express the government's counter-inflationary objectives; and attempts to cap sterling's value at an unannounced rate in the past - as in 1977/78 and 1987/88 - have led to reductions in interest rates which were not warranted by the behaviour of domestic monetary conditions. These observations suggest that it might be important for any exchange rate objective to be announced, although inconsistencies in policy may, even then, not be avoided. The 1987/88 experience, in particular, has led to claims that membership of the ERM would lead to a sacrifice of control over UK short-term interest rates (which would fall towards the EC average). In such circumstances, greater reliance would have to be placed either on other techniques of monetary control or on fiscal policy.

In the circumstances of the 1990s, however, no other form of monetary control appears viable. Financial innovation and deregulation, coupled with the removal of exchange controls, has rendered direct control of the banks' balance sheets largely unworkable. Overfunding is ruled out not only because it would lead to renewed distortions in the money market but also because it would fail to tackle the fundamental problem of the need to control credit expansion. A reserve assets ratio would not be capable of controlling monetary growth in itself but would, rather, provide a supplementary and unnecessary form of control over short-term interest rates.

Although financial innovation makes monetary control very difficult, strong growth of broad money, driven by an expansion of credit, has undoubtedly had very important effects on the real economy. There have been two periods in which broad money has been seriously affected by structural changes and deregulation in the financial system: between 1971 and 1973; and from 1980 to 1983, although this later episode proved to be the antecedent to sustained financial innovation. In both periods, the authorities attempted to play down the role of broad money and credit which ensued, arguing that such deregulation made the broad money aggregates difficult to interpret. Both periods, however, saw such financial changes have very real effects on the availability of credit and on the behaviour of the real economy.

As financial innovation may itself make changes in interest rates a less effective form of monetary control, and as control over interest rates may be sacrificed by ERM membership, the challenge for the authorities in the 1990s is a very difficult one. The implication is that a much more active role may be needed for fiscal policy.

Narrow money may be able to play some role as a monetary target in the 1990s but this seems largely to be as an ancillary source of information on concurrent developments in the real economy: its role as a leading indicator of inflation seems to be limited. The experience of the last decade demonstrates clearly that no one monetary indicator - broad money, narrow money, real interest rates, the behaviour of asset markets or the exchange rate - can be expected to capture all the information on monetary conditions. With such a wide variety of information available, coming to an overall conclusion about monetary conditions is difficult. The framework developed in Chapter 10 may be helpful in this process of aggregating the many sources of information taken into account when judging monetary conditions.

Appendix 1: Official Interest Rates, 1932 to 1989[1]

Date of change	New rate (per cent)	Date of change	New rate (per cent)
1932 30 June	2	1960 27 October	5^1/$_2$
		8 December	5
1939 24 August	4		
28 September	3	1961 25 July	7
26 October	2	5 October	6^1/$_2$
		2 November	6
1951 8 November	2^1/$_2$		
		1962 8 March	5^1/$_2$
1952 12 March	4	22 March	5
		26 April	4^1/$_2$
1953 17 September	3^1/$_2$		
		1963 3 January	4
1954 13 May	3		
		1964 27 February	5
1955 27 January	3^1/$_2$	23 November	7
24 February	4^1/$_2$		
		1965 3 June	6
1956 16 February	5^1/$_2$		
		1966 14 July	7
1957 7 February	5		
19 September	7	1967 26 January	6^1/$_2$
		16 March	6
1958 20 March	6	4 May	5^1/$_2$
22 May	5^1/$_2$	19 October	6
19 June	5	9 November	6^1/$_2$
14 August	4^1/$_2$	18 November	8
20 November	4		
		1968 21 March	7^1/$_2$
1960 21 January	5	19 September	7
23 June	6		

181

Date of change	New rate (per cent)	Date of change	New rate (per cent)
1969 27 February	8	1975 7 February	$10^3/4$
		14 February	$10^1/2$
1970 5 March	$7^1/2$	7 March	$10^1/4$
15 April	7	21 March	10
		18 April	$9^3/4$
1971 1 April	6	2 May	10
2 September	5	25 July	11
		3 October	12
1972 22 June	6	14 November	$11^3/4$
		28 November	$11^1/2$
		24 December	$11^1/4$
13 October	$7^1/4$		
27 October	$7^1/2$	1976 2 January	11
1 December	$7^3/4$	16 January	$10^3/4$
8 December	8	23 January	$10^1/2$
22 December	9	30 January	10
		6 February	$9^1/2$
1973 19 January	$8^3/4$	27 February	$9^1/4$
23 March	$8^1/2$	5 March	9
13 April	8	23 April	$10^1/2$
19 April	$8^1/4$	21 May	$11^1/2$
11 May	8	10 September	13
18 May	$7^3/4$	7 October	15 *
22 June	$7^1/2$	19 November	$14^3/4$
20 July	9	17 December	$14^1/2$
27 July	$11^1/2$	24 December	$14^1/4$
19 October	$11^1/4$		
13 November	13 *	1977 7 January	14
		21 January	$13^1/4$
1974 4 January	$12^3/4$	28 January	$12^1/4$
1 February	$12^1/2$	3 February	12 *
5 April	$12^1/4$	10 March	11
11 April	12	18 March	$10^1/2$
24 May	$11^3/4$	31 March	$9^1/2$
20 September	$11^1/2$	7 April	$9^1/4$
		15 April	9
1975 17 January	$11^1/4$	22 April	$8^3/4$
24 January	11	29 April	$8^1/4$

Date of change	New rate (per cent)	Date of change	New rate (per cent)
1977 13 May	8	1982 13 July	12
5 August	7^1/$_2$	2 August	11.5
12 August	7	18 August	11
9 September	6^1/$_2$	31 August	10.5
16 September	6	7 October	10
7 October	5^1/$_2$	14 October	9.5
14 October	5	4 November	9
25 October	7	26 November	10-10.25
1978 6 January	6^1/$_2$	1983 12 January	11
11 April	7^1/$_2$ *	15 March	10.5
5 May	8^3/$_4$ *	15 April	10
12 May	9 *	15 June	9.5
8 June	10 *	4 October	9
9 November	12^1/$_2$ *		
		1984 7 March	8.75-9
1979 8 February	14 *	15 March	8.5-8.75
1 March	13 *	10 May	9-9.25
5 April	12 *	27 June	9.25
12 June	14 *	9 July	10
15 November	17 *	12 July	12
		9 August	11.5
1980 3 July	16 *	10 August	11
24 November	14 *	20 August	10.5
		7 November	10
1981 10 March	12 *	20 November	9.75-10
		23 November	9.5-9.75
16 September [2]	14	1985 11 January	10.5
1 October	16	14 January	12
14 October	15.5	28 January	14
9 November	15	21 March	13.5
3 December	14.5	29 March	13-13.5
		2 April	13-13.25
1982 22 January	14	12 April	12.75-13
25 February	13.5	19 April	12.5-12.75
12 March	13	12 June	12.5
8 June	12.5	7 July	12-12.5

Date of change	New rate (per cent)	Date of change	New rate (per cent)
1985 16 July	12	1988 2 February	9
30 July	11.5	17 March	8.5
		11 April	8
1986 9 January	12.5	18 May	7.5
19 March	11.5	3 June	8
9 April	11	6 June	8.5
24 April	10.5	22 June	9
27 May	10	29 June	9.5
14 October	11	5 July	10
		19 July	10.5
1987 10 March	10.5	9 August	11
19 March	10	26 August	12
29 April	9.5	25 November	13
11 May	9		
7 August	10		
26 October	9.5		
5 November	9	1989 24 May	14
4 December	8.5	5 October	15

Notes:

1. The official interest rate is defined as:
   Bank Rate (from 30 June 1932 to 12 October 1972)
   Bank of England's minimum lending rate to the market (from 13 October 1972 to 19 August 1981)
   Retail bank base rate (from 20 August 1981 onwards)

2. The first time, under the Bank of England's new arrangements, that base rates were changed.

* Indicates that MLR was administered, not determined by formula.

Appendix 2: Monetary Policy Developments

1970

April   LCBs were asked to limit the increase in sterling lending to the private sector and overseas to 5% over the twelve months to March 1971. Other banks were allowed 7% growth. Within the guidelines, lending should be directed to exporters; there should be no increase in lending for personal consumption. A further call for special deposits was made raising their level to 2½% of eligible liabilities for the LCBs and 1¼% for the SCBs.

July   Banks were requested to reduce the rate of growth of lending, which was growing faster than that consistent with the April guidance.

October   A further call for special deposits was made raising their level to 3½% of eligible liabilities for LCBs and 1¾% for SCBs.

1971

January   Foreign currency borrowing to finance domestic expenditure was to be for a term of at least five years.

March   Quantitative credit controls were eased. It was requested that lending in restricted categories should not rise beyond 107½% of the March 1970 level for clearing banks, and 109½% for other banks, in the second quarter of 1971.

May   'Competition and Credit Control' (CCC), a consultative docu-
              ment, was published. It was suggested that the authorities
              would place less emphasis on direct control of lending to the
              private sector. Instead, the intention was to place greater
              emphasis on variations in interest rates to influence the de-
              mand for credit. These were to be backed up, if needed, by
              calls for special deposits.

June   It was requested that, pending the introduction of the new
              credit control arrangements, lending by clearing banks should
              not exceed 110% of March 1970 levels by mid-September.
              The limit for other banks was 112%.

July   Hire purchase controls were removed.

August   Measures taken to discourage inflow of capital from abroad,
              including restrictions on the payment of interest on new non-
              resident sterling balances.

September   New credit control arrangements, broadly along the lines of
              CCC, became effective from mid-September. Reserve assets
              ratio introduced.

December   Measures taken to restrict foreign capital inflows were
              removed.

1972

June   Sterling was floated.

August   Banks were asked to ensure that finance was available to
              sustain industrial expansion. If necessary, this should be at the
              expense of finance to property companies.

October   Bank Rate replaced by Minimum Lending Rate (MLR). This
              was determined by formula: it was to be ½% above the
              average rate of discount for Treasury bills at the most recent
              tender, rounded to the nearest ¼% above. The Bank reserved
              the right to suspend the formula.

| November | Special deposits called from banks and finance houses equal to 1% of eligible liabilities. |

December   A further call for special deposits, making a total of 3% of eligible liabilities.

1973

July   A further call for special deposits, making a total of 4% of eligible liabilities.

September   Banks asked to restrict personal credit, to restrict further lending on property and financial transactions and to discourage interest arbitrage activities. Banks asked to limit interest paid on deposits of less than £10,000 to $9\frac{1}{2}$% to protect building society inflows.

October   Minimum term for foreign currency borrowing to finance domestic expenditure reduced to two years (from five years).

November   Further call for special deposits, making 6% of eligible liabilities.

December   Supplementary Special Deposits scheme (SSD, or 'corset') introduced. Banks were required to place supplementary special deposits with the Bank of England if their interest bearing eligible liabilities (IBELs) grew faster than a specified rate (8% for the first six months).
Hire purchase controls reintroduced.
The balance of the November special deposits call ($\frac{1}{2}$% on 27 December and $\frac{1}{2}$% on 2 January) was revoked. This left special deposits at 5% of eligible liabilities.

1974

January   Special deposits reduced to $4\frac{1}{2}$% of eligible liabilities.

April   Special deposits reduced to 3%. The SSD scheme was to be
               continued for a further six months, with IBELs allowed to
               grow by 1½% per month.

November   SSD extended for a further six months, with the allowed
               growth again 1½% per month.
               Banks and finance houses asked to maintain restraint on lend-
               ing to persons, to property companies and for purely financial
               transactions.

1975

February   SSD scheme suspended.
               Guidance on lending was maintained.
               Request to banks not to pay more than 9½% on deposits under
               £10,000 was withdrawn.

December   D. Healey, Chancellor of the Exchequer, announced that Do-
               mestic Credit Expansion (DCE) should be £9 billion in
               1976/77.

1976

January   Special deposits reduced to 2%.

February   Special deposits raised to 3%.

April   (6th, Budget) D. Healey, Chancellor of the Exchequer, an-
               nounced that, after two years in which M3 had grown more
               slowly than GDP, he would expect their growth rates to come
               into line in the 1976/77 financial year.

July   Healey announced that for the financial year 1976/77 as a
               whole, money supply (M3) growth should amount to around
               12%.

September   Special deposits to be raised to 4%.

October   Special deposits to be raised to 6%.

November   SSD scheme reintroduced. Base was the average level of
            IBELs on August, September and October make-up days.
            Rate of growth 3% for first six months and ½% per month for
            further two months. Penalties were to be: for growth of IBELs
            3% or less above limit, 5% of excess to be placed in SSDs;
            growth 3-5% above limit, 25% of excess to be placed in SSDs;
            5% and above, 50% to be placed in SSDs.

December   The UK borrowed from the IMF and sent a 'Letter of Intent'
            in which the authorities agreed to limits on DCE of £9 billion
            in 1976/77; £7.7 billion in 1977/78 and £6 billion in 1978/79.
            £M3 growth of 9-13% in 1976/77 was thought to be com-
            patible with the DCE limit.

1977

January   Special deposits reduced to 2%.

March   Special deposits raised to 3%.

May   SSD scheme continued for a further six months. Base was the
            average level of IBELs on the April to June make-up days.
            Growth of ½% per month to be allowed.

August   SSD scheme suspended. Growth of DCE and £M3 both within
            target.

October   Official intervention to 'cap' sterling was withdrawn and the
            currency strengthened substantially.

1978

April   (11th, Budget) £M3 target range 8-12% for 1978/79. Targets
            to be rebased once every six months.

May   MLR formula terminated. In future, MLR to be determined by
            administrative decision.

June   SSD scheme reactivated. Base period six months from No-
                vember 1977/April 1978, permitted growth 4% to August/Oc-
                tober 1978. Same penalty rates as with November 1978
                scheme.
                Special deposits reduced to 1½%.

July   Special deposits raised to 2%.

August   SSD scheme continued for a further eight months. Base period
                September/November 1978; allowable growth 1% per month.

September   Special deposits raised to 3%.

November   Growth of £M3 below 8-12% target range in six months
                April-October 1978. Target range for six months October-
                April remained 8-12%.

1979

February   Special deposits reduced from 3% to 1% because of pressure
                on reserve assets; to be restored to 2% on 9 March and 3% on
                30 March.

March   1% recall of special deposits due on 9 March suspended. 1%
                recall on 30 March delayed to 8 May. In addition, special
                deposits were reduced to zero between 19 and 30 March. A
                1% recall on 23 April was announced to take the level to 2%,
                then to 3% with the 8 May recall.

April   SSD scheme continued for a further three months. Penalty free
                growth 1% per month.

June   (12th, First Conservative Budget) Announcement of relaxa-
                tion of exchange controls. SSD scheme continued for a further
                three months. Penalty free growth again 1% per month. £M3
                target range 7-11% from mid-June 1979.

July   Temporary reduction of special deposits to ½%. Recalls of
                ½% on 3 August and 1% on 13 August to return rate to 2%.

Recall of ½% on 3 August subsequently delayed to 10 September.

September   (23rd) Announcement that all remaining exchange controls will be removed with effect from 24 October.

November   SSD scheme continued for a further six months. Penalty free growth again 1% per month.
£M3 growth of 2% in October, took annualised growth since mid-June to 14%, above the 7-11% range. Target range was extended for a further six months (i.e. to mid-October 1980).

1980

January   Temporary reduction in special deposits from 2% to zero, effective from 16 January. Restoration to 1% on 8 February and 2% on 7 March.

February   Special deposits recall due on 8 February delayed to 8 April; that for 7 March delayed to 14 May.

March   Monetary Control Green Paper published.
(26th, Budget) MTFS announced, with a progressive reduction in money supply growth. Target range for £M3 to be 7-11% in 1980/81 with the target period defined as the fourteen months mid-February 1980 to mid-April 1981. Progressive reduction in £M3 growth with target ranges declining by 1% in each of the subsequent years to 4-8% in 1983/84. SSD scheme to be discontinued after mid-June.

April   Special deposits call due on 8 April delayed to 16 June.

May   Cancellation of 1% special deposits recall due on 14 May.

June   Cancellation of 1% special deposits recall due on 16 June. SSD scheme discontinued.

September   Publication of Bank of England papers on 'The Measurement of Liquidity' and 'The Measurement of Capital'.

November   Publication of a background note 'Methods of Monetary Con-
            trol' following on from discussions in response to the March
            'Green Paper'. Reserve assets ratio to be abolished. Future of
            cash ratio to be considered. Bank to discuss with the banks
            collection of data on retail deposits. Three changes to be made
            to Bank's intervention in the money market: (i) intervention
            will place a greater emphasis on dealing in bills rather than
            'discount window' lending; (ii) aim will be 'to keep very short
            term interest rates within an unpublished band'. The Bank
            might cease to announce MLR; (iii) 'the Bank's operations
            would be broadly intended to offset daily cash flows between
            the Bank and the money markets'. Technique of deliberately
            over-issuing Treasury bills to be abandoned.

1981

January   The minimum reserve assets ratio was reduced from 12½% to
            10% of eligible liabilities.

March   (10th, Budget) New target range for £M3 6-10% for 14 months
            mid-February 1981 to mid-April 1982. Reserve assets ratio to
            be phased out. Introduction of index-linked gilts available to
            pension funds, life insurance companies and friendly societies.
            (12th) Publication by the Bank of 'Monetary Control: next
            steps', following on from the background paper 'Methods of
            Monetary Control' published in November 1980. Require-
            ment for the LCBs to hold 1½% of their eligible liabilities in
            deposits at the Bank to be replaced by the requirement for all
            recognised banks and licensed deposit-taking institutions to
            hold non-operational non-interest bearing deposits with the
            Bank. The LCBs will maintain, as well as these deposits, 'such
            balances as are necessary for clearing purposes'. Bank had
            placed greater reliance on dealing in bills rather than discount
            window lending since November 1980. Bank to extend list of
            banks whose bills are eligible for rediscount at the Bank.

August   (5th) Publication by the Bank of 'Monetary Control Provi-
            sions' following on from 'Monetary Control: next steps'.
            Level of non-operational non-interest bearing deposits to be

set at ½% of eligible liabilities. Level to be changed each six months in relation to average eligible liabilities in previous six months. Special deposits scheme retained, applying to all institutions with eligible liabilities of £10 million or more. New, extended, list of 'eligible banks' (i.e. those banks whose bills are eligible for rediscount at the Bank) published. Eligible banks required to keep specified ratios of secured money with the discount houses and/or secured call money with money brokers and gilt edged jobbers.

(20th) New arrangements for monetary control take effect. MLR suspended. Minimum reserve assets ratio abolished.

1982

March   (9th, Budget) Target range of 8-12% set for M1, £M3 and PSL2. Target period 14 months mid-February 1982 to mid-April 1983.

1983

March   (15th, Budget) Target range of 7-11% set for M1, £M3 and PSL2. Target period 14 months mid-February 1982 to mid-April 1983.

October   Nigel Lawson, new Chancellor of the Exchequer (after the re-election of the Conservative government in June) in his speech at the Mansion House discusses his review of monetary policy. Narrower measures of money linked more closely to future inflation.

1984

March   (13th, Budget) Target ranges set for M0 of 4-8% and £M3 of 6-10%. Target period 14 months mid-February 1984 to mid-April 1985.

1985

January   (14th) MLR re-introduced, at the rate of 12%, for one day only.

March   (19th, Budget) Target ranges set for MO of 3-7% and £M3 of 5-9%.

May   Announcement in the Treasury's 'Economic Progress Report' that target ranges for monetary growth are to relate to the twelve month growth rate, rather than the annualised rate of growth since the start of the target period. Target periods are now to be for financial years.

September   (21st to 22nd) Meeting in New York at the Plaza Hotel of the G7 Finance Ministers. The meeting agreed that the dollar was fundamentally overvalued and that a further fall in the value of the dollar (which had peaked in February 1985) would be appropriate. The meeting came to be known as the Plaza Accord.

October   (17th) Nigel Lawson announced in his Mansion House speech that the 5-9% £M3 target for 1985/86 had been set 'too low' and that it would be suspended. Overfunding was dropped as a policy and the full funding rule was restated and re-emphasised. External finance of the PSBR was to be considered an equally valid form of funding the PSBR as sales of government debt to the UK non-bank private sector.

1986

March   (18th, Budget) After the suspension of the £M3 target in the previous year, a new target range of 11-15% for 1986/87 was set. This was well above the earlier MTFS target for that year of 4-8% growth. Target range of 2-6% growth set for MO in 1986/87. Money GDP was forecast to grow by 6.75% in the financial year.

October   (22nd) Speech by Robin Leigh-Pemberton, Governor of the Bank of England, at Loughborough University in which he outlined reasons for less importance being placed on the behaviour of the broad monetary aggregates. The speech

1987

paved the way for the final abandonment of broad money targets in the Budget of the following year.

February   Meeting of the G6 Finance Ministers at the Louvre in Paris. The meeting decided to manage key exchange rates within unannounced target bands. Sterling was considered to be 'marginally too low'.

March   (17th, Budget) Final abandonment of target ranges for broad money supply growth. Target of 2-6% set for the growth of M0 in 1987/88. Money GDP forecast to grow by 7.5% in 1987/88.

November   In the Chancellor's Mansion House Speech the timing of the 'full funding' objective was relaxed, so that full funding need not necessarily be achieved over the course of just one financial year. This was in response to the heavy foreign exchange intervention in the period, which threatened to make the full funding objective unattainable. In the event, the lower than expected PSBR led to an outturn very close to full funding.

1988

March   Sterling was allowed to appreciate above DM3.00/£.

March   (15th, Budget) M4 replaced M3 as the authorities' preferred measure of the broad money supply. As M4 includes deposits with building societies, debt sales to the non-bank, non-building society private sector replaced debt sales to the non-bank private sector in the 'full funding' calculation.

October   In the Mansion House Speech the Chancellor reaffirmed that the full funding rule need not necessarily apply over the course of just one financial year. Given the move from a PSBR to a PSDR the government's funding objective was now best described as 'unfunding the PSDR' rather than 'funding the PSBR'.

1989

March   (14th, Budget) Target range of 1-5% set for the growth of M0 in 1989/90. Money GDP forecast to grow by 8% in 1989/90.

June   UK agrees, at the Madrid Summit, to start Stage One of the Delors plan for European Economic and Monetary Union on 1 July 1990. This involves the UK becoming a member of the European Exchange Rate Mechanism by the end of Stage One - for which no time limit has been set.

October   (26th) Nigel Lawson resigns as Chancellor of the Exchequer and is replaced by John Major. Sir Alan Walters resigns as the Prime Minister's Economic Advisor.

1990

March   (20th, Budget) Target range of 1-5% set for the growth of M0 in 1990/91.

Glossary of terms

Asset Management: The process whereby banks adjust the volume of their loans to equal the supply of deposits (the opposite process is termed *liability management*).

Bank Return: A weekly return from the Bank of England (released at 3 p.m. each Thursday) giving the balance sheets of the Bank of England's Issue and Banking Departments.

Banking Sector: The banking sector was replaced by the *monetary sector* at the end of 1981. It comprised those institutions included on the statistical lists of banks and discount market institutions, together with the Banking Department of the Bank of England. Inclusion on the statistical lists was based on informal appraisal of a bank's size and reputation and was usually closely linked with the granting of authorised bank status for exchange control purposes.

Base Drift: If a new *monetary target* has a base level which is higher than the mid-point of the previous target, base drift is said to occur.

Bill Arbitrage: Alternatively referred to as bill *round-tripping*. Hard arbitrage refers to the practice of borrowing on bills in order to place the funds on deposit (at the same maturity) at a profitable margin. Such arbitrage inflates both bank lending to the private sector and broad money. Soft arbitrage involves switching to bill finance from other forms of finance (e.g. a base rate related overdraft); it does not inflate bank lending and broad money.

Bill Leak: The level of bills held by the non-bank private sector.

Bill Mountain: The portfolio of commercial bills held by the Bank of England. As the amount of intervention by the Bank of England in the money market increased in the mid-1980s, the quantity of bills held by the Bank increased substantially, reaching a peak of £14.3 billion in February 1985. It fell back to £2.4 billion at the end of June 1989.

Broad Money: Broad money refers to money held as a form of savings as well as money held for transactions purposes. It provides a measure of the private sector's holdings of relatively liquid assets - i.e. those which could be converted with relative ease and without capital loss into spending on goods and services. *M4* is currently the most widely used measure of broad money; data for *M5* are also published.

Bulldog Bonds: Bonds issued by overseas institutions and denominated in sterling.

Cash Ratio Deposits: These are non-interest bearing deposits which all banks must keep with the Bank of England. They are essentially a tax on the banks and are designed to provide income and resources for the Bank. They do not form any part of a system of *monetary base control*. The level is adjusted twice a year and is at the rate of 0.45% of *eligible liabilities*. The average level of eligible liabilities in the period April to September is used to ascertain the level of cash ratio deposits from October onwards (the new level has to be held by the end of October). The average level of eligible liabilities in the period October to March is used to ascertain the level of cash ratio deposits from April onwards (the new level has to be held by the end of April).

Certificates of Deposit (CDs): CDs are issued by both banks and building societies. They are bearer certificates of short initial maturity. They have been used by banks and building societies alike as an important tool of *liability management*.

Certificates of Tax Deposit (CTDs): CTDs provide an instrument in which funds awaiting the payment of tax can be temporarily invested. The interest rate paid depends on the time for which the CTD is held and is higher for larger deposits (over £100,000). CTDs can be withdrawn for cash at a penal rate of interest. They can be used to settle all tax liabilities apart from PAYE. The main holders are UK industrial and commercial companies.

Competition and Credit Control (CCC): This was the consultative document published in May 1971 which suggested that the authorities should place less emphasis on direct control of lending to the private sector and, instead, place greater emphasis on variations in interest rates to influence the demand for credit. Measures broadly along the lines envisaged in CCC were introduced in September 1971.

Contingent Liability: A liability which is contingent on some other event. For example, a bank underwriting a bill will only have the liability to pay should the original drawer of the bill default.

Corset: See *Supplementary Special Deposits*.

Covered Interest Rate Differential: The differential between interest rates on instruments in different currencies after allowing for forward cover in the foreign exchange market.

Delors Plan: A three stage plan for achieving *European Economic and Monetary Union*.

Discount Houses (& LDMA): The group of institutions whose traditional activity is the discounting of bills issued either by companies or the Treasury. The nine discount houses forming the London Discount Market Association (LDMA) are: Alexanders Discount; Cater Allen; Clive Discount; Gerard and National; Greenwell Montagu Gilt Edged; King and Shaxson; Seccombe, Marshall and Campion; Union Discount; and S G Warburg.

Discount Window: The term used to describe the mechanism through which the Bank of England lends to the money market in order to relieve shortages of cash.

Disintermediation: The process whereby business which was previously intermediated by the banking system becomes channelled through other institutions. 'Cosmetic' disintermediation occurs if the bank still acts as an intermediary but the business does not appear on its balance sheet.

Divergence Indicator: The divergence indicator is a measure of the relative strength of each currency in the *Exchange Rate Mechanism*.

Domestic Credit Expansion (DCE): Domestic Credit Expansion is equivalent to the sum of the domestic counterparts to broad money growth plus bank lending in sterling to overseas.

Eligible Liabilities: The eligible liabilities of the UK *monetary sector* comprise basically their sterling sight and time deposits net of balances held with certain approved institutions. Specifically, eligible liabilities comprise: sight deposits (except those of overseas offices); time deposits, other than those of overseas offices, with an original maturity of two years or less; CDs issued; promissory notes, bills and other short-term paper issued; items in suspense; 60% of credit items in the course of transmission; and net sterling liabilities to overseas offices (an overall net claim not being treated as an offset). From this total is subtracted the sum of: 60% of debit items in the course of collection; balances with the Bank of England (excluding special deposits and cash ratio deposits); secured and unsecured money with the LDMA; and secured money at call with money brokers and gilt edged jobbers.

Equity Withdrawal: A term normally used in relation to the housing market. It is said to occur if net new loans for house purchase exceed net private sector expenditure on housing.

Eurocurrency Deposits: Deposits with a bank that is not located in the country in whose currency the deposit is denominated. For example, dollars deposited in a London bank are called eurodollars; sterling deposited in a New York bank is called eurosterling.

European Currency Unit (ECU): The ECU is a basket of European currencies. The basket contains fixed amounts of each component currency. Currently, one ECU is equal to:

	0.6242	Deutschemarks
plus	1.332	French francs
plus	0.2198	Dutch florins
plus	151.8	Italian lira
plus	3.431	Belgian/Luxembourg francs
plus	0.1976	Danish krone
plus	0.008552	Irish punts
plus	6.885	Spanish pesetas
plus	1.393	Portuguese escudos
plus	1.44	Greek drachmas
plus	0.08784	Pounds sterling.

European Economic and Monetary Union (EMU): European Economic and Monetary Union covers both *European Economic Union* and *European Monetary Union.*

European Economic Union: European Economic Union is generally understood to be an unrestricted common market. There would be no internal barriers to the free movement of persons, goods, services and capital within the EC. The 1986 Single European Act and the package of reforms commonly referred to as the '1992' programme go some way towards achieving this state of economic union.

European Monetary Union: European Monetary Union is generally understood to mean a European Community in which there are no margins of fluctuation between individual members' national currencies and exchange rate parities are irrevocably locked.

European System of Central Banks (ESCB): The second stage of the *Delors plan* sees the establishment of the European System of Central Banks (ESCB). The ESCB would progressively assume the responsibility for an EC-wide monetary policy.

Exchange Equalisation Account (EEA): The account at the Bank of England through which official operations in the foreign exchange market are transacted.

Exchange Rate Mechanism (ERM): The Exchange Rate Mechanism of the EMS is a system which sets limits on the movements of member countries' currencies against each other. For each currency in the ERM a central rate against the *ECU* is set. On the basis of these central rates, a system of central bilateral rates is derived. For each currency, fluctuations of +/- 2.25% around this central rate (+/- 6% at the moment for the Spanish peseta) are allowed. All EC member countries participate in the ERM with the exception of the UK, Portugal and Greece.

Financial Statement and Budget Report (FSBR): Otherwise known as the 'Red Book', this is published each year at the time of the Budget and contains the government's economic forecasts, fiscal and monetary objectives.

Fundamental Equilibrium Exchange Rate (FEER): This is the level of the real exchange rate index that produces an equilibrium level for the current account balance that is exactly matched by structural capital flows. If the current account balance is at this level then there will be no need to attract short-term, speculative capital inflows which may be more dependent on expectations of short-term exchange rate movements or short-term interest rate differentials.

Funding: The policy whereby the authorities offset the effect on the broad money supply of the public sector borrowing requirement (or debt repayment) and the effect of the underlying change in the foreign exchange reserves by selling government debt to the UK private sector (apart from banks and building societies) and the overseas sector. Overfunding is said to occur if the net effect of these flows is to reduce the growth of the broad money supply; underfunding occurs if the net effect is to expand the broad money supply.

G5: The Group of Five countries: France, Great Britain, Japan, the United States and West Germany.

G7: The Group of Seven countries: *G5* plus Canada and Italy.

Gilt edged stocks (Gilts): Stocks, issued by the government, normally paying a fixed amount of interest (in the form of a 'coupon') per year and having an original maturity of several years.

Intermediation: The process whereby funds are channelled, via an intermediary, from one sector of the economy to another. For example, banks may act as intermediaries between the personal sector and the company sector.

Liability Management: The process whereby banks adjust the volume of their deposits in order to accommodate changes in the demand for loans (the opposite process is termed *asset management*).

'Lifeboat': The term used to refer to the joint operation by the Bank of England and the clearing banks in 1973 to support the 'secondary' banks.

Louvre Accord: The agreement by the Group of Seven *(G7)* countries, made on 22 February 1987, that their currencies were within ranges broadly consistent with underlying economic fundamentals and that they should aim for broad stability of exchange rates.

M0: M0 is a measure of *narrow money*. It is also termed the wide monetary base as it includes all the possible components of a monetary base measure. These are notes and coin in circulation with the public, banks' holdings of cash (termed either *vault cash* or *till money*) and bankers' operational balances at the Bank of England. M0 is currently the authorities' targeted measure of narrow money.

M1: A narrow measure of money comprising notes and coin in circulation with the public and the sterling *sight deposits* of the UK private sector. Sterling sight deposits can be classified as either interest bearing or non-interest bearing. Adding just non-interest bearing deposits to notes and coin in circulation with the public gives the measure non-interest bearing M1 (or nib M1). Data for M1 have not been published since June 1989 but data for nib M1 are still available. The classification of the Abbey National Building Society as a bank from 12 July 1989 meant that deposits with it would have been included within M1 from that date. The large break in the series of data for M1 as a result of this move led the Bank of England to cease publication of the M1 measure of the money supply. As building societies do not attract significant amounts of non-interest bearing deposits, nib M1 was not significantly affected by the development.

M2: A specially devised measure of transactions balances which comprises non-interest bearing M1, private sector interest bearing retail sterling bank deposits, private sector holdings of retail building society shares and deposits and National Savings Bank Ordinary Accounts.

M3 and M3c: Between April 1987 and June 1989, the term M3 was used to describe the measure of the money supply previously referred to as *sterling M3 (£M3)*. This measure comprised: notes and coin in circulation with the public; private sector sterling sight and time deposits with banks; and private sector holdings of sterling bank certificates of deposit. Between April 1987 and June 1989 the term M3c was used to describe the measure of the money supply previously referred to as M3. This measure comprised M3 plus private sector holdings of foreign currency bank deposits. Data for M3 and M3c have not been published since June 1989. The classification of the Abbey National Building Society as a bank from 12 July 1989 meant that it would have been included within M3 from that date. The large break in the series of data for M3 and M3c as a result of this move led the Bank of England to cease publication of these two measures of the money supply (and *M1*).

M4: M4 is currently the most widely used measure of *broad money*. It comprises notes and coin in circulation with the public *plus* private sector sterling sight and time bank deposits *plus* private sector holdings of sterling bank CDs *plus* private sector holdings of building society shares and deposits *minus* building society holdings of bank deposits, bank CDs, and notes and coin. As M4 includes deposits with building societies it was unaffected by the conversion of the Abbey National Building Society to a bank in July 1989.

M4c: M4c is similar in concept to *M3c*. It comprises M4 plus deposits in currencies other than sterling placed with UK banks and building societies by the rest of the UK private sector.

M5: M5 is the broadest measure of the money supply. It comprises all the components of *M4* plus holdings by the UK private sector (excluding building societies) of money market instruments (bank bills, Treasury bills, local authority deposits), CTDs and National Savings instruments (excluding certificates, SAYE and other long-term deposits).

Monetary Base: The monetary base is defined as a subset of the monetary liabilities of the Bank of England. The three components which may be included are: notes and coin in circulation with the public; notes and coin held by the banks; and bankers' operational deposits at the Bank of England. *M0*, the wide measure of the monetary base, includes all three components.

Monetary Base Control: A method of monetary control which relies on the authorities influencing the level of *monetary base*.

Monetary Sector: The UK monetary sector comprises: all recognised banks and licensed deposit-takers (LDTs); the National Girobank; the trustee savings banks; the Banking Department of the Bank of England; and those banks in the Channel Islands and the Isle of Man which have chosen to comply with the current monetary control arrangements. The monetary sector replaced the *banking sector* at the end of 1981. Broadly, it differs from the banking sector in that it includes all recognised banks and LDTs (rather than just those on the statistical list), the trustee savings banks and the National Girobank. As the liabilities of these institutions are no longer so predominant in the definition of the monetary aggregates, the term has now been replaced simply by the term 'banks'.

Monetary Statistics: A monthly press release from the Bank giving new and revised data on some of the tables in the *Bank of England Quarterly Bulletin*.

Monetary Target: A target, normally expressed as a range (say, 5-9%), for the growth of one or more measures of the money supply.

Narrow Money: Narrow money refers to money balances which are readily available to finance current spending, i.e. for 'transactions purposes'. *M0* is currently the authorities' targeted measure of the narrow money supply; nib *M1* and *M2* are the two other measures of narrow money for which data are currently published.

Off Balance Sheet Business: This is banking business which is effectively carried out by a bank but which is not recorded on its balance sheet. For example, a bank may underwrite a bill which is then sold to the non-bank private sector. The bank is effectively acting as an intermediary but the business does not appear on its balance sheet.

Operational Deposits: These are deposits of the clearing banks held at the Bank of England which are used for settling transactions between themselves and the Bank. The clearing banks have a target for the level of operational deposits they hold at the Bank of England. Operational deposits are included within the *M0* measure of the narrow money supply.

Original Maturity: The original maturity of an instrument is the term to maturity when the instrument is issued.

Overfunding: See *Funding*.

Plaza Accord: The agreement between the Group of Five *(G5)* countries reached at the Plaza Hotel on 22 September 1985. The main element of the Accord was that a further fall in the value of the US dollar would be desirable.

PSL1: PSL1 was a measure of private sector liquidity published up to and including March 1987. It included all the components of *£M3* (apart from private sector sterling time deposits with an *original maturity* of over two years) as well as private sector holdings of money market instruments (bank bills, Treasury bills, local authority deposits) and certificates of tax deposit.

PSL2: PSL2 was renamed *M5* in April 1987.

Purchasing Power Parity (PPP): The PPP exchange rate is that rate at which the prices of goods in different countries are equalised.

Reserve Assets Ratio: Between September 1971 and August 1981, banks were required to keep a certain proportion of their *eligible liabilities* as reserve assets. The ratio was 12 ½% for the period up to January 1981, when it was reduced to 10%. It was temporarily reduced to 8% for most of March and April 1981 and abolished in August 1981. Reserve assets comprised:

(a) balances at the Bank of England (other than special deposits or supplementary special deposits);
(b) British government and Northern Ireland Treasury bills;
(c) secured money at call with the London discount market;
(d) British government stocks with a residual maturity of less than one year;
(e) local authority bills eligible for rediscount at the Bank of England;
(f) commercial bills eligible for rediscount at the Bank of England, up to a maximum of 2% of *eligible liabilities*.

Residual Maturity: The remaining term to maturity of an instrument. For example, a bill with an *original maturity* of three months issued two months ago has a residual maturity of one month.

Round-Tripping: The process whereby funds raised in one market are deposited in another to yield a profit. For example, a company may issue a bill and deposit the proceeds in the money market to yield a higher return (this process is also referred to as *bill arbitrage*).

Sale and Repurchase Agreement (REPO): An agreement whereby instruments are sold with an agreement to repurchase them at a specified future date.

Seasonal Adjustment: The process whereby recurrent variations in a series of data are removed.

Securitisation: The process whereby intermediation which was previously carried out by the banking sector is replaced by intermediation in the securities markets. For example, banks may securitise their portfolio of residential mortgages which are then traded as a mortgage-backed security.

Seignorage: The profits accruing to a government from the ability to issue non-interest bearing cash as a method of financing its budget deficit.

Sight Deposits: Deposits which are withdrawable without notice. Sight deposits which are non-interest bearing consist predominantly of current (chequable) accounts. Sight deposits which are interest bearing include both current accounts and money market deposits which are withdrawable on demand.

Special Deposits: The authorities can call on the banks to place a certain percentage of their *eligible liabilities* in a special deposit at the Bank of England which is non-interest bearing. They have not been called since 1980. These deposits did not count as reserve assets when the reserve assets ratio was in place.

Sterilised Intervention: When the authorities intervene in the foreign exchange market there will be an initial effect on the money supply: if the authorities sell sterling and buy foreign currency then the broad measures of the money supply are increased. If the authorities offset the monetary effect of this intervention by selling government debt, sterilised intervention is said to take place. The full *funding rule* in the UK ensures that foreign exchange intervention is sterilised in this manner.

Sterling M3 (£M3): £M3 was renamed *M3* in 1987.

Supplementary Special Deposits (SSD): The Supplementary Special Deposit Scheme was a scheme which imposed penalties on the banking system for expanding their interest bearing *eligible liabilities* at a rate faster than that prescribed by the Bank of England. The scheme operated in three periods: December 1973 to February 1975; November 1976 to August 1977; and June 1978 to June 1980.

Tender: An offer to buy at a fixed price. For example, the *discount houses* at the weekly Treasury bill tender will offer to take up so many bills at a certain price.

Term Structure: The relationship between interest rates (and/or yields) at different maturities. For bonds, this is often expressed as a *yield curve*.

Till Money: The quantity of notes and coin held by banks. Alternatively termed vault cash.

Time Deposits: Deposits for which notice has to be given before they can be withdrawn without penalty.

Town Clearing: The town clearing facility enables a cheque for more than £10,000, drawn on an office of a London Clearing Bank located within a specified area of the City, to be presented by any such other office at the town clearing for settlement on the same day. The settlement takes place after the banks have closed for business.

Treasury Bills: Short term bills (normally of three months maturity) issued by the government.

Underfunding: See *Funding*.

Vault Cash: See *Till Money*.

Wholesale deposits: Large deposits bearing an interest rate in line with market rates: for example, CDs.

Yield Curve: A curve showing the relationship between yields on bonds at different maturities. It is one of the most popular ways of expressing the *term structure*.

Index

1992 100, 105

Abbey National Building Society 26, 29, 87
acceptance facilities 85
Antibes 107
Artis, M.J. 149
asset management 32, 87, 197 *See also*
  liability management
asset prices 13, 37, 151, 156-7, 159, 179

balance of payments:
  as a contraint on demand management 1;
  deterioration in late 1980s 19, 121;
  relationship with external and foreign
  currency counterparts to M4 62-3
bank bills 30
Bank Rate 72, 161-2, 184, 186
banking supervision 101
bank lending to the private sector:
  as a counterpart to broad money 3, 5, 83;
  direct controls on 2, 4, 86, 89, 162, 185,
  186
  See also credit, lending to the private sector
Bank of England 28, 30, 34, 44, 47, 72, 75,
  92, 94, 95-6, 110, 118, 119, 187, 191:
  liabilities of 26; Banking Department's
  Balance sheet 48-9; Issue Department 57,
  59; purchases of bills 68; Governor of the
  86, 90, 93; balance sheet 95-6; operations
  in the money market 161-75, 184; as
  banker to central government 163, 170
Bank of England Discussion Paper (Number
  47) 35
Bank of England Quarterly Bulletin 59,
  175:
  December 1977 21; September 1981 175;
  December 1981 13; March 1982 175;
  June 1982 35; December 1982 53; June
  1983 175; September 1986 118, 125,
  152; December 1986 35, 97; May 1987
  35; August 1988 175; May 1989 175;
  August 1989 175; November 1989 175
Bank Return 197
banking sector 197
banks:
  capital issues by 62-4; profits of 63; and
  residential mortgage market 13, 33, 87;
  deposits with 23-32; overseas 85; balance

sheets 95, 178
banks' and building societies' balance
  sheets 32-3, 55-6
Barrell, R. 150
base drift 197
Base rates 14, 115, 173, 183-4
Basle/Nyborg agreement 144
Belgium 131, 177
Belgian/Luxemourg franc 110, 139, 140,
  141, 143
Big Bang 75
bill arbitrage 197
bill leak 85, 86, 198
bill market 167-9
bill mountain 170, 171, 198
bills:
  private sector holdings and PLSI 13
Bismarck 105
Brittan, S. 113
broad money 4, 29-33, 82, 97, 151, 178,
  179, 196-7, 198:
  targets for 4, 67, 82, 93-4, 154; demand
  for 32-3; supply of 32-3; counterparts to
  55-64, 90; and inflation 82-3; and
  nominal incomes 89, 154-5
Budget:
  March 1972 4; June 1979 8; March 1980
  8, 12; March 1981 50; March 1983 14;
  March 1984 15, 38; March 1985 15, 116;
  March 1986 16; March 1987 17, 82, 89,
  118; March 1988 69, 120-1
building societies:
  deposits with 23-32; cartel arrangements
  of 33, 87; and mortgage market 87
Building Society Act 1988 28, 88
bulldog bonds 198

Cable and Wireless 169
capital controls 131-2
  See also exchange controls
capital inflows 137, 186
cash in circulation:
  See notes and coin in circulation
cash dispensers 45-6
cash ratio deposits 49, 192, 198
central government 163, 164, 170
Central Government Borrowing
  Requirement (CGBR) 171:
  as a counterpart to M0 48-9
certificates of deposit (CDs) 25, 29, 32-3,

87, 198
See also liability management
certificates of tax deposit (CTDs) 30, 57,
   74, 198
cheque accounts 23:
   high interest 27, 88
civil service dispute 13
clearing banks 161-2, 166, 173, 174, 185,
   186, 192
commercial bills 57, 72, 170, 171
See also bill mountain
Committee of Central Bank Governors
   100, 101
companies:
   deposits held by 28
competing currencies 107-9, 111
Competition and Credit Control 32, 89, 95,
   162, 186, 199
composite rate tax 88
Congdon, T. 80, 93-4, 97, 98
conjuctural convergence 132
consumer boom 90
consumer spending 90, 97
contingent liability 199
corporate finance 88
corporate sector 87, 128
corset:
   See Supplementary Special Deposits
cosmetic disintermediation 85
Council of Economic and Finance Ministers
   100
Council of Ministers 106
covered interest rate differential 199
credit:
   availability 20, 90; demand for, and
   interest rates 21, 92; demand for, and
   monetary growth 32, 83, 97, 178; direct
   controls on 92-3, 178
See also bank lending to the private sector,
   lending to the private sector, mortgage
   lending, mortgage market
credit cards 23, 104, 110
cross-border trade 104
current accounts:
   interest bearing 26, 27; non-interest
   bearing 26
See also M1, sight deposits
current account (of the balance of
   payments) 61-2, 97, 137-8, 147

Danish krone 139, 140, 141, 143
Davies, G. 113
Davis, E.P. 149
Delors:
   Committee 100, 103, 104; Report 100-3,
   106-7, 109, 112, 131; plan 100-3, 105,
   108, 109, 127, 177, 196, 199
demand management 1, 10
Department of the Environment 156
Deutschemark 139, 140, 141, 143, 147
See also sterling exchange rate
direct controls on the banking system 85
See also Supplementary Special Deposits
   scheme
discount houses 72, 73, 161, 162, 163, 165,
   167, 168, 169, 171, 199
discount window 72, 169, 199
disintermediation 85-6, 199
divergence indicator:
   See under Exchange Rate Mechanism
Divisia money 28, 34
Domestic Credit Expansion (DCE) 3, 6, 61,
   188, 189, 199
domestic demand 132, 145, 146
Dornbush, R. 111
Durham speech 93
See also Leigh-Pemberton
Dutch florin 139, 140, 141, 143

economic studies of the demand for money
   3
See also M0, M1, Sterling M3
Economic and Monetary Union (EMU)
   99-113, 127, 196, 200
eligible banks 193
eligible liabilities 49, 96, 170, 200
employment 1
equity market 156-7
equity prices 159
equity withdrawal 200
eurobond market 87
eurocurrency deposits 200
European Community 99:
   definition of the money supply 31-2;
   internal market 99, 103; interest rates in
   99; structural funds of 106
European Council 102, 103
European Currency Unit (ECU) 200:
   Treasury bills 58, 128; mortgages 91; and
   EMU 109-11; bond market 109-10;

sterling component of 128, 135, 138-40;
construction of 139-40
See also Exchange Rate Mechanism
European Economic Union 100, 201
European Monetary System 17, 19-20, 97,
100, 121, 127, 177
European Monetary Union 99, 201
European System of Central Banks 101-2,
201
exchange controls:
removal of UK controls 8, 13, 30, 85, 86,
178, 190-1; removal of EC 108, 131-2,
177; in France and Italy 110, 128, 131-2,
177
Exchange Equalisation Account (EEA)
57-8, 164-5, 201
Exchange Rate Mechanism:
UK membership of 17, 19-20, 21, 80, 97,
99, 100, 102, 121, 124, 127-50, 177-8,
201; and Delors plan 100-1; parity grid
135, 140, 141; central rates 139;
divergence indicator 135, 140-44, 199;
conventional adjustment process in 144-5
See also Walters critique
Exchequer transactions 164-5, 167
external and foreign currency counterparts
33, 59-62, 84
external finance (of the PSBR) 69, 75, 79,
194

Fforde, J.S. 5, 21
Finance Act:
1983 87; 1985 87, 88
financial deregulation 3, 20, 82, 85, 89, 97,
178
financial intermediation 84
financial innovation 13, 20, 24, 85, 89, 90,
91, 93, 97, 178
Financial Statement and Budget Report
(FSBR) 201:
1980/81 21; 1981/82 12; 1982/83 13;
1985/86 125; 1987/88 18, 120, 125
Financial Times All Share index 156
fiscal policy 4, 6, 8, 12, 33, 83, 97, 103,
106-7, 124, 145-8, 178
Foot, M.D.K.W. 53
foreign currency deposits 30-1
foreign exchange reserves 68-69, 75,
119-21, 165:
to finance a balance of payments deficit 1,

62; and broad money 6, 33, 58, 62, 65;
and narrow money 48-9; pooling of 101
'fortress Europe' 129
FOTRA gilts 75
France 105, 112, 129
French franc 140, 141, 143, 147
Funabashi, Y. 118, 125
fundamental equilibrium exchange rate
(FEER) 137, 201
See also Williamson
funding 202:
full funding 65, 67, 69, 79, 195; narrow
definition of 66, 67, 68; broad definition
of 66, 67, 68; policy 6, 33, 65-80, 94;
unfunding 69, 80, 195; underfunding 68,
79; overfunding 67-8, 70, 76-8, 79, 80,
83-4, 94, 170, 194;
pause 163
See also gilts, National Debt, Treasury bills

G5 202
G7 20
Germany, West 105, 129, 132, 134, 136-7:
life insurance companies 131-2
Giavazzi, F. 149
gilts 57, 70, 72, 75, 76, 77, 94, 164, 168,
202:
reverse auctions for 76; assessing real
return on 158
Goodhart, C.A.E. 53, 89, 92, 97, 98, 116,
124, 138, 150
Greece 100, 103, 106, 111, 131
Greek drachma 139, 140, 141, 142, 143
Green Paper on Monetary Control 10, 14,
191

Healey, D. 5, 188
high-powered money 95-6
See also monetary base control
hire purchase controls 186,187
H.M. Treasury 44, 45-7, 160:
model of the economy 46-7; paper on
EMU 106, 107-9, 112; Economic
Progress Report 194
Holtham, G. 113
Hotson, A.C. 53
house prices 156-7, 159

industrial and commercial companies:
holdings of CTDs 74

inflation 37, 94:
  trend in the 1950s and 1960s 1; and real
  interest rates 3; expectations of 3, 10;
  zero inflation as objective of policy 12; in
  the 1980s 97; and EMU 107-8; and ERM
  129-30, 132-5, 144-8; differential between
  UK and EC 131-5, 177; and monetary
  tightness 159-60
  See also broad money, narrow money, M0,
  M3, Sterling M3
interbank market 171-5
interest bearing eligible liabilities (IBELs)
  85, 187, 188, 189
intermediation 202
interest rates:
  official interest rates, 1932 to 1989 181-4;
  nominal interest rates and monetary policy
  2, 3; real interest rates 3, 13, 90, 151,
  157-9, 179; as a means of controlling
  monetary growth 4, 91, 97; volatility of
  52, 128; long-term 71, 78; setting
  short-term interest rates 95, 178; very
  short-term 163, 171
  See also Bank Rate, Minimum Lending
  Rate
International Air Transport Association 110
International Monetary Fund (IMF) 3, 58,
  189:
  letter of intent to 6, 189; and fixed
  exhange rates 102
Ireland 106, 131
Irish punt 139, 140, 141, 143
Italian lira 139, 140, 141, 143, 147
Italy 111, 129:
  budget problems 100; trade with rest of
  EC 105

Johnston, R.B. 44-7, 53

Keynesian policies 10

Lawson, N. 10, 15, 17, 20, 21, 22, 37, 38,
  41, 42, 53, 80, 98, 104, 107, 112, 116, 118,
  124, 125, 193, 194
Legal Tender Laws 109
Leigh-Pemberton, R. 22, 97, 98, 102, 106,
  112, 116, 117, 124, 125, 131, 149, 194
lender of last resort:
  and the ECU 111; Bank of England as
  161-2

lending to the private sector 84, 89, 94, 185
liability management 4, 32, 85, 87, 90, 202
  See also asset management
lifeboat 86, 202
Lilley, P. 90, 97
Lipsey, R.G. 98
local authorities 74, 164, 170, 171
Loehnis, A. 112
London Clearing banks (LCBs)
  See clearing banks
London Interbank Offered Rate (LIBOR)
  173
London International Financial Futures
  Exchange (LIFFE) 175
Loughborough lecture 16, 22, 84, 89, 90,
  97, 194
  See also Leigh-Pemberton
Louvre Accord 17, 118, 119, 121, 195, 202
Luxembourg 110

M0 27, 29, 96, 202:
  targets for 7, 15, 18, 19, 29, 38, 116, 120,
  153-4, 159, 193, 194, 195, 196; definition
  of 24-6, 96; amount outstanding 28; and
  changes in the banking system 38-40; and
  inflation 38, 41-4; demand for 39, 44-7;
  and interest rates 39, 47-9; counterparts of
  48-9
M1 4, 7, 9, 14, 25, 26, 203:
  interest bearing component 14, 25, 26; nib
  M1 28; targets for 9, 14, 38, 193
M2 203:
  amount outstanding 28; definition of 25,
  26-9
M3 69, 79, 195, 203:
  and inflation 4, 41; counterparts of 5;
  targets for 6, 188; definition of 24
M3c 203
M4 27, 67, 69, 79, 195, 203-4:
  amount outstanding 28; definition of 24,
  29, 58; M4 private sector 29, 30, 56, 59,
  72; counterparts to 33, 55-64; and money
  GDP 94, 154-5
M4c 204:
  amount outstanding 28; definition of 25,
  30-2
M5 204:
  amount outstanding 28; definition of 25,
  30
Madrid Summit 1989 102, 177, 196

Major, J. 20, 196
Mansion House speech:
  October 1983 37, 41, 53, 193; October
  1984 38, 53, 124; October 1985 80, 194;
  October 1986 16, 117; November 1987
  79, 80, 195; October 1988 79, 80, 195;
  October 1989 80, 92
Medium Term Financial Strategy (MTFS)
  8-12, 37, 76, 81, 83, 115, 117, 130, 191,
  194
Micossi, S. 149
Miller, M. 149
Mills, T.C. 42, 53
Minimum Lending Rate (MLR) 6, 8, 115,
  162, 163, 169, 184, 186, 189, 194
monetary base 204:
  definition of 26; Swiss approach to 49;
  and broad money 96
monetary base control 49-53, 204:
  non-mandatory schemes 50-1, 96;
  mandatory schemes 51-2
monetary sector 204
'Monetary Statistics' 59, 204
monetary targets 5-6, 9, 81, 204
money:
  functions of 23; definition of 23-4
money GDP 13, 14, 16, 18, 84, 155, 194,
  195, 196
  See also M4
money market 72, 95, 161-75
money multiplier 94
Morgan Guaranty 136, 149
mortgage lending 13:
mortgage market 20, 87-8, 91, 156

narrow money 4, 17, 24-9, 37-53, 151, 179,
  205:
  and inflation 15, 21, 28-9
  See also M0, M1, M2
National Debt 70, 71, 78
National Debt Commissioners 70
National Institute of Economic and Social
  Research (NIESR) 134, 147, 149, 150
National Savings 30, 34, 57, 70-1, 164
National Savings Bank Ordinary Accounts
  27
Netherlands 111
nominal GDP:
  See money GDP
non-deposit liabilities 33, 62-4, 84

Norman, P. 98
North Sea oil 138
note circulation 165
notes and coin 23:
  in circulation with the public 24, 25, 27,
  29, 32, 34, 48, 50, 52, 96 ; held by banks
  (till money or vault cash) 24, 25, 48, 57,
  96, 207

OECD 136, 138, 148, 149
off balance sheet business 205
oil market 116:
oil prices 41, 116, 118, 152
open market operations 161
operational balances (or deposits) 25-6, 40,
  48-51, 96, 163-5, 192, 205
optimum currency area 105
original maturity 205
other public sector 73:
  repayment of debt 74
overfunding:
  See funding policy
overheating 19
overseas sector 57, 164:
  sales of public sector debt to 65, 73; sales
  of gilts to 75

Pepper, G. 95-6, 98
personal savings 71
personal sector 28, 87
Plaza Accord 17, 118, 194, 205
Portugal 100, 103, 106, 111, 131
Portuguese escudo 139, 140, 141, 142, 143
private sector 164, 165:
  external capital transactions 62; sales of
  public sector debt to 65; demand for
  credit 84
PSL1 13, 205
PSL2 7, 9, 14, 15, 37, 193, 205
public corporations 74, 164, 170, 171
Public Policy Centre 138, 150
public sector:
  external capital transactions 62
public sector borrowing requirements
  (PSBR) 3, 62, 65-7, 69, 70, 76, 78, 79, 80,
  83, 170:
  PSBR/GDP ratio 9, 11, 76; financing 56-8
public sector debt repayment (PSDR) 65,
  69, 70, 71, 72, 76, 80, 83, 94, 124, 147
Public Works Loan Board (PWLB) 74,

170-1
purchase and resale agreement 168, 206
purchasing power parity (PPP) 136-8, 205

quantity theory of money 9

Radcliffe Committee 21
regional transfers 103, 106
reintermediation 93
reserve asset ratio 94-5, 178, 186, 190, 192, 205-6
residual maturity 206
retail deposits 28
Reuters 167
Riddell, P. 124
round tripping 206

sale and repurchase agreement:
  See purchase and resale agreement
Scottish clearing banks (SCBs):
  See clearing banks
Seasonal adjustment 206
secondary banking crisis 86
securitisation 88, 206
seignorage 111, 206
sight deposits 206:
  interest bearing 26, 27, 34; non-interest bearing 26, 27, 34
  See also current accounts, M1
Single European Act 1986 100, 104
Single European market 105
snake 4
sovereignty 105:
  loss of as a result of EMU 105; loss of as a result of ERM 130
Spain 100, 111, 131, 140
Spanish peseta 139, 140, 141, 143
special deposits 95, 170, 185, 187-93, 207
Stephenson, M.J. 42, 53
sterilised intervention 144-6, 207
  See also foreign exchange reserves
Sterling commercial paper 30
sterling exchange rate:
  as a monetary indicator 13, 14, 15, 16, 37, 38, 99, 115-25, 151-3, 179; capping DM/£ rate 117-24, 127, 130, 144, 178; DM/£ rate and ERM entry 135-8; DM/£ rate and the Lourve Accord 17-9, 21, 68; fixed value of $/£ rate 1-3; floating rate 1972-73 4; index 6, 118-9, 128, 152-3,

177; in EMU 99-100, 102; volatility 121-2, 128
  See also European Currency Unit, Louvre Accord
Sterling M3 (£M3):
  data for 24; targets for 6, 7, 8, 9, 10, 12, 14, 15, 16, 37, 38, 81, 82, 115, 116, 117, 189, 190, 191, 192, 193, 194; counterparts of 30, 67, 81-2; and funding policy 67; and inflation 4, 41, 81-2; and money GDP 81-2
stock market crash 18, 19, 120
Strasbourg Summit 1989 104
structural change in the financial system 13, 14, 20, 24
Supplementary Special Deposits Scheme (SSD) 4, 8, 12, 13, 52, 85, 86, 92, 93, 187-91, 207
supranational budget control 106-7
swaps 88, 104

Tax Exempt Special Savings Accounts (TESSAs) 71
Taylor, M.P. 149
Temperton, P. 124
tender 207
term structure 174, 207
Thygesen, N. 103, 107, 112
till money:
  See under notes and coin
time deposits 23, 27, 207
town clearing 207
transactions balances 26, 39-40
  See also M2
Treasury
  See H.M. Treasury
Treasury bills 30, 57, 70, 72-4, 162, 164, 165, 169-70, 208
Treaty of Rome 103:
  amendments to 103-4

underfunding
  See funding policy
unemployment 45
United Stated of America 106, 129, 136
user cost of money 34

VAT 8
vault cash
  See under notes and coin

velocity of circulation 9:
of sterling M3 12, 13, 14, 15; of M0 15,
 16; of broad money 84, 90, 94
Walters, Sir Alan 20, 144, 150, 196
Walters critique (of ERM) 144-8
wholesale deposits 208
wholesale funds 87
Williamson, J. 136-8, 149, 150
Wren-Lewis, S. 150

yield curve 208

Zollverein 105